Earning a Living
Outside of Managed
Mental Health Care

Earning a Living Outside of Managed Mental Health Care

50 Ways to Expand Your Practice

Edited by Steven Walfish

American Psychological Association
Washington, DC

Published by
American Psychological Association
750 First Street, NE
Washington, DC 20002
www.apa.org

To order
APA Order Department
P.O. Box 92984
Washington, DC 20090-2984
Tel: (800) 374-2721; Direct: (202) 336-5510
Fax: (202) 336-5502; TDD/TTY: (202) 336-6123
Online: www.apa.org/books/
E-mail: order@apa.org

In the U.K., Europe, Africa, and the Middle East, copies may be ordered from
American Psychological Association
3 Henrietta Street
Covent Garden, London
WC2E 8LU England

Typeset in Meridien by Circle Graphics, Inc., Columbia, MD

Printer: Edwards Brothers, Ann Arbor, MI
Cover Designer: Watermark Design Office, Alexandria, VA

The opinions and statements published are the responsibility of the authors, and such opinions and statements do not necessarily represent the policies of the American Psychological Association.

Library of Congress Cataloging-in-Publication Data

Earning a living outside of managed mental health care : 50 ways to expand your practice / edited by Steven Walfish.
    p. cm.
 ISBN-13: 978-1-4338-0809-8
 ISBN-10: 1-4338-0809-9
1. Counseling psychology—Vocational guidance. I. Walfish, Steven.
 BF636.64.E24 2010
 158'.3023—dc22

                        2009046058

British Library Cataloguing-in-Publication Data
A CIP record is available from the British Library.

Printed in the United States of America
First Edition

To my parents, Jack and Ethel Walfish, who helped to instill in me a strong work ethic and a compassion for people, and to Mary, who always has and always will be the love of my life. She has helped to fill my life with warmth, love, and purpose.

Contents

Introduction: Practice Possibilities Outside
of Managed Care   *3*
Steven Walfish

Seven Keys to Developing Your Dream Non–Managed
Care Practice   *8*
David Verhaagen

I

Family Psychology   *19*

1. Premarital Counseling   *21*
    Susan Gamble

2. Teaching Marriage Skills   *25*
    Susan Heitler

3. Conducting Family Interventions With
    Substance Abusers   *28*
    Michaele P. Dunlap

4. Roles for Psychologists in Collaborative
    Divorce Practice   *32*
    Lauren Behrman

5. Assessing Those Seeking to Adopt and Working With
    the Adoption Triad   *36*
    Nancy M. Sidun and Debbie Daniels-Mohring

6. CBT Stands for Canine Behavior Therapy: Helping Dog
    Owners Become Better Parents   *40*
    Brad Rosenfield

II

Psychoeducational Psychology 45

7. Conducting Academic Readiness Evaluations 47
   Myles L. Cooley

8. Psychoeducational Testing 51
   Gary M. Eisenberg

9. Coaching for Attention-Deficit/Hyperactivity Disorder 54
   Peter C. Thomas

10. Vocational Counseling 58
    Mary Gresham

11. Improving Interviewing Skills 61
    Jeffrey Jones

III

Health Psychology 65

12. A Fledgling Private Practice in Reproductive Medicine 67
    Lucille Keenan

13. Smoking Cessation: Cognitive Behavioral Strategies With Hypnosis 71
    Marc B. Lipton

14. Cognitive Therapy Groups for Weight Management 75
    Nona L. Patterson

15. Neurotherapy 78
    Kirk D. Little

IV

Business Psychology 81

16. Executive Leadership Coaching 83
    Nicole A. Lipkin

17. Responding to Trauma in the Workplace 87
    Elizabeth K. Carll

18. Employee Assistance Programs 90
    David R. Starr

19. Stress Management for Corporations 94
    Daniela E. Schreier

20. Consulting to Family-Owned Businesses 97
    Kathleen V. Shea

V

Services to Government *101*

21. Vocational Rehabilitation Assessments *103*
    David Lutz

22. Completing Social Security Disability Assessments *106*
    Molly C. McKenna

23. Evaluating Pilots and Air Traffic Controllers: Psychologists and the Federal Aviation Administration *110*
    Douglas C. Haldeman

24. Public Safety Services *114*
    Stephen F. Curran

25. Psychological Evaluations for State Agencies *118*
    Marla W. Deibler

VI

Services to Organizations *121*

26. Working With Developmentally Disabled Adults *123*
    Frank Froman

27. Assessment of Men and Women Entering Religious Life *127*
    Thomas G. Plante

28. Consulting With Health Care Organizations *130*
    Edward A. Wise

VII

Finance *135*

29. Coaching Traders and Investors *137*
    Steven J. Hendlin

30. Consulting With Financial Planners *141*
    Brad Klontz

VIII

Teaching and Supervision *145*

31. Supervision of Psychotherapy Providers *147*
    T. J. Price

32. Integrating University Teaching Into Independent Clinical Practice *150*
    Valerie L. Shebroe

33. Teaching Online *153*
    Mitchell W. Hicks

34. Conducting Workshops for Teachers and Educators *156*
    Tish Taylor

35. Combining Treatment and Professional Training Within
    a Private Practice Model *159*
    Mark Gilson

IX

Specialty Groups *163*

36. Pregnancy Support Groups *165*
    Gina Hassan

37. Assertiveness Skills Training Groups *168*
    Laurie Little

38. Mind–Body Skills Training Groups *171*
    David O. Aspenson

X

Forensic Psychology *175*

39. Serving as a Guardian Ad Litem *177*
    Steven N. Shapse

40. High-Conflict Divorce *180*
    Jeffrey Zimmerman

41. Assessment of Competency *184*
    Eric G. Mart

42. Serving as an Expert Witness *187*
    Marcia Knight

43. The Role of the Assessment Psychologist
    in Immigration Evaluations *191*
    Ray Kamoo

44. Evaluations of Professionals and Professional Practice *195*
    Lisa R. Grossman

XI

Products 199

45. Developing Software for Social Service Programs *201*
     Genie Skypek

46. Developing a Brand Around a Theme: One's Own Enchanted Self *204*
     Barbara Becker Holstein

XII

Positive Psychology 209

47. Assessing and Counseling Gifted Children and Adults *211*
     Stuart Dansinger

48. Developing a Sport Psychology Practice *215*
     Mitchell A. Greene

49. Retreats for Personal Growth *219*
     Kathy Martone

50. Tantric Sexuality Education *222*
     David Yarian

EPILOGUE *225*

INDEX *229*

ABOUT THE CONTRIBUTORS *239*

ABOUT THE EDITOR *243*

Earning a Living Outside of Managed Mental Health Care

Steven Walfish

Introduction
Practice Possibilities Outside of Managed Care

Most mental health professionals (MHPs) would prefer to have a fee-for-service practice in which they see a client for assessment or psychotherapy and are then paid by check or credit card at the time of service. However, most practitioners, especially graduate students and early-career professionals, are unsure of how to develop a practice that is not dependent on managed care and insurance.

Many MHPs have developed their entire practice to be independent of managed care and health insurance. Others have created a hybrid model (Walfish & Barnett, 2008) in which a portion of their practice activities is insurance-based and the remainder falls outside the purview of managed care. These proportions can vary depending on practice location (rural vs. urban), prevailing market conditions, and whether the MHP possesses an entrepreneurial mind-set to recognize opportunities and has the ability to bring these opportunities to fruition.

Two books are essential reading for MHPs who wish to develop a managed care–free practice: *Breaking Free of Managed Care* (Ackley, 1997) and *Saying Goodbye to Managed Care* (Haber, Rodino, & Lipner, 2008). These authors discuss the attitude shift necessary to overcome anxieties of not being dependent on insurance and offer suggestions for earning a living outside of managed care.

I have conducted two surveys among members of American Psychological Association (APA) Division 42 (Independent Practice) in an attempt to identify income-generating practice strategies that fall outside of managed care. The first survey (Walfish, 2001) included a sample of 179 psychologists. Participants were asked to name three specific activities in their current clinical practice that did not fall under the purview of a managed care company. The responses were reviewed and synthesized into individual practice activities. A total of 180 activities were identified that were rationally grouped into 10 separate categories. The second study was a replication of the first and conducted with Jane Le (Le & Walfish, 2007). The 141 psychologists in this second sample were able to identify 158 practice strategies in which they received income for their efforts.

Presenting each of the strategies identified in these surveys is beyond the scope of this chapter.[1] However, Exhibit 1.1 presents a listing of three sample practice strategies within each of the broad general categories found across the two studies.

The results of these surveys suggest that a number of practice opportunities are available for MHPs to use their assessment, consultation, and psychotherapy skills outside the restrictions of managed care. These are not traditional psychotherapy practices with third-party insurance paying the majority of the psychologist's fee. Plante (1996) and Ware (2001) have suggested that when considering employment or income-producing strategies, those practicing in the field of psychology should think not solely about the degree they have earned but also consider the skill set they possess. Walfish and Barnett (2008) expanded on this concept by suggesting that psychologists apply their skills in research, assessment, consultation, and psychotherapy, looking for opportunities, and developing the mind-set of an entrepreneur (Baron & Shane, 2008) so that they can generate income without relying on managed care. The diversity of skills is reflected in the clinical practice activities identified by the survey participants.

Organization of the Book

This book highlights the work of 50 creative and skilled psychologists. They represent the "everyday psychologist" practicing in all parts of the country. The purpose of this book is to demonstrate how the skill sets of MHPs, developed through graduate training, continuing education, clinical practice, and recognizing needs in the community, can translate

---

[1] Those interested in receiving complimentary copies of the two studies may contact me at psychpubs@aol.com. I will forward them by e-mail attachment.

EXHIBIT 1.1

Samples of Non–Managed Care Activities of Psychologists in Independent Practice
Business psychology
   Disability evaluations for individuals attempting to return to work
   Executive coaching in corporations
   Mediation of disputes in small businesses
Consultation to organizations
   Conducing a wellness group for clergy
   Critical incident debriefing for emergency service providers
   Helping to train new volunteers at a local rape crisis assistance/prevention agency
Fee-for-service activities
   Career counseling and assessment
   Psychotherapy (through contract) for school students
   Remarital assessments
Forensic psychology
   Evaluations for individuals on probation and parole
   Mediation services for divorcing couples
   Psychotherapy with victims of crime
Group psychotherapy
   Group psychotherapy for adolescents
   Group psychotherapy for individuals undergoing separation or divorce
   Group psychotherapy for singles
Health psychology
   Counseling and education with couples struggling with infertility
   Hypnosis for pain control
   Psychological evaluation and psychotherapy in worker's compensation cases
Psychoeducational services
   Parenting guidance for children with learning disabilities
   Psychological evaluations for the presence of attention-deficit disorder/attention-deficit/hyperactivity disorder
   Psychological evaluation to determine the presence of mental retardation
Services to government
   Consultation to Social Security Administration reviewing cases of disability applicants
   Fitness-for-duty assessment for police
   Psychological consultant to state regulatory boards
Teaching and supervision
   Individual case consultation to other psychotherapists
   Supervision of potential PhD/PsyD graduates for licensure hours
   Workshops and seminars on relationships for the general public
Miscellaneous
   Conduct a research service to individuals writing journal articles
   Consult for colleagues on ethical and forensic matters
   Peer review to determine the necessity of treatment for an insurance company

into income-generating services or products. Most of the practice activities described are not eligible for insurance reimbursement. Readers are encouraged to see whether they can replicate the activities of these MHPs in their own practices. Readers may find that an exact practice activity will not work for them; nonetheless, portions of a given activity may apply or help generate other ideas.

I encourage readers who are inspired to incorporate some of the practice activities highlighted in this book to seek out the expert contributors as consultants (their websites and e-mail addresses are provided in the list of contributors), enroll in continuing education classes, read related books and journal articles, join relevant professional associations, subscribe to Internet mailing lists related to the practice activity, and obtain necessary supervision. MHPs have an ethical obligation not to practice outside their areas of expertise. Becoming excited about a new practice area should be followed by diligent learning of the skill. Time must be taken to obtain training and supervision as necessary. Of special importance is becoming familiar with ethical issues that apply in nontraditional practice areas.

The book opens with advice from Dave Verhaagen, a psychologist who has helped build a successful large group practice that is completely fee-for-service. He provides sage advice and guidance on how to develop a practice that accepts no insurance—and thrives. The next 12 chapters present the practice activities, services offered, and products developed by innovative and creative psychologists. The sections are rationally grouped, but overlap clearly exists. Placement in one category rather than another was an arbitrary decision on my part. The authors were asked to do the following: (a) identify themselves and their practice arrangement; (b) describe the activity and what percentage of their practice is spent in this activity; (c) identify how they became interested in doing this type of work and what types of training experiences they had to become proficient; (d) describe why they like the activity and which aspects, if any, of the activity may be unpleasant or annoying; (e) describe business aspects of the activity; (f) provide suggestions if a psychologist would like to develop this strategy into his or her practice; and (g) identify which books, journal articles, websites, or professional societies the reader might consult to learn more about this practice area.

With Appreciation

I first thank the contributors to this book. They are creative and skilled psychologists who generously agreed to share their expertise and practice wisdom with their colleagues. Without their kindness, this book would not have been possible.

Second, I thank Linda McCarter, acquisitions editor at APA, for seeing the value in a book like this and for her encouragement, patience, and support.

Finally, I thank my wife Mary O'Horo. As my life partner, she has encouraged me, continues to encourage me, and I have no doubt will always encourage

References

Ackley, D. (1997). *Breaking free of managed care.* New York, NY: Guilford Press.

Baron, R., & Shane, S. (2008). *Entrepreneurship: A process perspective.* New York, NY: Thomson.

Haber, S., Rodino, E., & Lipner, I. (2008). *Saying good-bye to managed care: Building your independent psychotherapy practice.* Charleston, SC: BookSurge.

Le, J., & Walfish, S. (2007, August). *Clinical practice strategies outside the realm of managed care: An update.* Paper presented at the meeting of the American Psychological Association, San Francisco, CA.

Plante, T. (1996). Ten principles of success for psychology trainees embarking on their careers. *Professional Psychology: Research and Practice, 27,* 304–307.

Walfish, S. (2001, August). *Clinical practice strategies outside the realm of managed care.* Paper presented at the meeting of the American Psychological Association, San Francisco, CA.

Walfish, S., & Barnett, J. (2008). *Financial success in mental health practice: Essential tools and strategies for practitioners.* Washington, DC: American Psychological Association.

Ware, M. (2001). Pursuing a career with a bachelor's degree in psychology. In S. Walfish & A. K. Hess (Eds.), *Succeeding in graduate school: The career guide for psychology students.* Mahway, NJ: Erlbaum.

David Verhaagen

Seven Keys to Building Your Dream Non–Managed Care Practice

Many years ago, just before managed care came trouncing through the world of mental health, I was part of a growing, thriving group practice. Business was good; our quality of life was high. Then managed care appeared on the horizon. The owner of the practice, panicked by the coming onslaught of managed care, sounded the alarm. He became insistent that we fill out lengthy applications, join panels, and prepare ourselves for the inevitable financial and professional spanking we were going to receive. Meetings became filled with tedious discussions about what was going to happen to the field and how we could survive. Forms with decision trees and dozens of boxes were created. New bureaucratic lingo was introduced. It was miserable.

For a number of reasons—that mind-set among them—the practice disbanded. A couple of us decided to start our own group, learning our lessons from this experience about what we did *not* want. Top of the list: We did not want to play the managed care game. So, for nearly a decade, we haven't. And guess what? We have done better than we could ever have imagined.

This chapter is about building your dream therapy practice free of the burdens of managed care. Some of the focus here is on group practices because that is my experience and expertise; however, these principles can also apply to solo practitioners. Whether in group or solo practice, you absolutely can build your dream practice without the oppression of managed care.

The Seven Keys

When we interview clinicians for our practice, one of the first things we tell them is that we are not on any managed care panels. Almost always, we get this response: eyebrows raised, then a smile, then something like a confused grimace. If you could read their thoughts, they would probably be, "What? I like the sound of that . . . but how?"

When we tell them how, we end up running some of them off. The short answer is that we go for it headlong with no halfhearted commitment, throwing caution to the wind. The truth is that you have to be a bit of a risk taker to be successful at our place—or any non–managed care practice. Agency work is much safer with a set salary and benefits. Managed care private practice is a little riskier but still relatively safe. Non–managed care private practice, however, is like doing the trapeze without a net. It's pretty scary. But when done well, the payoff is much bigger.

When you open a practice, there is a lot at stake: financial investment, reputation, annual income. No wonder so many seek safety in the arms of managed care. It won't treat you well, but if you cozy up to it, it will at least give you basic food and shelter and let you live. Building a non–managed care practice is riskier, and there are no guarantees. There has to be something that sets you apart from the rest. Over the years, we have found seven keys to making it happen:

1. Create a special experience.
2. Think of yourself as a brand.
3. Connect emotionally and relationally.
4. Give killer presentations.
5. Build niches.
6. Be OK with losing referrals.
7. Think abundance, not scarcity.

Notice that I did not say you need to be a top-notch clinician who provides top-notch service. I assume that is a given. The items on the list are not self-evident, however. In fact, some practitioners would disagree with a few of them. In our experience, all seven are important. I am confident that if you do all or most of these things, you can build your dream practice without being involved with managed care. So let's take a look at each of these keys to the game.

Create a Special Experience

My client stood in the hall and looked around with the one eye that wasn't covered by his jet black hair. He wore a hooded sweatshirt, a studded belt, tight jeans, and canvas shoes. To look at him, my client was one of the last people you'd expect to give a compliment. But still he said it.

I like this place, he said. It's fun.

Fun.

When have you ever heard a psychology practice described that way? For many professionals, it is almost unthinkable that a place of psychotherapy would be—or even should be—described as fun. Yet that's exactly what most people would say about Southeast Psych. When we showed up at the American Psychological Association (APA) Convention and just played the Wii at our booth and paraded Darth Vader around for pictures, people asked us why we were there. Mostly we were just there to have fun.

When we started Southeast Psych (http://www.southeastpsych.com), we knew it was important to have core values that would guide and shape the culture of the practice. Our vision was to create an experience that made psychology cool and fun, so we came up with four core values that we've stuck with to this day. They make up the acronym FIRE: fun, innovation, relationships, and excellence. For us, fun comes first, and it helps create a special experience that clients can't find anywhere else.

The office fairly reeks of fun from the time you walk in the door. There are movie posters in the halls. In the corner, a life-size Darth Vader stands down the hall from Spider-Man and Wonder Woman. A mannequin painted blue with a bug-eyed chicken on his head (don't ask; it doesn't make sense) lurks in the conference room, as does a full-size cardboard C3PO. To keep the British robot company, a real working version of R2D2 occasionally roams down the hallway, beeping and chirping away. On the wall beside each clinician's office is a caricature of him or her as a superhero—Superman, Batman, Green Lantern, Wonder Woman, and so on.

In our push to create an even greater special experience, we took one large part of our waiting area and created a classy looking bookstore and coffee shop for our clients called *Insomnia*. Inside, a big screen television shows *Animal Planet, Home and Garden,* or *CNN,* depending on the clientele at the time. A full-time barista offers clients coffee or hot chocolate or water free of charge, along with some nice conversation. It's an unexpectedly special experience just in that little bookstore.

In another waiting area, another large screen TV plays *The Incredibles* and other fun movies. Throughout the office, there are paintings for sale on the wall by local artists. Kids huddle around an XBox to play football or racing games in another room. In other words, the office is soaked in fun, immersed in levity.

So why do all this? Because we believe in the value of fun. We believe it is good for our staff members, and they seem to think so as well. Our turnover is ridiculously low, and morale is incredibly high. We also believe it is good for our clients because it creates an experience of true positive psychology. In fact, research has confirmed our experience and has found that entertaining and fun workplaces have more loyal customers and employees (Gostick & Christopher, 2008).

You can create a special experience at the reception counter, in the waiting room, on your website, and in your psychotherapy office. The way the office is furnished, the human interactions, and the little touches all count. Whether you have a large practice like ours or a one-office suite, it can be distinctive and extraordinary. Everything could feel special, as though value is being added at every turn. If you are a client, why would you want to go anywhere else?

Your culture does not have to be like our culture. In fact, for many psychologists, ours would not work at all. It wouldn't fit you or your personality. However, you should be highly intentional about what kind of culture you want. You should pick a culture and a tone that works well for you, but one that is highly unique and special. If you are going to start your ideal non–managed care practice, then focus on the cultural architecture. Simply put, this is the careful, deliberate design of your culture. Give your clients—and your staff—a special experience from the time they walk in the door, and it will pay huge dividends for you.

Think of Yourself as a Brand

I have two teenage daughters, one of whom is strongly attached to all things Disney—*Radio Disney, The Disney Channel, High School Musical* in all its incarnations, and so on. She has an emotional connection with this brand. I am amazed and impressed by how much thought and effort Disney puts into building their brand. One product promotes another; one experience builds on another; one personality boosts another. All of this is done purely by design. None of it is unintentional. We could learn a lot from Disney and other companies who brand themselves well.

I have an emotional connection to Apple products and Volkswagens. These aren't just computers and cars; they are parts of my life. For you, there may be a brand of something—shoes, food, drink, electronics, and so on—to which you have grown attached over the years. If so, think for a moment about why you are attached to it. Be specific about the reasons.

If you think of your practice as a brand, then you begin to consider how to get clients and potential clients emotionally connected to that brand. From *Married to the Brand* (McEwen, 2005), we learn that consumers get attached to brands because of four factors:

1. *Confidence*—They trust the brand. For a practice, this means that clients and potential clients believe you are going to provide the highest standard of care. The only way to create this confidence is to deliver on the promise. If you are starting a group practice, hire only the best people. Keep your clinicians and your front office staff well trained. Make sure the cultural tone is aggressively protected. If you are in solo practice, keep yourself as sharp as possible. If you are good, get better. Immerse yourself in new learning. Take your continuing education seriously. Push yourself to be the best you can be.

2. *Integrity*—Loyal customers believe they will be treated fairly by the brand. Practically speaking, this means that clients can expect honest and fair rates and tons of respect when they call and when they walk in the door.

3. *Pride*—Customers are proud to be associated with it. This seems like it would be harder to accomplish because of the confidential nature of psychological services. However, as the stigma related to psychotherapy begins to decrease, it becomes more apparent that some people enjoy the affiliation with top-notch practices. For example, we have such good relationships with some of the private schools in town that it has become a matter of pride to be associated with us. They invite us to do parent workshops and in-services each year; they ask us to consult on ways to improve support services for students with learning differences; families refer their friends to us. Because we frame psychology in positive terms and strive to provide the best experience and the best service, there is a pride that people feel in being associated with us.

4. *Passion*—Customers find the brand to be a perfect fit for their needs. People often ask us how we have been able to build a successful group practice without being on any managed care panels. This is a big part of the reason. Our clients have come to believe that we are the best fit for them, and because of that, they are willing to pay for the good service they receive.

When you think of yourself as a brand, it changes how you do business. You see your work as a unified experience. How you market, how you build relationships, how you design your office, and all the rest fit together. You want your name to be synonymous with high quality. Certainly, this way of thinking lends itself nicely to a group practice, but even solo practitioners can benefit from thinking of themselves as a brand. Expanding on the special experience principle, thinking of yourself as a brand means you make your services indispensable to your referral sources, clients, and potential clients. You are not just some name on a managed care provider list. You offer something that is a cut above.

Connect to Key Referral Sources

Many solo practitioners and group practices approach marketing like eating broccoli: it's good for you, you really should do it, but it isn't all that pleasant. They show up at doctor's offices with brochures in hand, hoping to catch a busy doc in between patients. They send out mass letters trying to drum up referrals from whoever will read it. They attend networking luncheons, and so on.

At our practice, we do a fair amount of traditional marketing. We send out letters announcing new clinicians or new group offerings. We advertise on National Public Radio and in the Yellow Pages. We do office drop-ins, and all the rest. But to be honest, all of this yields less business for us than a different kind of approach.

For the past several years, we have encouraged our clinicians to form genuine, authentic relationships with other professionals in the community. We refer to this as *connecting* rather than marketing. When we talk about connecting, we mean we are forming genuine relationships to serve those individuals and organizations, even if we don't receive referrals from them. It is part of our mission to get psychology into the hands of as many people as possible to enhance their lives. We offer presentations to their schools and organizations free of charge, we offer to provide them with resources, and we invite them to social events. We find all sorts of creative ways to serve others through psychology. Here are a few of our connecting efforts from recent years:

- We set up a free crisis network for private schools. Students could call us in a crisis situation, and we would advise them on next steps. We have received calls from a parochial school where a student detailed a suicide plan during confession, a small school that had a beloved teacher unexpectedly die, and another school that had a student making threats on campus.
- We cosponsored a fundraiser for a not-for-profit counseling agency in the community.
- We have offered a public agency and a few schools a number of free assessments each year for families who cannot afford to pay.

- We have provided an intern to do an extensive literature review for an organization working on a special project.
- We have provided an advanced graduate intern to lead a group at a school free of charge.
- We have provided APA–approved continuing education trainings to local clinicians at low cost or even no charge.

Over the years, we have made dozens of connections with local professionals, including some who would be considered competitors. We have had doctors and teachers and executives over to our houses for parties and get-togethers. We have built solid friendships and ongoing relationships with many in the community. We know that this benefits us by making them more likely to send us referrals, but our mind-set is that we will do it for an agency or individual, regardless of whether we benefit from it.

If I had to summarize this in three words, it would be: *relationships, relationships, relationships.*

Give Killer Presentations

One evening Trey Ishee, a psychologist in our practice, was going out the door to do a presentation on attention-deficit/hyperactivity disorder at a local school. He noted, "Every time I do this sort of thing, the phone starts ringing off the hook." Later that week, he told me that he had gotten six referrals from that presentation alone. Trey is a skillful and knowledgeable presenter, and this has helped him become one of the most successful private practice clinicians in town. Nearly all our clinicians who have been highly successful in practice development are strong presenters. For some, this comes naturally; others have to work at it. Still, the ability to give a strong presentation is a nearly essential part of developing a practice.

We have a "speakers bureau" that is honestly nothing more than a brochure with suggested topics on which our staff members can provide presentations to different organizations. Yet calling it a speakers bureau and having some appealing, ready-made topics generates a lot of calls. We emphasize these five elements for all our presentations:

1. *Have top-notch, regularly updated content.* Don't just pull out a 5-year-old presentation. Update it. Keep it current. Make it fresh.
2. *Use humor and fun.* Make the presentation a blast. Tell funny stories. Banter with your audience. Be playful.
3. *Use strong visuals.* Use PowerPoint or Keynote with strong graphics whenever possible. Surprise your audience visually. Emphasize key phrases.

4. *Don't charge for it.* Give it away. If you do a good job, it will come back to you several times over.
5. *Have a standard statement for clinicians to promote the practice.* Make it short and concise, hitting all the key points you need to emphasize in under a half minute. When I start a presentation, I usually lead with something like this: "Hi, I'm Dave Verhaagen, and I'm a psychologist with Southeast Psych. We are a group practice in Charlotte with more than a dozen psychologists in two locations. Our goal is to get psychology into the hands of as many people as possible to enhance their lives, and that is why we love to give presentations. You can check us out at southeastpsych.com."

There it is in 20 seconds or less. We encourage our clinicians to use PowerPoint slides with our logo and watermark, but otherwise we don't reference the practice again at any point during the presentation. This feels honest to us. It allows us to promote the practice up front, and then spend the rest of the time presenting the best material our research interns can find. The presentation should not feel like a commercial or a marketing pitch.

Present the best material in a dynamic way. Be fresh. Be funny. Be fascinating. Do all of that, and referrals will come.

Build Niches

Charlotte is the 19th largest city in the country, and, like most larger cities, it has its sizeable share of mental health providers. With so much competition, why would a physician, a school administrator, a physical therapist, or any other professional going start referring to you in the first place? Many psychotherapists position themselves as generalists who are willing and able to see a wide range of clients, with the hope that throwing out a big net will yield a large number of referrals. This may work for some, but I suggest that you think smaller, not bigger. More specifically, I mean you should be more tightly focused on who you want to see and how you will build your practice.

To use our practice as an example again, we have a few generalists, but mostly we have clinicians who have clearly defined niches. When a professional comes across a young woman with an eating disorder, they think of Heidi Limbrunner. When they meet a deaf person or someone with auditory processing problems who is going through a difficult time, they think of Barrie Morganstein. When they have a middle-grade kid who is having problems with social skills, they think of Frank Gaskill. As for me, more than 95% of my clients are 15- to 23-year-old young men, most of whom are angry, depressed, and typically using some kind of illegal substance. I have a narrow niche, and so it goes for most people in our practice.

Our rationale is that you want your name and face to be associated with a type of client. It could be an age range (e.g., children), a gender, a modality (e.g., couples therapy), a presenting problem (e.g., anxiety disorders), or even all of the above. A 12-year-old who is getting picked on at school? He should see Frank Gaskill! A feuding couple on the brink of splitting up? Send them to Jonathan Feather! A young woman who can't follow the instruction in her college classes? She needs to see Barrie Morganstein! An angry, pot-smoking adolescent boy? Go see Dave Verhaagen!

If you do good work with a certain kind of client, then position yourself to be the go-to person for that referral. Have one, two, but no more than three specialty areas. Work hard to make it so that when a referring professional encounters someone who needs help in your area of expertise, they automatically think of you.

Be OK With Losing Referrals

When we decided to build our practice without being on managed care panels, a few people said to us, "You are going to lose a lot of business." We didn't dispute that then, and we don't dispute it now. In an average month, about 60% of the new clients who call schedule an appointment, which means we lose approximately 40% of all prospective business. When we have surveyed the ones who don't schedule with us, we found a range of answers: It's too expensive, I didn't realize you weren't on my insurance panel, I don't think I really need to come in after all, I'll wait until after the first of the year, and so on.

There is a range of reasons for not coming in, and finances are definitely a factor for some people. We are fully aware that we are losing potential clients because of our decision to excuse ourselves from managed care. However, because we have created a special experience, have strong psychotherapists, have solid connections with community professionals, have well-defined niches, and regularly give killer presentations, the volume of referrals more than offsets the loss. It is OK if you lose potential business. *Do not freak out if you do not capture all of your referrals.* Not everyone can afford it, and not everyone is ready. If you generate a large volume of inquiries and referrals, you will not need to worry that you are losing some of them. The ones that stick will tend to be a good match for you, and your quality of life will be a lot higher.

Think Abundance, Not Scarcity

A few years back, I was interviewing a top-notch psychologist with a well-defined specialty area who was working in another large city. He was considering relocating to Charlotte, and we were talking about the possibility of him joining our practice. I'll call him "Jeff," and part of the conversation went like this:

> *Jeff:* So if I come to town, who will I be taking away business from?
>
> *Dave:* What do you mean?
>
> *Jeff:* If I am doing well, then that means that I am taking business away from someone else. Who is my competition in town?
>
> *Dave:* Hmmm. Well, we really don't think about it that way.
>
> *Jeff:* How do you think about it?
>
> *Dave:* We think there is plenty of business for everyone, that many people who need mental health services do not get them, and that anyone who is doing good work is likely to do well.
>
> *Jeff:* I don't really see it that way. I think we have to be honest and say there is only a limited amount of resources, and that if one person is doing well, that means someone else is losing business.

Needless to say, we didn't hire him. He was certainly qualified, but his mind-set was a total mismatch for us. He was thinking scarcity; we were thinking abundance. How you think about this makes a huge difference in your practice development. Scarcity thinking gets professionals more negative; abundance thinking makes them more positive. I received an e-mail from a solo practitioner who expressed "paranoia" (her word) over our new office in her part of town. Her thinking was that we might come in and gobble up all of the referrals. My thinking is that we should both do well. I told her I think of it as the Wild West, with plenty of gold and land for everyone.

Those who think scarcity are more likely to get scarcity, and those who think in abundance are more likely to have more. This, of course, is not a guarantee. There are a lot of anxious, scrappy psychotherapists who do well and plenty of self-confident types who do not. For the most part, however, the belief that there is plenty opens up your head to the possibilities. It is an optimistic and positive way of thinking. It frees up the opportunity to serve and collaborate with others, including your competitors. It motivates you to find ways to tap into untapped markets and referral streams.

When you think abundance instead of scarcity, it keeps you from operating out of fear. If you had a client who had some good skills and a great idea for a business but was fearful that it might not fly, my guess is that you would encourage her to step out, take a risk, and believe in herself. That would certainly be good advice to follow.

References

Gostick, A., & Christopher, S. (2008). *The levity effect: Why it pays to lighten up*. San Francisco, CA: Wiley.

McEwen, W. (2005). *Married to the brand: Why consumers bond with some products for life*. New York, NY: Gallup Press.

FAMILY PSYCHOLOGY

Susan Gamble

Premarital Counseling

S everal years after obtaining my license in California, I decided to embark on starting my own private practice. I currently own and operate a private practice in Pasadena on a part-time basis. Initially, my private practice income was a supplement to my work as a learning disability specialist, an instructor at two colleges, and my work at private for-profit hospitals. Currently, my private practice and University of Phoenix teaching position are supplementing my "income" from my new full-time job as a stay-at-home mom of twins.

My practice has had many components and variables based on juggling my busy work schedule and now caring for young children. In addition to general psychotherapy, I chose to market those aspects of the psychology field I enjoyed the most, which include couples psychotherapy, psychological and psychoeducational testing, and supervision of psychotherapists.

Out of my love for family, couples psychotherapy, and a spouse who works in the wedding industry, an interest in premarital counseling arose for me. I had enjoyed my few encounters into my husband's work where I could see his clients experience the stressful preparation for marriage with joy and excitement. This was definitely a different side of life compared with the inpatients with whom I worked. There was also my own disappointment with the church-required "marriage preparation" course. I also attended a 4-week workshop where I learned more about a healthy marriage from the 30-minute talk by a clergyman than the hours and hours of talk from the couple who were leading the course but were clearly using this "ministry" to deal with their own issues!

Premarital counseling is a time-limited counseling relationship focusing on aspects of preparation for the wedding day and the future marriage. Depending on the clients' needs, the referral source, and the time frame available, couples may be seen anywhere from four sessions to several months of sessions. The work can include, but is not limited to, managing stress related to wedding preparation, improving communication skills, increasing awareness or working on family-of-origin issues, preparing for the merging of two households, and understanding differences that exist between the partners. Spiritual and religious aspects of marriage can be addressed, depending on the couple's preferences and the clinician's training in this area.

Because members of an engaged couple are not "diagnosed" with a problem, for this practice activity, no insurance is involved. To attract potential clients, one can add premarital counseling on a psychotherapist website as a service provided and can include a web page specifically discussing this activity. Be sure to include a variety of key words (e.g., premarital counseling, premarital therapy, wedding preparation) on your website to assist couples in finding your service. Beyond Internet and other typical marketing sources (e.g., Yellow Pages, other clinicians), making connections with other wedding professionals can be invaluable. Ministers, officiates, churches, and synagogues are generally the primary focus. Many religions require some form of marriage preparation. A private clinician can provide these services completely to the couple or be an adjunct to what is provided by the church, synagogue, or officiant. Providing a brochure on the purpose and benefits of premarital counseling that the referrer can give the couple is a helpful marketing tool. In addition, other wedding professionals (e.g., wedding coordinators, photographers, florists) can be referral sources, and a clinician can market oneself by participating in bridal shows or advertising on bridal planning websites and in local wedding magazines. The goal of this marketing is twofold: to obtain referrals and to increase awareness of the service.

Many couples do not budget for premarital counseling, and bridal preparation books and websites often do not address it as a topic. However, compared with the large sums of money they are paying for the wedding, the hourly amount a clinician charges may feel like a drop in the bucket. Most of my clients have been self-referred because of their own interest and sought out the service independent of their other wedding planning. Setting up a number of sessions in that first phone call, based on the time available until their wedding and their relationship concerns, can help couples feel comfortable with the additional cost.

Generally, couples tend to seek out this service a few months before the wedding. This can be a challenge when working with a couple with significant issues to be addressed. During the last few months of wedding preparation, the couple can be busy tying up the details, putting down large deposits or final payments on services, and having multiple events to attend. Having evening and weekend sessions available is essential for this population. In addition, having less frequent but extended sessions can help the couple meet the requirements of an officiate or clergy, without affecting their wedding planning schedule.

Premarital counseling can be a wonderful adjunct to a practice. It can break up a day filled with clients who have anxiety, depression, and conflicted relationships with individuals who express love, joy, and excitement. To add this service to your practice successfully, consider your office environment. Although clinicians do not need to remove the psychotherapy and mental illness components from their office environment, they do need to tone it down. Additional, reading materials in the waiting room should include relationship books, wedding magazines, and magazines that look at issues of health, fitness, and home. Because of confidentiality, clinicians already avoid having clients spend time together in a waiting room. With this population, you may want to avoid scheduling a couple near an appointment of individuals with severe mental illness or highly conflicted couples and families. When a couple is going in to see a premarital counselor, they do not want to see the last couple playing out their conflict in the parking lot.

To prepare for work in this area, a clinician's background should include training and experience with systemic approaches to psychotherapy or training and experience in other approaches specifically geared toward working with couples. An excellent resource for training in couples work is the Milton H. Erickson Foundation (http://www.erickson-foundation.org/), which holds a couples psychotherapy conference each year. Some helpful journals in this area include the *Journal of Marriage and Family* and the *Journal of Family Psychology*. Assessments of couples can be used in the course of premarital counseling, and a good review of these tools may be found in Larson, Newell, Topham, and Nichols (2002). Readings on the topic that can be helpful for the clinician, the couple, or both include Gottman (1999), Gottman and Silver (2000), Schnarch (2009), and Wallerstein and Blakeslee (1996). John Gottman's books, especially Gottman and Silver (2000), can be useful tools for bibliotherapy during the sessions, with exercises and manageable chapter lengths.

References

Gottman, J. (1999). *The marriage clinic: A scientifically-based marital therapy.* New York, NY: Norton.

Gottman, J., & Silver, N. (2000). *The seven principles for making marriage work: A practical guide for the country's foremost relationship expert.* New York, NY: Three Rivers Press.

Larson, J., Newell, K., Topham, G., & Nichols, S. (2002). A review of three comprehensive premarital assessment questionnaires. *Journal of Marriage and Family, 28,* 233–238.

Schnarch, D. (2009). *Passionate marriage.* New York, NY: Norton.

Wallerstein, J., & Blakeslee, S. (1996). *The good marriage: How and why love lasts.* New York, NY: Grand Central.

Susan Heitler

Teaching Marriage Skills | 2

I am a psychologist in private practice whose marriage therapy treatment strategy includes a heavy dose of skills training. I write books for marriage therapists and for couples. I have been invited by many state therapist associations to give continuing education workshops on conflict resolution and marriage communication skills.

In addition, based on my book *The Power of Two*, I have written a workbook plus a curriculum for couples' marriage skills workshops. Lastly, I work for Torque Interactive Media, which offers Internet-based games and workshops where couples (and psychotherapists) can upgrade their collaborative dialogue and conflict resolution skills.

In the 60% of my time (3 days a week) that I devote to clinical work, primarily with couples, my skills-oriented treatment strategy rests on the assumption that if people knew better, they would do better. Backward-looking family-of-origin work strengthens people's understanding of where they learned their mistaken interaction patterns. However, for improvement in these patterns, most clients need explicit skill building. The three-part combination of teaching skills, exploring the family-of-origin sources of mistaken habits, and guiding couples to resolution of issues that have divided them has enabled my clinical practice to flourish free of managed care.

I focus most of the remaining 40% of my work hours on disseminating information about marriage skills to the general public and to marriage therapists. I have been particularly interested in developing online marriage skills-training materials that (a) teach couples the communication, emotional regulation, and conflict resolution skills that can enable them to enjoy a harmonious marriage and (b) boost psychotherapist effectiveness on conducting marriage treatment. Psychologists especially need training materials like these because of the dearth of marital and family therapy training offered in most psychology graduate schools.

My own interest in these areas began early on in my clinical training with the realization that psychotherapy is the art of helping people to resolve their conflicts, so psychotherapists need to be experts in conflict resolution. When the psychology literature did not offer this expertise, I turned to the literature on business negotiation.

I love teaching communication and conflict resolution skills because the results are so immediate and so gratifyingly obvious. I love when couples enter a session surrounded by clouds of tension and leave laughing together. I love hearing older couples in marriage workshops tell younger ones, "You are so fortunate. If we had learned these skills when we first married, we would have been spared years of needless tensions."

Insurance companies are often reluctant to pay for problems that are labeled *marriage dysfunction.* Diagnosing the problem as depressive and anxious reactions—which almost inevitably result when there have been marriage problems—and listing marriage therapy as the treatment modality is one solution. Alternatively, psychologists can choose not to accept insurance and instead charge clients directly for treatment. I use the latter option.

The main downside of offering marriage skills workshops is the significant marketing effort necessary to get a referral flow established. Also, workshops generally need to be scheduled during non–work hours. That generally limits workshops to weekday evenings or weekends, which can intrude on the psychotherapist's own leisure and family time. However, offering workshops one or two nights a week, one weekend a month, or every other month (or a combination of these) can substantially boost earnings. Many workshop participants decide that they want to continue their learning after their initial exposure to marriage skills training and may request further sessions with the workshop leader.

Most marriage education courses, including Power of Two Workshops, focus on skill development rather than on the content of couples' contentious issues. They also generally use a group format. Marriage workshops therefore tend to be a most appropriate, and least expensive, option for couples who mainly need a skills upgrade rather than help settling urgent conflicts or exploring deeply rooted problems.

Workshops and therapy can be used together, but they are not mutually exclusive. Marriage therapists may encourage their clients to attend a workshop to accelerate their treatment. Workshop leaders may likewise refer couples for therapy during or after completion of the course. It can be helpful to orient new clients initially to both options. That way, the therapist and couple can decide together if and when each option is appropriate.

With regard to related business opportunities, psychotherapists who are able to teach collaborative communication and conflict resolution skills can market to divorce lawyers, who tend to be a virtually untapped referral source. These attorneys can refer couples who prefer to fix rather than abandon their marriage and also postdivorce couples who need to be able to coparent more cooperatively.

Leading workshops actually can yield higher per-hour income than marriage therapy. One of the clinicians in our practice recently reported that teaching a workshop with five couples—her preferred workshop size—yields more than double what she earns per psychotherapy hour.

As I mentioned earlier, marketing is vital for building a marriage workshops program. Marketing can be targeted to engaged couples seeking premarital education, established couples seeking marriage enhancement, couples in therapy, as well as to specific high divorce-risk groups such as empty nesters and parents of special needs children. Marketing strategies can include posting flyers at obstetrics and gynecology practices, hairdressers, gyms, and wedding dress stores and using Internet or radio ads.

To conduct skills-oriented premarital or marriage therapy, one must first become expert in emotional regulation, cooperative communication, and conflict resolution skills. In addition to books, psychotherapists can download the free articles from my website (http://www.Therapy Help.com) and learn from free online games (e.g., http://www.po2.com, http://www.poweroftwo.org).

To teach workshops, psychotherapists can design their own course materials. It is preferable, however, to start with one of the many excellent existing curricula rather than to reinvent the wheel. The Smart Marriages website (http://www.SmartMarriages.com) offers an overview of the full field of marriage education, including listings of existing marriage education curricula. The Power of Two Marriage Skills Workshops program may also have opportunities for psychotherapists who want to teach Internet-based courses.

The bottom line: A good marriage enhances life's blessings—longer life, more happiness, health, wealth, and enjoyment. Communication and conflict resolution skills play a huge part in sustaining successful marriages. Psychologists have much to learn, and potentially much they can earn, in this important area.

Michaele P. Dunlap

3 Conducting Family Interventions With Substance Abusers

I am a clinical psychologist in a private practice group in Portland, Oregon. My partners and I supervise early career psychologists and work with adults, couples, and families. Treatment of alcoholics, addicts, and their relationships has formed 40% to 50% of my practice for more than 25 years. I have worked in a dual-diagnosis hospital and managed and provided treatment in a state-certified treatment program. I hold a Certificate of Proficiency in the Treatment of Alcohol and Other Psychoactive Substance Use Disorders from the American Psychological Association (APA) College of Professional Psychology. My practice is managed care–free. Many services I provide to chemically involved people and their families are paid out-of-pocket because people are aware of risks to privacy when they use a third-party payer. Conducting interventions is a subset of my work with addiction issues.

Intervention is a process in which people concerned about the behavior of a drug user or problem drinker focus their intention to change the user's behavior. Overall, there is good evidence that interventions can change the course of self-destructive behaviors, but the process is seldom without complications.

Hard-Sell Intervention

Hard-sell intervention by legal authorities and employers can be both coercive and effective. Hard-sell interventions may be ineffective when a user resists the coercion and accepts consequences of jail time or job loss. When interveners are friends or family, the intervention process is usually less coercive. Family interventions typically rely on relationship pressure and persuasion to prompt change in the user's behavior. However, family interventions with adolescents can be coercive when parents have legal authority to enroll the adolescent in a treatment program without the child's consent.

Some "specialists" focus only on interventions, offering their services on the Internet, arriving in a community to conduct a process in which they (a) meet with family and friends to discuss the history of the user's behavior, (b) rehearse roles to be taken by the family members and friends who participate in the intervention, (c) facilitate the intervention itself in the home of the user or in some other safe and familiar place, and (d) facilitate transportation to treatment and enrollment of the user. Fees for these services may be substantial. Treatment programs to which the user is referred or taken may be among the most expensive. Involving "specialists" can give a family the sense that they are following an "approved mode." However, following an intervention specialist's crisp prescriptive explanations for how an intervention "should be done" can sometimes backfire and lead to recriminations that reverberate through families for years. When beginning any intervention process, the motives and motivation of all parties must be fully considered.

Soft-Sell Intervention

As a psychologist trained in the complexity of addictive processes and family dynamics, I offer intervention services as a fluid and individualized process. I help family members support their loved ones toward detoxification, enrollment in appropriate inpatient or outpatient treatment, and mutual-help programs such as Alcoholics Anonymous, Smart Recovery, or Women for Sobriety. Interventions to support behavior change are sometimes sought by family members who "see a problem developing." Such early interventions can be extremely effective.

Family members may be self-referred through my print or Internet visibility or referred by a friend, physician, or mental health colleague. I charge for my time at my usual per-session rate. I encourage and support family members to do much of the research that gathers information about local, regional, and national treatment options to determine costs, availability, and program philosophies. Treatment programs' availability and affordability can vary widely and change frequently.

Preparation for the intervention process is focused first on the family members as "clients" and second on the behavior of and treatment venues appropriate for the drug or alcohol user. The process involves gathering history and descriptions of the problem behaviors and assessment of family members' willingness, ability, and resources to intervene. Family members seeking to change the user's behavior first need an understanding of the complexity of addictive behavior. Creating that understanding is an important professional task. Even the best-intentioned attempt to change a user's behavior can be sabotaged when family members do not understand that treatment is a process rather than a cure and that relapse may be an inevitable part of the process of change away from self-destructive behaviors. To be helpful to the family, the professional needs to know both the current state of affairs in the family and user's lives and what change attempts, treatments, or approaches have already been tried. The family needs to understand the variety of models and approaches to changing substance abuse behavior and to have a clear sense of which approach is most likely to help in their particular situation. Before the intervention, I work with family members to explore treatment options, whether inpatient, outpatient, private therapy, or mutual help, and we discuss the availability and affordability of treatment. Problems can arise when there is a large gap between family resources and the cost of appropriate treatment.

We consider approaches that may convince the user to enter a supported change process. Intervention only happens after family members have created the best plan they can to support the user toward change. The intervention itself may involve a family meeting in which I participate or more private conversations between the user and family members who have prepared an approach and strategies during their meetings with me.

Models of intervention in substance abuse are frequently based in disease theory. In the disease model, the user is ill and needs to be convinced to accept treatment for the illness. In contrast to the disease model, a harm-reduction model acknowledges that drug problems can be the result of serious life problems as well as a source of harm to oneself and others. This approach allows professionals who support interveners to assess each situation and to help create plans for treatment suited to the individual. While preparing for an intervention in the harm-reduction model, family members are coached in a nonjudgmental and collaborative approach that helps both the user and family explore the barriers to change and to choose among an initial range of options such as abstinence, moderation, or other short-term goals. When options are offered and change has begun, users frequently opt for abstinence after finding that moderation "doesn't work" for them.

To support family interventions, the professional must understand both addictive behavior and family dynamics. Experience with inpatient or outpatient substance abuse treatment is useful. Training in intervention processes and knowledge of treatment options is required. A biopsychosocial intervention supports both the family and the alcohol or drug user. Helping families intervene to improve the lives of those they love is rewarding work.

Resources

Denning, P. (2000). *Practicing harm reduction psychotherapy: An alternative approach to addictions.* New York, NY: Guilford Press.

Horvath, T. A. (2004). *Sex, drugs, gambling & chocolate: A workbook for overcoming addictions.* Atascadero, CA: Impact.

Marlatt, G. A. (1998). *Harm reduction: Pragmatic strategies for managing high-risk behaviors.* New York, NY: Guilford Press.

Miller, W. M., & Rollnick, S. (1987). *Motivational interviewing: Preparing people to change addictive behavior.* New York, NY: Guilford Press.

Lauren Behrman

4 | Roles for Psychologists in Collaborative Divorce Practice

M y professional journey has taken me through Veterans Administration and private psychiatric hospitals, outpatient clinics for children and adults, early childhood intervention programs, therapeutic nursery schools, diagnostic clinics, special education programs in elementary schools, and a postdoctoral program in child, adolescent, and family psychoanalytic psychotherapy. I began an independent solo practice in psychology part time 22 years ago while also working part time as a supervising psychologist at the Jewish Board of Family and Children's Services. With the onset of motherhood, I left my institutional affiliation and have been solely in part time private practice for the past 15 years while raising three children.

In the early years of independent practice, I spent 80% of my time treating and evaluating children and 20% of my time treating adults. Because the school-age children with whom I worked were in school until 3 p.m., my days were filled in the after-school hours, often into the evening. As my children transitioned into full days of school, I wanted to be spending after-school hours with them. At the 2000 American Psychological Association Convention in Washington, DC, I was searching for a practice niche that would allow me to move more of my practice into daytime hours and free myself from managed care. In a workshop on alternatives to litigated divorce, I first encountered a form of forensic coparent counseling and collaborative divorce team practice that captured my attention.

My current practice is now completely free of managed care and approximately 50% of my time is spent in these out-of-the-courtroom forensic activities. In this chapter, I highlight the collaborative divorce team practice that accounts for approximately 25% of my billable hours. Collaborative divorce team practice is a relatively new field that has grown out of the collaborative law movement. The collaborative divorce model is a paradigm shift in the culture of divorce—a shift away from seeing divorce as a battle to be fought and toward looking at it as a problem to be solved. It is a process in which each divorcing spouse is represented by his or her own attorney, and the two attorneys work together with their clients to reach a settlement without going to court. The attorneys actually sign an agreement stating that they will not go to court, and both must leave the case if either of the clients seeks litigation.

In collaborative divorce team practice, there is recognition that divorce is not simply a legal problem but a complex family transition and challenge on multiple levels. In many cases, a full interdisciplinary professional team is formed that consists of mental health coaches for each of the divorcing spouses, a neutral financial specialist, and a neutral child specialist. Together, the team functions to assist the couple in making a lasting agreement covering their parenting and financial plans to make a smooth transition for their family. As a psychologist on a collaborative team, one can function either as a divorce coach or a neutral child specialist. My training and skill set allows me to function in both roles on different cases. As a neutral child specialist, the psychologist meets with the divorcing parents individually, together, and with their children. We help them address their children's needs in this process and develop a parenting plan that will best fit their family. The child specialist brings these insights to inform the team in working with this family. In the role of divorce coach, the psychologist can work in either a one- or two-coach model. In the one-coach model, the coach functions as a process facilitator for the team and family. The coach meets separately and together with the divorcing couple and attends all legal meetings as a neutral participant who takes responsibility for the integrity of the process. In the two-coach model, each member of the divorcing couple has his or her own coach. In this model, the coaches may work individually with their client and in four-way coaching meetings with the other spouse and their coach. At times, the coaches are brought into the legal meetings to help contain the affect and facilitate the process.

To learn how to do this work, a number of additional professional trainings are required. The primary professional organization is the International Association of Collaborative Professionals (IACP), which offers introductory and advanced training for psychologists along with attorneys and financial professionals. Groups of collaborative professionals at the state level have formed that also offer training and networking opportunities. A 40-hour mediation training is required, and a basic 1-day introduction to family law for nonlawyers is required as well. Ongoing training is required to shift one's perspective to work in this way and to address the complexities of working within these multiple systems.

Referrals come from mental health colleagues working with couples and individuals who are looking for alternatives to litigation, as well as attorneys and financial professionals who bring cases from their practices. Referrals can also come from anyone in the community who is or knows someone contemplating divorce (e.g., friends, family members, clergy, school personnel, hairdressers). There are workshops and supports to build and market collaborative practice, and the IACP and state chapters maintain websites with the names of trained collaborative professionals in their area. Marketing one's collaborative practice begins with developing a clear, succinct message to deliver that describes your collaborative practice. Educating people about collaborative work by giving formal presentations in the community and telling people with whom you come in contact about the work is also a source of referrals. One can also send mailings to colleagues, attorneys, school personnel, physicians, and pediatricians describing this work. Hourly rates are commensurate with what the market bears for professional services in the divorce arena and are usually somewhat higher than psychotherapy fees. This is because the work is within the legal arena, and our fees for this work reflect the different role we take on, which brings with it more travel, need for flexibility in scheduling, and greater liability risk. Fees are collected at the time of service.

I have found the work to be challenging, stimulating, and rewarding. Helping parents resolve their disputes with a minimum of acrimony preserves their ability to coparent after divorce and protects children from being caught in the middle of parental conflict. In addition to a settlement, the team helps the divorcing parents develop conflict-resolution, joint decision-making, and problem-solving skills to take with them into their postdivorce lives. Working with professionals in related disciplines counteracts the isolation that one can find in a solo private practice and broadens and deepens your perspective.

To begin exploring this area, I recommend visiting the IACP website (http://www.collaborativepractice.org). Find the nearest local collaborative practice group in your area and contact them to find out when information meetings or trainings for new professionals are scheduled. If none exists in your area, you might want to locate practicing collaborative attorneys and explore the possibility of starting a practice group.

The IACP sponsors an annual convention open to both members and nonmembers every October. One may also gain knowledge and understanding of this area through reading books such as *Collaborative Divorce: The Revolutionary New Way to Restructure Your Family, Resolve Legal Issues, and Move on With Your Life* by Pauline H. Tesler and Peggy Thompson (2007) and *The Collaborative Way to Divorce: The Revolutionary Method That Results in Less Stress, Lower Costs, and Happier Kids—Without Going to Court* by Stuart G. Webb and Ronald D. Ousky (2007).

Nancy M. Sidun and Debbie Daniels-Mohring

5

Assessing Those Seeking to Adopt and Working With the Adoption Triad

L ess than 20 years ago, most adoptions were domestic and traditional confidential or closed adoptions. In these adoptive
families, the birth and adoptive parent(s) had no contact
with each other and only shared nonidentifying information
through an agency or facilitator. The adoption agencies tended
to match children and parents. Today, however, the trend is
to offer, encourage, or require an array of open adoption
alternatives for domestic adoptions. *Open adoptions* are most
commonly defined as those in which the birth parents or
other family members and adoptive parents share with each
other some sort of information about themselves and have
some sort of contact before or after the adoption takes place.

In addition to closed and open domestic adoptions, international adoptions have tripled since 1990. These adoptions
present a new challenge for adoptive families, because frequently the adopted child is of a different race and culture
than their adoptive parents; therefore, the adoption is visible
because nonmatching families stand out.

It is estimated that between 2% and 4% of Americans
have adopted children; that 200,000 children are adopted
yearly, domestically and internationally; and that there are
5 million adoptees in the United States. Experts have empha-
sized the importance for mental health professionals to understand the complexities of working with adoption issues and

adoption triad members (adoptees, adoptive parents, and birth parents). Unfortunately, adoption issues are rarely addressed in graduate psychology programs despite psychologists being involved in all levels of the adoption process, from assessment to treatment.

Assessment

Over the past 20 years, I (D. Daniels-Mohring) have developed a niche of providing psychological assessments for prospective adoptive parents. I also provide educational training for adults wishing to adopt children from the foster-care system. These activities comprise approximately 10% of my overall clinical time. I became interested in adoptive families after struggling with infertility. My husband and I were gathering information concerning adoption when we became pregnant, but I had, by that time, developed a relationship with a local adoption agency and started a dialogue with regarding the agency's need for assessments. All international adoptions and many domestic adoptions require a written psychological assessment of adults desiring to adopt a child. In addition, when agencies are conducting home studies and run into concerns, they often need further clinical assessment to decide whether to proceed with a particular individual or couple.

My assessments include the Minnesota Multiphasic Personality Inventory—2, a two-generational family history, and a clinical interview. I also review a copy of an autobiography written by each prospective adoptive parent. Unless a local department of social services requests the evaluation, the reimbursement is always self-pay. I only bill for my actual time spent interviewing, writing the report, and scoring. This usually amounts to 2 hours per evaluation. I meet with the individual or couple to review the results and discuss any concerns or questions I may have. I then write a brief (two- to three-page) report that is mailed to the adoption agency.

I enjoy this activity because of my commitment to adoptive families. It is an interesting change from doing clinical work and has provided an arena for developing a relationship with local agencies and departments of social services. The unpleasant parts of this activity are twofold: First, I must be very organized and efficient to make this activity cost-effective. Additionally, the rules for assessments differ from country to country, so attention to details of where the report must be notarized, what must be included, and so forth is important. Third, when findings are negative and I must tell prospective parents that I cannot recommend they proceed with the adoption, the discussion is often difficult and painful. Because my role is ultimately to advocate for the adoptee, the feedback is oriented around the best interest of the child. I often recommend that the couple or individual seek psychotherapy to help them deal with the issues that are impeding their readiness for adoption.

I would suggest that psychologists considering providing assessment services do the following:

1. Schedule informational meetings with local adoption agencies and departments of social services.
2. Tell the agency about the service you are willing to provide and make the process as seamless for them as possible. Most of these agencies do not have licensed clinical psychologists on staff and are looking to form relationships with those in private practice who are willing to work with them in a way that does not add to their workload.
3. Offer to provide training for the agency or for prospective adoptive parents on issues relative to their agency.
4. Make sure that you have received training in adoption issues and are familiar with the laws and regulations of the program with which you are dealing.

Working With the Triad

I (N. Sidun) started my work as a clinical psychologist more than 20 years ago, never having been introduced to the issues of adoption and never having considered the challenges for members of the adoptive triad. It was not until I became a member of an adoptive triad myself that I realized the depth of the issues that members face. The adoption experience affects every member of the triad, from attachment and identity development, to the concept of family, to relationships with peers and intimate relations. One of the greatest obstacles to the triad members finding solutions to these challenges is finding a mental health professional who understands adoption.

I have found through the years since my "awakening" and subsequent seeking of knowledge and training regarding adoption issues that my practice always consists of members of the adoption triad. I find working with adoption issues to be gratifying, in part because my clients are so grateful that someone understands their dynamics and challenges but perhaps more important because I feel like I am giving them quality care. Unfortunately, I've heard too many stories from my clients about times when they felt either not understood or, worse, damaged by previous therapeutic experiences.

Recently, I was working with a young adolescent girl from an open adoption. As this adoptee entered her adolescence, her biological parents wanted a more substantial relationship with her. Her adoptive parents were conflicted, wanting to support their daughter's connection to her biological parents but uncertain how to proceed and protect their daughter. Psychotherapy consisted of both family and individual work. The complexities of the issues were profound. Because of my knowledge about adoption, I was able to assist both the adoptee and her adoptive parents successfully though this journey.

Although training in adoption issues is not found in formal doctoral programs, training opportunities are available. The American Psychological Association (APA) Annual Convention has hosted continuing education workshops on adoption issues. Currently, APA's Division 17, Counseling Psychology, has an Adoption Research and Practice Special Interest Group that is open to any member interested in adoption issues. Professional journals have addressed adoption; specifically, a special issue of *The Counseling Psychologist* in 2003 and in 2009 a special issue of *International Social Work* on intercountry adoption appeared. Finally, an outstanding resource is Javier, Baden, Biafora, and Camacho-Ginerich's (2006) *Handbook of Adoption: Implications for Researchers, Practitioners, and Families* (published by Sage).

Brad Rosenfield

6

CBT Stands for Canine Behavior Therapy

Helping Dog Owners Become Better Parents

On a blazing summer day, I met my first dog, Peppy, my neighbor's new 2-pound Chihuahua. Peppy would have been irresistible to any 3 year old, especially one who had never had the opportunity to pet a dog. I still vividly remember the euphoria of gently stroking the tiny dog's head, his helpless, big brown eyes staring at me . . . and then the vicious bite that Peppy administered to my young hand!

Between the pain, the gushing blood, and my limited vocabulary, I could only scream "Why? Why?" Indeed, why had Peppy bitten me? I would later solve this mystery.

As a clinical assistant professor at Philadelphia College of Osteopathic Medicine and a clinical associate at the University of Pennsylvania's Adult Attention-Deficit/Hyperactivity Disorder (ADHD) Treatment and Research Program, most of my patients and students are of the two-legged variety. Nonetheless, as part of my private practice, I have also had the distinct pleasure of applying some techniques gathered from radical behaviorism to assist a large number of dog owners in resolving a wide variety of behavioral disorders in their beloved pets. To the knowledgeable psychologist, some of these disorders have familiar names, such as separation anxiety, depression, and pica. Thankfully, other diagnoses are not so familiar in our human patients, such the dreaded varieties of aggression: dominant, territorial, and predatory.

Diagnoses aside, the plethora of canine behavioral problems respond well to proper behavior modification. Initial assessment and training sessions are conducted in the home, which allows for the entire social and physical environment to be properly assessed and modified. The fees for this service are the same as I charge for psychotherapy in my private practice and are payable at the time of service. This avoids billing and third-party payer involvement.

Years of undergraduate and graduate work in operant and classical conditioning, research into the neurology of dogs, and my love for the species have led me to develop a unique neurobehavioral model of dog behavior. Techniques emanating from this model have been invaluable in helping dogs and their families. Outcome has been so positive that all referrals come from an assortment of veterinarians and satisfied former clients. Having an extensive background clinical psychology is also valuable in this line of work. More than 50% of clients have volunteered that at least one family member in the home has a diagnosed psychological disorder or that they could benefit from family therapy. Personality disorders in dog owners can also impede implementation of otherwise effective treatment recommendations. Ironically, effective treatment for dogs often involves addressing the obstacles that clinical problems produce. Although space constraints prevent adequate elucidation here, some simple examples of overcoming human obstacles to treatment effectiveness include setting alarms for training sessions (to aid forgetful owners with ADHD), cognitive reframing (to reinterpret a dog's urination behavior as "untrained" vs. "hostile and dominant"), or communication skills (both human–human and human–animal) to deescalate conflict or narcissistic reactance that can derail practice sessions.

It is not surprising that these clinical problems have escaped the notice of previous "dog trainers," thereby dooming treatment to failure. Consequently, because I have been able to problem solve these impediments, I receive many referrals from concerned veterinarians when other trainers fail.

Although I have never formally advertised, I have developed a simple and effective marketing strategy to facilitate referrals from veterinary professionals, based on fostering close, mutually beneficial professional relationships, as well as social psychological and behavioral principles. I have also been fortunate to be associated with James Bianco, VMD, a genius in the field who has created Ardmore Animal Hospital, a truly state-of-the-art veterinary facility with a superb staff of veterinary professionals.

Although my primary career is still a professor–cognitive therapist, many nights and weekends are consigned to my four-legged patients. Behavioral problems are the most frequent reason that people abandon their dogs to an uncertain fate in shelters. It is gratifying to know that helping a family to ameliorate their dog's behavior problems will likely save a life and prevent the grief associated with losing a pet, which can be the emotional equivalent of losing a family member.

However, this service can be dangerous. Dogs can bite, and the biter can range in size from a 2-pound Chihuahua to a lethal 165-pound mastiff. In fact, I am the only behaviorist or trainer I know who has not been bitten in his or her entire career. Additionally, liability may be an increasing risk because a plethora of attorneys advertise for dog-bite cases. However, even this risk brings opportunity because attorneys occasionally call on me for expert assessment and legal testimony. Providing expert testimony requires extensive understanding of dog behavior and professional experience to be able explain the fundamental human–animal interaction that may result in a bite injury.

Although good psychologists take pride in the fact that their interventions are brief and effective, producing satisfactory, objective results in an average of two to three sessions makes family therapy for dogs a different but much more efficient business model than traditional psychotherapy.

Most gratifying is the opportunity to train other professionals and provide regular consultation services to assist budding behaviorists to help dogs and their families. I have developed a formalized training program, including educational material, training videos, mentoring, and a proven marketing plan—a virtual "how to" for establishing one's own dog-training business. The program is designed to enable professionals to establish an evidence-based behavioral practice and generate referrals so that they can help to improve relationships between pets and their people and, ultimately, to save lives.

For additional information, see the following selected references or feel free to contact the author. He doesn't bite.

Professional Societies

Association of Pet Dog Trainers: http://www.apdt.com
International Association of Canine Professionals: http://www.dog pro.com
American Veterinary Society of Animal Behavior: http://www.avsab online.org/avsabonline

Books

Donaldson, J. (2005). *The culture clash.* Berkley, CA: James and Kenneth.

Miller, P. (2008). *The power of positive dog training.* Hoboken, NJ: Wiley.

Pryor, K. (2002). *Don't shoot the dog! The new art of teaching and training.* Gloustershire: Rignpress Books.

Silvani, P., & Eckhardt, L. (2005). *Raising puppies and kids together: A guide for parents.* Neptune City, NJ: TFH.

PSYCHOEDUCATIONAL PSYCHOLOGY

II

Myles L. Cooley

Conducting Academic Readiness Evaluations 7

'm a clinical psychologist in full-time private practice in a suburb of West Palm Beach, Florida. I began a part-time private practice more than 30 years ago following brief employment at a community mental health center. When my practice became full time, I shared office expenses for many years with two other psychologists. For the past 10 years, I've leased my own office suite and have been in solo practice. Until recently, I employed a part-time receptionist–secretary. I decided to decrease my expenses, however, and I eliminated this position. I now perform all administrative tasks myself. This was made possible several years ago by dropping participation in all managed care plans. The paperwork and appointments have substantially decreased, which provides the available hours during the week for administrative tasks.

Conducting kindergarten readiness evaluations is mostly seasonal, occurring between January and June as parents contemplate school and grade choices for the school year beginning in the fall. Although all children are eligible for kindergarten in public and private schools in respective states by a certain fall date, parents and preschool teachers occasionally question the readiness of some children. This work comprises less than 5% of my practice. There is a relatively limited demand for this service. First, the demographics of South Florida mean fewer young children as a percentage of the total population compared with many other areas of the country. Second, apparently only a small percentage of parents of prekindergarten children have questions about their children's readiness.

My interest in conducting these evaluations evolved from parents' requests to help them make decisions about kindergarten enrollment. Parents may have a general awareness of their child's academic, behavioral, social, and emotional skills, but they lack information about the importance of each of these domains in predicting kindergarten success. Much of the uncertainty surrounds children who appear skilled or advanced in one area but delayed in another. Adding to parents' confusion are different emphases placed on skills by teachers and parents. Research indicates that teachers believe social–behavioral skills are more important for readiness, whereas parents tend to emphasize academic skills (Ackerman & Barnett, 2005).

Studies have shown that kindergarten readiness tests do not have much predictive validity because they typically assess a single domain of behavior or skill. There are simply too many variables that can contribute to kindergarten success. Consequently, a more valid evaluation consists of an assessment of a child's cognitive, developmental, social, and behavioral skills. Some of this assessment is conducted by administering the tests that measure cognitive ability and basic literacy and conceptual skills. I use subtests from the Woodcock–Johnson Tests of Achievement III, Diagnostic Assessments of Reading—Second Edition II, and the Bracken School Readiness Assessment—Third Edition. Another part of the assessment involves a parent interview that solicits information regarding a child's social skills and tendencies toward compliance versus oppositional behavior. It is helpful to know which schools parents are considering because expectations, standards, and curricula for each school can vary significantly. Verbal or written information from the child's preschool teacher can also be an important piece of information in completing the assessment. Typically, the assessment can be conducted in 90 minutes.

Much of the satisfaction from doing these evaluations comes from educating parents about what is more and less important for kindergarten success. Assessing the various functional domains and generating a conclusion provides parents with a comprehensive understanding and rationale for their decision. Evaluations also offer an opportunity for myths to be dispelled, for example, that holding back or red shirting 5-year-olds will definitely be advantageous throughout their school years.

Another source of satisfaction is the ability to identify developmental problems that were not a part of the presenting question. Teachers and parents frequently report that a child may not be ready for kindergarten because of immaturity. Developmental maturity is variable and can be a bona fide reason for lack of readiness. However, I've found that the word *immaturity* is too frequently used as a catch-all by preschool teachers for significant developmental delays or weaknesses (e.g., attention-deficit/hyperactivity disorder, dyslexia). If not identified and addressed, some of these weaknesses will continue to cause difficulties in school regardless of how old the child is or what grade he or she is in. Identifying these difficulties at 5 years old can expedite necessary intervention.

Identifying developmental delays and disorders is where the value of training in child–developmental–clinical psychology plays a large role. This training is essential to distinguish our evaluations from those of teachers or other educators. As a result of our advanced training, we're more capable of identifying more serious developmental problems that might be exhibited.

These evaluations provide a good deal of professional satisfaction. Parents who present with the issue of kindergarten readiness for their child have typically been in a quandary regarding this decision for several months. Combined with the confusion created by differing opinions of teachers, other parents, in-laws, and the media, parents are motivated for some expert clarification. They usually appreciate these assessments' comprehensive, educated perspective. From a business perspective, the procedure couldn't be simpler because there is no billing or insurance involved. Parents pay for the evaluation during the consultation when feedback is offered. If parents want a written evaluation, there is an additional fee.

Referrals are generated primarily through word of mouth from parents as a result of other psychoeducational evaluations I've conducted with children. Referrals are also generated from schools that have previously received my evaluations. This is another reason for the value of training and experience in psychoeducational assessments. It creates credibility among parents and teachers. Psychologists interested in this work are advised to develop a reputation in the community among parents and schools as someone who is an expert in developmental, psychological, and educational issues of young children. This can be accomplished by offering to give talks to parent groups at preschools, community recreation centers, and religious institutions.

The following resources would be helpful for psychologists interested in these evaluations:

- Type Kindergarten Readiness Assessment into Google search. Protocols from various state departments of education can be reviewed.
- Education.com: http://www.education.com/reference/kinder gartenreadiness
- Gesell Institute: http://www.gesellinstitute.org (In my opinion, their bias is in favor of holding children back.)

- Parents as Partners for Kindergarten Readiness (Waikele, HI Elementary School): http://www.waikele.k12.hi.us/parent%20 information/kindergarten_readiness.html
- Ackerman, D. J., & Barnett, W. S. (2005). Prepared for kindergarten: What does readiness mean? New Brunswick, NJ: National Institute for Early Education Research. Retrieved October 29, 2009, from http://www.nieer.org

Reference

Ackerman, D. J., & Barnett, W. S. (2005). *Prepared for kindergarten: What does readiness mean?* New Brunswick, NJ: National Institute for Early Education Research.

Gary M. Eisenberg

Psychoeducational Testing 8

I operate a child clinical practice in Boca Raton, Florida, that is strongly rooted in psychoeducational testing. Approximately 50% of my time is spent in this activity. The other 50% is spent conducting psychotherapy and conducting workshops for professionals related to developmental disabilities in children. The overwhelming advantage of psychoeducational testing is that insurance companies will not pay for it.

I offer a plethora of psychoeducational and psychological test batteries. Contrary to some of the psychologists who complete a one-size-fits-all comprehensive battery for every patient, I customize my testing and fee to the referral question at hand. Most of my evaluations focus on evaluating for the presence of attention-deficit disorder (ADD), attention-deficit/hyperactivity disorder (ADHD), a learning disability, or autism.

ADHD evaluations involve a thorough history, IQ testing, screening for learning disabilities, screening for personality issues, and interview with an individual outside of the home (preferably the teacher). In addition, the Continuous Performance Test (CPT; Integrated Visual and Auditory, or IVA) and Conners' Rating Scales are administered to both teacher and parent. This battery is usually administered in four parts, starting with an interview with at least one parent and the child. Testing takes place over one longer testing session (2 hours) and usually occurs in the morning. An advantage of psychoeducational testing is that no negotiation has to take place about taking the child out of school. To be tested, the child must be removed from school. This allows the child psychologist an income-producing activity during the school day. This is important for practice development because daytime hours can be hard to fill in a child psychology practice. A second and briefer session may be needed to complete the testing. In addition, the child takes the CPT (a computer-based test) and the parent completes the Conners' scale under the supervision of the secretary whom I have trained. After all testing and interviews are completed, I schedule another meeting to meet with the parents to review the results. In the case of a teenager, he or she is also included in this feedback session.

Learning disability testing follows the same process just described but adds another 2-hour testing session for achievement and processing tests. Usually, the Woodcock–Johnson Tests of Cognitive Ability and Tests of Achievement are administered as part of this test battery.

Evaluations are also conducted to evaluate for the presence of autism. The method to complete this evaluation varies depending on the child's age and level of functioning. Generally, a full history from the parent is again required. An IQ test is necessary to assess intellectual potential and to estimate functioning level. High-functioning autistic children often have learning disabilities, so the learning disability tests described earlier may be incorporated in the assessment. Teacher observations of the child's behavior are essential to gather. A series of questionnaires is also completed by the parent, including the Asperger's Syndrome Diagnostic Scale, Children's Atypical Development Scale, Pervasive Developmental Disorder Behavior Inventory, and problem checklists as needed.

The advent of my psychoeducational testing practice grew out of my interest in child psychology. I believe that assessment is an essential service that child psychologists must offer in their practices. My practice has by and large been developed through personal contact with pediatricians and schools. I have found that the best means of promotion is to find any way and any excuse to make telephone contact with the child's doctor, teacher, school counselor, or other school personnel. The ostensible purpose is to inquire as to their observations of this child or perhaps discuss interventions. At other times, with parental permission, the individual is provided the test results. The underlying purpose is always to make myself and the services I offer known to these gatekeepers in hope of generating additional referrals.

I have found that direct marketing by approaching such individuals and "selling" one's services by and large falls on deaf ears. A busy practice begets a busy practice. Hence, it is better to approach these individuals when you are treating a patient whom you have in common. Talking directly with these professionals will make for a better professional connection.

Financially, these test batteries are charged out in a lump sum and not by the hour. The parents are told what the fee will be after the initial session. Parents are more likely to be flexible in paying after they have developed a rapport with the doctor. In addition, this practice charges a weekend differential should parents prefer not to take their child out of school.

Many parents are indignant and incredulous that these charges are not covered by insurance companies. This is the biggest source of tension for the secretary and the office. Testing is also termed *educational testing*. Insurance companies have no CPT five-digit code for educational testing. Hence, we bill it out as educational testing 90899. We also make specific reference on this bill to the fact that these are learning disability–based tests. *Learning disability* is a buzzword that will cause insurance companies to reject payment. Parents are forewarned that this will happen. Many times, if the child does have a DSM-IV diagnosis, such as ADHD, the insurance company will pay for the interviews. This includes the initial interview and the follow-up feedback interview. Sometimes, they will pay for the brief testing related to ADHD only, which might include the Conners' inventories and Continuous Performance Test (IVA).

Psychoeducational testing is a specialty. Should one wish to begin such a practice, he or she should seek supervision from an expert in the field. Further training can also be obtained by taking the continuing education (1-day course) offered on the Woodcock–Johnson tests by Riverside Publishing. The Woodcock–Johnson is an essential part of a learning disability evaluation. Hence, the manuals and interpretive books that come with the Woodcock–Johnson are essential to be learned and mastered. Supplemental books from the Woodcock–Johnson are also available.

Psychoeducational testing nicely rounds out my practice. I do all of the test administration myself. I am aware that some psychologists hire a psychometrist to administer many of these tests. Although the testing itself may sometimes be boring, it is often engaging to do this "detective work." Ultimately, psychoeducational testing is a hypothesis-checking procedure in which the psychologist eventually narrows down the issues to a clear diagnosis. The testing can at times be mindless (given that I have done this more than 2,000 times), but it can be a nice diversion from an afternoon of intensive psychotherapy.

Peter C. Thomas

9 Coaching for Attention-Deficit/ Hyperactivity Disorder

am trained as a school psychologist. After working 9 years for a local school system, I began a private practice. I have always shared office space with other professionals. Because of my training, a majority of my practice is taken up in conducting psychoeducational evaluations and psychotherapy with children, adolescents, and families. I perform custody evaluations as well. For about 10 years, I have directed and my wife has managed a coaching program called FOCUS (From Organized Coaching Ultimate Success). This is a service for adults and adolescents, most of whom suffer from an attention-deficit/hyperactivity disorder (ADHD) or an executive dysfunction. It accounts for about 1% to 3% of my income.

Many of the evaluations I am asked to complete are for the purpose of determining whether a child has a learning disability or ADHD. Over the years, as my practice has grown and the research in ADHD has expanded, it became obvious that many of the parents of children I was seeing also had the same disorder. The disorganization in the home caused by this often exacerbated these children's troubles. As parents became more aware of the similarities between their own and their child's behavior, they often sought relief from their symptoms. However, even when medication was prescribed, it was insufficient for changing long-standing behavioral patterns. Many of these parents needed daily support with their organization and planning skills. Psychotherapy alone was ineffective because it was not consistent enough. Exploring available resources revealed a coaching program developed by Edward Hallowell, MD, author of several books on ADHD, including *Driven to Distraction.* This program is oriented to helping people learn to problem solve effectively while modeling appropriate organizational structure.

Training was fairly simple. My wife and I spent 3 days learning his methodology. This included instruction from Dr. Hallowell and several coaches. Interaction with other participants interested in beginning a coaching program in their area of the country and role-playing the process prepared us for what lay ahead. Time was spent on the business aspects of a coaching business as well. Each participant received a packet of forms to be used or modified for his or her own purposes.

The coaching program is relatively straightforward. The charges are very affordable. This is because it is not psychotherapy. I do not provide the coaching services myself. The model involves hiring and training other individuals to be the coaches. This form of coaching is distinctly different from what many think of as life coaching. In its purest form, it is an organizational and training vehicle for individuals who need external support to get through their daily routine. The coach maintains a record of each contact and specific client objectives addressed each day. When the clients call the coach, they begin by providing their three top objectives to be met that day. The coach helps the client develop an organized plan of action by walking him or her through the process one step at a time. This modeling of problem-solving techniques ends with the coach providing the client with encouragement to get started and follow through. A majority of the clients find that over time, they begin to internalize the organizational techniques they practice daily with their coach. After several months of coaching, the rate of contact may be cut back according to the client's acquisition of these new skills. Eventually, many clients are able to coach themselves. However, there are some clients who use this service over several years. Coaching works well with people with many diagnoses that can disrupt their ability to concentrate, organize, and follow through. I have found it to be successful with individuals with an ADHD, depression, or problems interfering with efficient processing and executive functioning. After the initial contact with the client, which takes approximately 1 hour, the coaching process requires 5 to 10 minutes per day, 5 days per week. When I began this program, all coaching was performed over the telephone. With the proliferation of the Internet, we have been using e-mail, depending on the client's preference.

There is no need for an office visit, although there have been times when a client wants to engage in psychotherapy to explore aspects of his or her life that require more in-depth treatment. Under these circumstances, coaching becomes an adjunct to psychotherapy. This is an aspect of the coaching service that can be marketed to other clinicians as well.

Referrals come from psychotherapists, psychiatrists, my own practice, and other clients. Most aspects of this service are conducted over the telephone or Internet. After completing questionnaires and signing a contract, the client "meets" with his or her assigned coach over the phone. Billing transactions are by credit card, and the client pays in advance in 2-week increments.

One time-consuming aspect of my involvement in this endeavor is finding, training, and monitoring the coaches. The coach does not provide answers as much as he or she elicits solutions from the client. This role requires individuals who are bright, organized, and have a facility to listen well. Some training or interest in psychology is helpful. If you have found individuals with these attributes, you can expect to spend about 4 hours training them. You will need to check in with them on a regular basis for several weeks after that and then on an as-needed basis. Some of my best coaches have been students in master's- or doctorate-level clinical or counseling programs. Because they generally only work with one or two clients, the coaches' time commitment is minimal and the pay attractive.

Several groups offer coaching training. Should a practitioner be interested in offering this type of service, I'd suggest going online to discover what is available. This is an area that is in its fledgling stage regarding credentialing. I like Hallowell's coaching model because it is straightforward, and my time involvement is not overly taxing. It is important to grasp current latest research on ADHD as well. This will help the practitioner understand how clients' symptoms affect them.

Marketing can be the most difficult aspect of getting this service up and running. I was lucky enough to know a number of psychiatrists who were looking for something to augment their patients' treatment. They were looking for a service that offered the daily contact and organizational supports. Other coaches have developed elaborate websites or advertise with online coaching organizations. Either way, practitioners interested in this work will need to think clearly about how they want to target a referral base and spend the upfront time necessary to educate potential partners on what you can do for them.

Resources

Hallowell, J., & Ratey, J. (1994). *Driven to distraction*. New York, NY: Simon & Schuster.

Quinn, P., Ratey, N., & Maitland, T. (2001). *Coaching college students with AD/HD: Issues and answers.* Bethesda, MD: Advantage Books.

Ratey, N. (2002). Life coaching for adult AD/HD. In S. Goldstein & A. Ellison (Eds.), *Clinician's guide to Adult AD/HD: Assessment and intervention.* London, England: Academic Press.

Ratey, N. (2008). *The disorganized mind: Coaching your ADHD brain to take control of your time, tasks, and talents.* New York, NY: St. Martin's Press.

Mary Gresham

10 | Vocational Counseling

n 1988, when I began my private practice in Atlanta, Georgia, my goals were finding an office group and referrals. In Atlanta, the most common arrangement in private practice is for a group of solo practitioners to share office space but to maintain separate businesses. That is the practice arrangement that I have had for 20 years, although the locations and groups have changed on occasion. I continue with that model now and am sharing space with a social worker and a psychiatrist.

I initially began to do career counseling and assessment as a way to become known in the community and to offer a service that many doctoral-level psychologists did not. During my graduate studies, I enrolled in two courses in career assessment and did a practicum and my predoctoral internship in college counseling centers. University counseling centers are a good way to get supervised experience in career counseling. In addition, I took time off from my doctoral studies and worked for a psychologist who had a contract performing disability evaluations for Social Security. As his employee, I tested numerous clients using intellectual and personality instruments and wrote reports addressing work-related skills.

I took it upon myself to order a library of books related to my new area of interest. I particularly found Rodney Lowman and Harry Levinson to be good sources on career assessment and career development topics. I ordered a battery of testing materials: Strong Interest Inventory, Campbell Interest and Skill Survey, Myers-Briggs, 16 Personality Factors, Minnesota Multiphasic Personality Inventory, the Wonderlic, and the Wechsler Adult Intelligence Scale. I joined the National Career Development Association and the Atlanta Society for Training and Development. In addition, I researched local programs and discovered that Atlanta offered the Johnson O'Connor Abilities Battery testing to which I could refer when necessary. I referred to them in lieu of my taking on the testing for artistic, mechanical, or musical skills.

At this point, I was ready to advertise. I called and sent letters to psychologists and other psychotherapists and told them that I was now offering this service and would be glad to work with any of their patients who may need career work. I was clear that I would limit my consultation to career issues only and that both the referring clinician and the client would receive feedback from me, if that was acceptable to the client. Because a number of psychotherapists knew me personally, I believe that they were more comfortable referring to me specifically for career work. Most of the other career counselors were not in clinical practice and were not doctoral-level psychologists. I developed a protocol that consisted of an initial interview in which I asked about the client's current concerns as well as family work history and messages from family members about work. I included the family material because I found it interesting, and it added a valuable dimension not usually covered in typical career assessment. I constructed a customized test battery for each client. I integrated the results into a written report and scheduled a feedback session. At the end of the feedback session, I gave the client a copy of the report. I charged by the test and also for the hours that I spent with the client directly. The work is strictly fee-for-service because it is not covered by health insurance. Some clients elected to continue working with me on career issues on an as-needed basis. In general, I enjoyed doing this work because it focused on an area that I find interesting: How do people decide what work to do, and how does it turn out for them? What do people need to make work changes? How can I help them with this?

I do believe that Freud had a good recipe for well-being: to love and work effectively. I also find it bothersome that so many people spend so much of the day in work settings that slowly decrease their vitality as humans. What I like about this work is the opportunity to make a difference in people's daily lives. I did not really dislike anything about the work. However, I have slowly eliminated the testing side of career counseling so perhaps that is a way of noticing that I must not have enjoyed the testing side as much as I enjoyed the personal interactions. I continue to do career work and am interested in it, but I generally approach it now through interview and verbal interactions. I still administer the Campbell Interest and Skill Surveys on occasion, sending it off for computer scoring. I use that survey with women clients who are going through a life change (primarily divorces) and are confused about reentering the workforce. Over the years as my psychotherapy practice grew, I gradually phased out marketing myself as a career counselor-psychologist, but I do believe it has been a useful part of both my skill development and practice building.

I interviewed a fellow psychologist, Dr. Rick Van Haveren, who recently started his practice as a career-oriented psychologist so that I could get more up-to-date information for this chapter. He has built a website that advertises his specialty (http://www.careernavigator.net) and explains his work and his services. Like me, he got his start in graduate school and university counseling centers. Unlike me, he primarily uses online testing services and occasionally does not meet his client in person until the feedback session, having done most of the initial work in a thorough telephone consultation. He offers two general packages and will work with an individual to design a custom program based on his or her specific needs.

What Rick likes about career counseling is that it tends to be focused, short-term work that is immediately helpful to a client. His work is targeted both to students and adults, and he feels gratified in his ability to assist clients in solving a defined problem. What Rick finds difficult about this work is the long preintervention interactions over the telephone in which he answers complex and lengthy questions explaining how his work differs from that of a career coach. A psychologist who wishes to develop this specialty needs to be prepared to differentiate himself or herself from the mass of career coaches in the field.

Like me, Rick recommends the use of the National Career Development Association's training programs to develop competencies that are often not taught in psychology programs. Members receive a quarterly journal, access to a database of helpful online resources, and notification of conferences, and certification is available to become a master career counselor or a master career development professional. Many of the members of this organization are not licensed as professional counselors and work in the corporate sector. These are good contacts to help you gain referrals for employees who may be having work issues and need more intervention than the workplace can provide. If you feel that you are interested in this kind of work, you will be able to stand out in the field as a PhD because the majority of career counselors are licensed at the master's level.

Jeffrey Jones

Improving Interviewing Skills 11

am a psychologist who has been practicing in the Atlanta area since I graduated from Emory University with my PhD in clinical psychology in 1988. My professional development has been characterized by an evolving interest and expertise in child, adolescent, and family intervention. Initially, I worked for a nonprofit community counseling center where I hoped to develop a general and varied practice. Because I was willing to work with children and adolescents and my colleagues preferred working with adults, I saw most of our young clients. There was a significant need to see these clients. I experimented with group therapy, first with adolescents and later with younger children and developed my own style of interpersonally oriented group work. Later, when I initiated private practice, my reputation and interest in working with younger clients continued.

It was in 1995 when a number of issues and perceptions came together to compel me to create Beyond Words Center (http://www.beyondwordscenter.com) and leave managed care. My mentors, Marshall Duke and Steve Nowicki, had just published a book, *Teaching Your Child the Language of Social Success*, in which they identified deficits in nonverbal communication as contributing to a lack of social success. At that time, I was dealing with some frustration in helping some of my clients who were not fitting well in the psychotherapy groups that I was leading. Although some clients responded well to process-oriented feedback, others did not. The former group members had the basic skills but were not using them. The latter group members did not seem to have a clue about the basic behaviors that were involved in being socially successful. In consultation with a dear friend and developmental pediatrician Alan Weintraub, MD, I began to understand the issues of children who were struggling with symptoms on the autistic spectrum. I had the thought that these children and adolescents needed a psychoeducational approach rather than process-oriented psychotherapy. In other words, they needed direct social skills training.

The idea was to continue my psychological practice while creating a psychoeducational adjunct to meet the needs of children and adolescents who need basic instruction in nonverbal and other social skills. I hired a young woman who had recently graduated from college, and I trained her and supervised her work. As a result, we were able to offer a relatively low fee for her services. We quickly outgrew our two-office space when two other employees were hired, in addition to another social skills teacher and a social worker. We developed an extensive curriculum and an intervention model that really worked. Our relationship with Emory University has continued, and we have a body of research that supports the efficacy of our approach. Beyond Words has grown to an organization consisting of two psychologists, four master's-level psychotherapists, an office manager, a bookkeeper, and four practicum students.

The original idea of separating clinical (process) and psychoeducational (training) interventions has changed at Beyond Words. We are now an organization of staff clinicians who conduct psychotherapy groups. Hiring the best and the brightest right out of college did not work out as a successful business model because we continued to lose wonderful and well-trained employees every year as they left to attend graduate school. The amount of energy required to train new people every year was daunting, and the loss of expertise kept the organization from growing. Although all of our groups are psychotherapy groups and we no longer offer "classes" in social skills, we continue to understand that the needs of our clients vary and continue to offer psychosocial training.

One remnant of the original model remains. At some point in the history of Beyond Words, we created a tangential program focused on helping children who struggle with nonverbal communication skills to be successful in interviews. Local private schools often require an interview for admission and in most cases the competition is fierce. We offer four-session groups in the late winter when the application process is in full swing. The idea is to help our young clients gain comfort and competence in this interview process.

The four-session Interviewing Skills Program begins with an assessment with both the parents and child, exploring the details of the pending interview or interviews, the strengths and weaknesses of the child, and the establishment of a contract. The instructor then spends time with the child exploring his or her perceptions and getting comfortable with the process. They leave with an assignment: to find out as much about the school(s) and the interview(s) as possible. The next three sessions can be accomplished individually or in a group. The second session begins with a review of the homework and a discussion of how to prepare for the interview and what to expect. Next, the basics of nonverbal communication skills are discussed and practiced with exercises and role-plays. Skills such as eye contact, sitting still, and speaking in a clear voice are practiced. If a group interview is pending, skills such as turn taking, active and supportive listening, sharing, and sportsmanship are included. The students leave with the assignment to work with their parents on developing appropriate questions to ask the interviewer. The third session begins with a review and discussion of the homework. Then videotaped mock interviews are conducted with a psychotherapist, unfamiliar to the child, in the role of the interviewer. In the final session, the tapes are reviewed and discussed. The child receives coaching, and skills are practiced in role-plays.

We have also developed individually tailored interviewing skills programs. Although our program was designed for children and adolescents, older clients have sought intervention in this area. College students with pending admissions interviews and adults seeking employment have sought out and received training from us. We have learned to modify our curriculum to meet individual needs. A recent example involves a businessman who had been receiving feedback that he was gruff in his dealings with clients and employees. A series of mock interviews was set up and videotaped and viewed with the client as he was provided with suggestions and observations.

Providing training in interviewing skills is by no means a big moneymaker. The need for the service is seasonal, and the demand is relatively small. However, by providing such a service, a psychotherapist can increase exposure to potential clients. The Interviewing Skills Program is an example of a relatively small addition to an existing program that was created on the basis of a perceived need in the community. There may also be a demand in the community for applying this concept to other areas, such as interviews for employment, college, or professional schools. A number of new clients in our group psychotherapy program have come from the interviewing skills program. Conversely, the Interviewing Skills Program has proved to be a valuable adjunct service for some of our regular clients. The work can be rewarding, because immediate feedback is available regarding the success of the interview. Sometimes, even if not accepted to the target school, parents have informed us let that they have noticed improvement in their child's general social skills.

HEALTH PSYCHOLOGY

Lucille Keenan

A Fledgling Private Practice in Reproductive Medicine

12

My son has brought more than joy to my life. He has started me down a career path. After 3 years of soul-wrenching infertility, my husband and I finally conceived through assisted reproductive technology (ART), specifically through in vitro fertilization (IVF). Although the end result—a beautiful, healthy, funny baby—was everything I'd hoped for, the process leading up to it was fraught with uncertainty, fear, feelings of inadequacy, and, stunningly, not much emotional support at the first clinic we went to, one of the leading infertility clinics in the nation. As I went through the process, I thought about how hellish it really was and wondered what it must be like for other women.

I earned a master's degree in counseling psychology from University of Southern Mississippi in 1994 and a doctorate in clinical psychology from George Washington University in 2006. In my downtime after delivering my son, I studied and passed the Examination for Professional Practice in Psychology and began planning the opening of my private practice, Cameron Park Psychotherapy and Assessment. About 6 months after the birth of our child, my husband started law school, and I started practicing part time. I am a solo practitioner in a building that houses only mental health professionals, a convenient walking distance from our house.

The commute is ideal, and the building was built specifically for the purpose of doing psychotherapy.

As a result of my own experience and based on the observation that there truly appears to be a dearth of qualified support in the community, I decided to form a specialty in reproductive medicine in addition to a general psychotherapy practice working with adolescents and adults. Captured under the rubric of reproductive medicine are issues that include infertility, pregnancy, postpartum depression, and attachment and bonding with a new infant. Assessment of anonymous egg donors, known egg donors, and gestational carriers is also part of a practice in reproductive medicine. About 50% of my time is spent on fertility-related work.

Although clients are each immersed in their own particular set of circumstances that interacts with their own personal psychology to form a unique experience, my own experience with infertility heightens my interest in this specialty area and gives me some understanding of what some infertile women may feel. Beyond the intense and personal nature of infertility, I found it and my associated emotions interesting from a clinical perspective. I had a somewhat unique opportunity to observe myself as I was winding down my own psychoanalysis. Looking back on that time, although I benefited greatly from my analyst's support, for this aspect of my life and only this aspect, I wish my analyst had been female and had been trained in reproductive mental health, because the concerns of an infertility population are quite specific.

When it came time to think about what I wanted to contribute to the profession, I knew I wanted to provide treatment to fertility patients, but I did not know where to begin. I sent out a query to the New Psych listserv about starting a fertility-related private practice and received good feedback. The best advice was to join the American Society of Reproductive Medicine (ASRM) and the ASRM mental health listserv, and to read *Infertility Counseling* (Covington & Burns, 2006). More advice followed: Attend the ASRM conference and use that opportunity to find a mentor. In fact, for formal mentoring, attending the ASRM conference is mandatory. Unfortunately, I was unable to attend because I could not leave my child at the time. Fortunately, however, I did query the ASRM mental health listserv and stated my interest in starting a fertility-related practice. Then one of those small, occasional miracles occurred. A local specialist in infertility was on maternity leave with her son and contacted me after seeing my query. She offered me informal mentoring and advice. We corresponded as we returned to work, and she eventually became my supervisor for the fertility portion of my practice. She works in a fertility clinic at an academic medical center and tends to provide a fair amount of referrals because this clinic is busy.

I draw from a number of previous experiences to inform my fertility-specific clinical work. My prior work includes psychotherapy groups, psychoeducational groups, and support groups; diagnosing and treating mental disorders; psychological assessment; sexual counseling; family psychotherapy; staff consultation and treatment team participation; and crisis intervention. All of these experiences are recommended for infertility counselors and listed in the ASRM qualification guidelines (http:// www.asrm.org/Professionals/PG-SIG-affiliated_Soc/MHPG/ MHPG_Guidlines.pdf). ASRM guidelines also include couples counseling, training in the medical and psychological aspects of infertility, as well as a minimum of 1 year of supervised experience providing infertility counseling.

My fertility-specific training thus far has consisted of observing my supervisor conduct psychological evaluations of anonymous egg donors and then performing the work in my own setting. In the near future, I will observe her perform known donor evaluations and gestational carrier evaluations and then conduct those evaluations independently. My supervisor has also referred fertility patients needing psychotherapy. As soon as I am trained in more aspects of fertility patient care and feel confident in my skills, I will market to fertility clinics, obstetrics and gynecology offices, and infertility agencies.

Evaluations are interesting because the population tends to be young and relatively psychologically and physically healthy. The primarily benevolent and altruistic motives of many women wishing to donate are heartwarming. Psychotherapy cases are difficult but rewarding because the work often involves life-and-death issues: grief work around giving up the dream of having a biologically related child or even bearing a child, losing a child in the last trimester, or repeated miscarriages or failed treatment cycles. Psychotherapy can assist a single woman in deciding whether to proceed with donor sperm or a help a couple negotiate the emotional intricacies of using a known donor for eggs or sperm.

Currently, I am not on any insurance panels. The clinic for which I do evaluations pays me directly through my credit card billing system. Many fertility patients are devoting considerable resources to their fertility treatment, and so finding money to pay full fee for psychotherapy treatment is difficult, even though the woman or couple may desperately be in need of services. To provide this psychotherapy, I am considering signing up with some insurance companies. However, my evaluations cannot be reimbursed by insurance.

I hold an undergraduate degree in advertising. I approached my private practice as a business and as a training opportunity because I am still pursuing licensure. I brainstormed business ideas with other psychologist friends who found themselves in the same position or a little further ahead. Acquiring a professional-looking website was one result of my discussions. I built my own website using Go-Daddy.com and their Website Tonight program. The program is designed to allow non–tech savvy people to edit their own materials easily. Additionally, I joined a public speaking support group, Toastmasters International, to enhance my ability to give prepared talks because I plan to visit clinics and market myself. My supervisor for my nonfertility practice is a specialist in couples therapy, an important skill when working with patients struggling with infertility. I also attend regional and statewide formal and informal meetings of psychologists and belong to a local chapter of PsychologistMoms@ YahooGroups.com, all with the purpose of networking and building my referral resources. I am activating my licensed professional counselor license in North Carolina so that I can bill Medicaid and other insurance companies that do not allow a provisional provider on their panels.

To repeat the best advice given to me when I first started out: Join ASRM and find a mentor or supervisor through the Mental Health Professional Group (MHPG) training program if you are considering this field. The work is fairly technical and specific to a population dealing with infertility and fraught with possibilities for legal action if one inadvertently operates outside the bounds of competence. The MHPG listserv within ASRM is helpful. Books I recommend are provided in the references that follow.

Resources

Covington, S., & Burns, L. (2006). *Infertility counseling: A comprehensive handbook for clinicians* (2nd ed). Cambridge, England: Cambridge University Press.

Domar, A., & Kelly, A. (2002). *Conquering infertility: Dr. Alice Domar's mind/body guide to enhancing fertility and coping with infertility.* New York, NY: Viking Penguin.

Ehrensaft, D. (2005). *Mommies, daddies, donors and surrogates: Answering tough questions and building strong families.* New York, NY: Guilford Press.

Lombardo, M., & Parker, L. (2007). *I am more than my Infertility: 7 proven tools for turning a life crisis into a personal breakthrough.* Orlando, FL: Seeds of Growth Press.

Peoples, D., & Ferguson, H. (2000). *Experiencing infertility. An essential resource.* New York, NY: Norton.

Marc B. Lipton

Smoking Cessation
Cognitive Behavioral Strategies With Hypnosis

13

have been in solo private practice for the past 37 years. I became interested in helping people stop smoking cigarettes based on my own experience with smoking. Upon graduating high school, I was awarded a National Science Foundation Grant to spend the summer before college at Roswell Park Memorial Institute in Buffalo, New York, a cancer research and training hospital. I spent the summer learning about cancer and watching in amazement people dying of lung cancer lying in bed smoking cigarettes. Before leaving for college, I confronted my father, a three-pack-a-day Camel smoker, with everything I had learned during the summer about the dangers of smoking. He didn't listen, became angry at my strident lecturing, and informed me he planned to continue smoking. As would any intelligent 17-year-old male angered by not being taken seriously by his father, I immediately started smoking as "payback" for his ignoring my advice. Twenty-three years later, I was smoking three packs of Marlboro Reds a day. I stopped smoking when my father died 9 hours and 20 minutes before his retirement at the age of 64 from pancreatic cancer. Writing this chapter is particularly timely because I am now 64 years old.

Providing individual, conjoint, family, and group psychotherapy can be rewarding but also frustrating because the efficacy of treatment is often hard to determine. Assisting people to stop smoking is gratifying from a number of perspectives. It provides a clear demonstration of the effectiveness of your intervention; the patient has either stopped smoking or not. Most important, getting people not to smoke cigarettes represents a greater contribution to their overall health status than any other psychological or medical intervention short of an acute resuscitation. Spending the time to develop and incorporate smoking cessation services into your private practice will have long-term benefits in helping you escape from dependence on managed care. Health insurance does not provide reimbursement for smoking cessation services. This has a benefit to your practice because you can charge a reasonable fee for your services even if your patient is insured by a managed care company with whom you participate for the provision of more traditional mental health services. Given the millions of adults who smoke cigarettes in the United States, there is a large number of potential patients.

From a clinical perspective, three populations of smokers will present themselves for your assistance. The first is a group of relatively healthy smokers who haven't tried to stop before and are looking for an "easy" fix using hypnosis. The second is a group of highly addicted people who have tried every program available to stop smoking and failed and are now, as a last resort, seeking hypnosis. The third group, sometimes self-referred but more often sent by their doctors, particularly cardiologists, oncologists, and pulmonologists, are those who have been formally diagnosed with a tobacco-related illness such as lung cancer, emphysema, or atherosclerosis and who are still smoking despite their life-threatening condition.

When initially contacted on the telephone I immediately convey the following: "I do not march you in the office and do hypnosis. Hypnosis is the cherry on the cake, not the cake. I am a clinical psychologist, and I spend our first session determining the best way to assist you and then develop a plan specifically tailored to help you stop smoking. The average person takes between two and four sessions to stop smoking."

The biggest pitfall that must be addressed with all clients asking for assistance to stop smoking relates to their expectations of hypnosis. I inform them that hypnosis can make the difference between success and failure but does not work at all unless all the other "ducks" are lined up correctly. I then perform the identical initial evaluation I do on any patient I treat. I take a mental status, a detailed psychosocial history, and evaluation for signs of any form of emotional difficulty with particular attention to issues of anxiety or depression because these disorders are incompatible with smoking cessation. Approximately 90% of those who continue to smoke after being diagnosed with serious ailments have significant issues with depression and anxiety. Similarly, the percentage of depression and anxiety in the second group of prior treatment failures is approximately 50%, and in the group of first attempters the percentages are much lower, about 30%. I refuse to continue to work toward smoking cessation with someone whom I determine needs treatment for anxiety or depression but declines to obtain help. I explain this to the patient on the basis that I would consider it unethical and a waste of his or her time, energy, and money because my experience has shown that long-term abstinence from nicotine is unlikely with untreated depression and or anxiety. I offer to provide treatment services or a referral to a colleague if that is his or her preference.

My approach in helping people to stop smoking is to inform them that they are about to embark on one of the hardest things they will ever do in their life, and they have to challenge themselves to tolerate their discomforts. I ask them to view themselves as "Rocky" fighting the "Russian," never giving up and resolving to win. I explain nicotine addiction, psychological addiction, cravings in the form of spontaneous recovery of a conditioned response, and emphasize that the day they stop smoking they are "ex-smokers" with the task of "entertaining themselves" until enough time passes for them to be craving-free rather than "trying" to stop smoking. I also suggest they set themselves up by telling everyone they respect that they are going to stop smoking and that they can "take it to the bank" that they will never be seen with a cigarette again. I train them in visualization and ask them to practice 20 minutes daily in preparation for hypnosis. I explain our hypnosis work as conditioned learning for the purpose of reaffirming their conscious resolve to remain nicotine-free. I suggest that they develop pride in their own capacity to tolerate discomfort and reassure them that their success at smoking cessation will generalize to other challenges in life requiring tough-mindedness and tenacity.

The primary issue in developing your specific approach to smoking cessation is to remember that you must increase motivation and tough-mindedness in your clients. Failing to do so, regardless of what else you incorporate, will not produce the success rate you are seeking. In this regard, it is essential that you evaluate your clients' defensive structure. I have found that denial and intellectualization protect people from feeling the danger of their potentially lethal habit. Breaking through these defenses is essential to increase the realistic fear that any smoker should have.

Approximately 15% of my practice hours are spent in helping people stop smoking. My hourly fee for smoking cessation is almost twice that provided by managed care insurance for individual psychotherapy. Regardless of income, clients almost universally respond when told the fee is $150 a session with, "Doc, with the amount of money I spend on cigarettes, I will make that up in no time."

Smokers know smokers, and once you succeed in helping one person stop smoking, they send all of their friends for treatment. I strongly suggest you work with the less difficult group of clients before sending a letter to local physicians informing them you can assist their patients to stop smoking. I started by sending letters to general practitioners, family physicians, and internists. I introduced myself as being trained in smoking cessation and expressed a willingness to provide treatment if they had patients desiring this. As my skills developed, I also sent letters to pulmonologists and cardiologists. Be aware that they will send you their most recalcitrant patients, and you will have to be well practiced in smoking cessation treatment before taking them on as clients.

If you have no training or exposure to hypnosis, I suggest you consult with a colleague who does to obtain supervision when first doing this work. You do not have to obtain certification as a hypnotherapist to do hypnosis for smoking cessation. All you need is a demonstration of various induction techniques and to select a smoking cessation script. There are many scripts that are easy to find. Remember, there is no magic in the "black box"; it is your relationship with your patients and your ability to educate and motivate that will help them stop smoking.

Cigarette smoking remains the leading preventable cause of death in the United States. There is no greater contribution you can make to the public health than to develop a smoking cessation program in your private practice. You can increase your income, gain freedom from the burdens and limitations of managed care, and add to the diversity of your clinical interests and activities.

If you would like more formal training or information about hypnosis, contact any of the following groups recommended by American Psychological Association, Division 30, Society of Psychological Hypnosis: American Board of Psychological Hypnosis (c/o Gary R. Elkins, PhD, ABPH, Department of Psychiatry, 2401 South 31st Street, Temple, TX 76508), American Society of Clinical Hypnosis (http://www.asch.net), International Society for Hypnosis (http://www.ish-web.org), and Society for Clinical and Experimental Hypnosis (http://www.sceh.us/).

Nona L. Patterson

Cognitive Therapy Groups for Weight Management

14

I have been in private practice over the past 16 years, after having worked at the local community mental health center for 3 years. I earned my doctorate in clinical psychology from the California School of Professional Psychology–Fresno in 1989, after having received a master's degree in psychology, with an emphasis in applied behavior analysis, from the University of the Pacific. I am a solo practitioner who shares an office suite and receptionist services with three full-time psychologists.

I became interested in obesity and weight management over the past 3 years as a consequence of becoming involved with performing preoperative psychological evaluations for bariatric surgery. In preparing myself to perform these evaluations, I did a great deal of research in the area of obesity and the components of effective weight management programs. I learned a great deal from these patients about what had worked for them in the past and what had not. I was amazed by the success that these individuals could have in losing such large amounts of weight, often more than 100 pounds, only to regain the weight in a short period of time. Over the past few years, I have developed interventions, handouts, and homework assignments to assist these patients in making changes in their behavior and cognitive thought processes. Many of these patients did not have a diagnosable "disorder" but could benefit from additional work to increase the likelihood of success following surgery. In addition, I was frustrated with the limited resources offered by the majority of the bariatric surgery with which practices I worked that offered "support groups" consisting of 40 to 50 people gathering in an auditorium once a month with a speaker. Many of the patients I saw complained that these support groups did not meet their needs. At the same time, patients in my practice often discussed concerns about and frustration regarding their attempts to lose weight. I found myself repeating information over and over again in a psychoeducational manner, but given patients' other issues, it was often hard to maintain the necessary focus and structure on their weight-related issues. Much like my past work among patients with borderline personality disorder, I found it difficult to teach the necessary skills in session and felt that the skills could be more efficiently and effectively taught in a group setting. During consultation groups with other psychologists performing bariatric evaluations, it became clear that we shared the same frustration in terms of lack of resources for these patients, and thus we decided to develop a program combining cognitive behavioral principles, mindfulness skills, and behavioral modification techniques.

In developing the group, we used the work of Judith Beck (2007) and Karen R. Koenig (2005). In addition, we incorporated mindfulness skills (Albers, 2003). The Center for Mindful Eating (http://www.tcme.org) is a great resource in terms of written materials, recorded audio education programs, and teleconferences. In addition, we have found the stories and metaphors from *Eating in the Light of the Moon: How Women Can Transform Their Relationship With Food Through Myths, Metaphors, and Storytelling* by Anita A. Johnston (2000) to be helpful as well.

The Take It Off/Keep It Off Program consists of two, 8-week workshops. Each workshop is led by two doctoral-level clinical psychologists and is limited to 10 participants. Take It Off is an 8-week workshop during which participants identify problem areas; learn to identify thoughts, feelings, and behaviors associated with eating and weight loss difficulties; and learn new cognitive, behavioral, and mindfulness skills. Keep It Off is an 8-week advanced workshop that builds on what was learned during the first workshop. Participants continue to refine cognitive, behavioral, and mindfulness skills; address the relationship between food and feelings; and explore body image and self-esteem.

The workshop costs $320 per 8-week group session, 50% due at the time of registration with the balance due at the first group session. It is important to have patients pay ahead of time given the nature of this group, because it is easy for patients to become discouraged and drop out. When they have prepaid, their likelihood of attending is increased even when discouraged.

We decided to break the group into two sessions, because we found patients hesitant to make a 16-week commitment. We have found that those who are active participants in the first 8 weeks are eager to sign up for the second group session. We market the group to bariatric professionals in the community as well as to mental health professionals and have found brochures in our own waiting rooms to be one of the most effective marketing approaches. We are also marketing to primary care physicians (PCPs), which allows us to develop further collegial relationships with family practice doctors. We send information to PCPs along with our bariatric presurgery psychological evaluations or with other correspondence with PCPs who seem eager for resources. In addition, we advertise the groups in a collaborative marketing publication that serves as a resource for professionals and clients providing information of available psychotherapy groups in the Charlotte, North Carolina, area.

The program is not intended for individuals with substance abuse problems or severe eating disorders. It is recommended that participants with these issues be enrolled in individual psychotherapy (either before or concurrent with participation in group) to address underlying issues associated with these patterns while using the group to learn healthy lifestyle skills. The biggest drawback of offering this program is the same as for any group: it is often difficult to get enough patients together to start a group at the same time. This is particularly true among this patient population. When overweight patients are motivated to get started, they do not want to wait a month or two because the motivation may have waned or they may have moved on to another treatment modality. In our practice, we have four psychotherapists and offer an evening and lunchtime group, with a new group available to start each month.

References

Albers, S. (2003). *Eating mindfully: How to end mindless eating and enjoy a balanced relationship with food*. Oakland, CA: New Harbinger.

Beck, J. S. (2007). *The Beck Diet Solution: Train your brain to think like a thin person*. Des Moines, IA: Oxmoor House.

Koenig, K. R. (2005). *The rules of normal eating: A commonsense approach for dieters, overeaters, undereaters, emotional eaters, and everyone in between*. Carlsbad, CA: Gürze.

Johnson, S. S. (2000). *Eating in the light of the moon: How women can transform their relationships with food through myth, metaphor and storytelling*. Carlsbad, CA: Gürze.

Kirk D. Little

15 | Neurotherapy

I am a licensed psychologist and co-owner with my wife, Laurie Little, of an independent practice in northern Kentucky with four full-time psychologists, a full-time billing coordinator, and a full-time receptionist. We have been in operation since 2002 and currently see approximately 900 new patients per year for assessment and treatment.

In 2006, I began offering neurotherapy, which is best understood as operant conditioning of the electroencephalograph (EEG). Also called EEG biofeedback, or neurofeedback, this procedure enables patients to observe their brainwaves on a computer screen, providing continuous feedback on how their brain is functioning. The EEG is first quantified and compared with a normative database (quantitative EEG; QEEG or "brain map"), and abnormalities are observed, helping to target specific problem areas for treatment.

The procedure involves connecting neurofeedback equipment to the patient with sensors. Safe and painless, the sensors are attached to the scalp with conductive paste. The brain's electricity is transmitted through the sensors to an amplifier, which translates the signal into a computer image.

By using neurofeedback to become aware of how their brain works, patients can learn to change and control their brain wave patterns to improve their brain function. This decreases their symptoms and improves their overall well-being. When the desired brain state is produced, a positive image is generated on the computer screen in the form of mind-conditioning games, such as racing cars or jumping fish. Thus, psychologists are well situated to perform this treatment because their standard training has given them the necessary understanding of conditioning and learning theory.

Neurotherapy has been shown through research and clinical experience to successfully treat patients with a wide variety of neurological and psychological disorders such as attention-deficit/hyperactivity disorder (ADHD), epilepsy, learning disabilities (LDs), substance use disorders, traumatic brain injuries, depression, anxiety, and insomnia. Many of my patients come to me after having tried standard psychological and psychiatric treatments with less than satisfactory results.

My two main areas of interest in practice have been neuropsychological assessment and pediatric health psychology. After having assessed and treated many children with ADHD and LDs, I became frustrated with the limits of what I was able to do to help reduce the core symptoms. I searched for ways to have a more powerful impact on patients' functioning and discovered I was able to do that through neurotherapy.

Before starting my work with patients, I went to a week-long intensive training with Joel Lubar, considered one of the fathers of neurotherapy, especially for children with ADHD, and the field's most prolific researcher. I also purchased equipment and practiced using it on myself for 6 months. I read the relevant literature and had Dr. Lubar supervise all of my work for 2 years. I also met all the requirements for certification by the Biofeedback Certification Institute of America (BCIA), which included completing hours of supervised neurotherapy experience and passing an extensive written examination.

Having a background in neuropsychology is good preparation for understanding brain–behavior relationships and functional localization, and the transition is easier if the psychologist has experience in neuropsychology or health psychology. It requires 2 years of extra training and supervision to become proficient, including a test if one chooses to earn BCIA certification.

Currently, 60% of my clinical time is spent on this activity. Because neurotherapy is considered experimental or unproven by insurance companies, despite much scientific evidence of effectiveness, it is not accepted by third-party payers. The QEEG or brain map is a one-time charge. The sessions are paid for on a fee-for-service basis. A typical course of treatment is 40 to 60 sessions, depending on the severity of the problem.

Marketing neurotherapy has been mostly done through my website and by contacting local physicians; former patients have also been a strong referral source. The physicians who have seen the positive effects from the treatment refer other patients. We have found that marketing to physicians directly, rather than to the general public, is most cost-effective. All patients who enter our office can read information packets that are displayed in the waiting room and may share them with others who they think may find the service to be helpful.

Resources

BOOKS

Schwartz, M., & Andrasik, F. (Eds.). (2005). *Biofeedback: A practitioner's guide* (3rd ed.). New York, NY: Guilford Press.

Demos, J. (2004). *Getting started with neurofeedback.* New York, NY: Norton.

Robbins, J. (2008). *A symphony in the brain: The evolution of the new brain wave biofeedback.* New York, NY: Grove Press.

Budzynski, T. H., Budzynski, H. K., Evans, J. R., & Abarbanel, A. (Eds.). (2008). *Introduction to quantitative EEG and neurofeedback: Advanced theory and applications* (2nd ed.). New York, NY: Academic Press.

Thompson, M., & Thompson, L. (2003). *The neurofeedback book.* Wheat Ridge, CO: Association for Applied Psychophysiology and Biofeedback.

PROFESSIONAL SOCIETIES

The International Society for Neurofeedback and Research: (http://www.isnr.org) and The Association for Applied Psychophysiology and Biofeedback (http://www.aapb.org) are the premier neurofeedback and biofeedback membership associations.

The Biofeedback Certification Institute of America (http://www.bcia.org) is the standard certification agency in the field for Biofeedback and Neurofeedback.

JOURNALS

The Journal of Neurotherapy is the official publication of the International Society for Neurofeedback and Research and is published by Routledge/Taylor & Francis (http://www.tandf.co.uk/journals/titles/10874208.asp).

Applied Psychophysiology and Biofeedback is the official publication of the Association for Applied Psychophysiology and Biofeedback and is published by Springer Netherlands (http://www.springerlink.com).

BUSINESS PSYCHOLOGY

Nicole A. Lipkin

Executive Leadership Coaching 16

E quilibria Psychological and Consultation Services, LLC, a private practice that I started, opened its doors in 2005. At the time, I was working at another organization as my "day job" but transitioned into a full-time private practice in less than a year. My business grew rapidly, and within 6 months I expanded into a group practice. We are now a midsized group psychology practice with four divisions: child services, adult services, forensic services, and business consultation and coaching services.

While managing the group practice, I have developed my personal practice to include organizational and business consulting, executive and leadership coaching, and team-building and assessment services for executives, leaders, and entrepreneurs. I spend approximately 40% of my time operating and growing all divisions of the business and 60% of my time providing direct services, including coaching, consultation, writing, and public speaking.

I am now building my executive and leadership coaching services for several reasons. First, coaching services fall outside of the claws of managed care. Coaching work is performed on a fee-for-service basis—either privately or through an organization that retains me to consult with them or coach one or more of their executives or leaders. Second, coaching is strength based and focuses on an individual's potential. We look at who they are, who they can be, and who they want to become. Third, coaches are exposed to talented and inspiring individuals who are seeking their help to perform at better levels. Given this strength-based approach, coupled with these other factors, I often leave coaching sessions feeling uplifted and invigorated. Fourth, coaching work is billed at a per-session or package rate and tends to be significantly more lucrative than general psychotherapy work. Fifth, coaching work allows for more flexibility than a traditional office-based practice. Most coaching is performed over the phone, allowing me to be in any location (e.g., overseas, on a beach, in the garden wearing flip-flops) as long as excellent phone service and equipment are available, and I can remain focused and attentive in my surroundings. Technology now can enable one to provide services nationally or internationally.

Although this is a positive, it can also serve as a challenge because psychologists are used to in-person work. Another challenge to note is that executives and leaders have problems too, and a variety of issues can surface (e.g., depression, anxiety, familial problems) in addition to their work-related goals. Coaches need to be careful not to take on the psychotherapist role and to know when to refer to treatment, even if they are capable of handling the psychological issue. Psychotherapy falls outside the scope of coaching work, and the line needs to be drawn at the beginning of the engagement.

I was equipped to begin this area of practice because of my educational background (PsyD, MBA) and various professional experiences. However, I wanted additional training to increase my confidence and develop my coaching-related knowledge base. I enrolled in the College of Executive Coaching, one of many educational programs geared toward developing coaching skills and advancing individuals in this profession toward certification through the International Coaching Federation. The certification is not mandatory but provides solid education and training to enhance coaching skills and adds another credential to help one stand out in an already popular and inundated field. The education and training includes in-person and telephonic classes, 50 hours of coaching experience, and completion of one's own coaching with a faculty member/coach.

As an executive coach, I help develop current and emerging leaders and high-potential talent in organizations that they work for or the businesses that they run. My philosophy is that people who are at the top of their game are in touch with their multiple "selves" as athletes, intellectuals, adventurers, artists, and leaders. My role is to be a thought partner or catalyst to hone these leaders' attributes so that they can reach new levels of personal and professional performance, talent, and success. When people's talents and inner attributes are fully realized and integrated, work becomes aligned with passion, and individuals and their organizations thrive. For example, I was able to help one of my client's overcome his personal and professional obstacles related to starting his own business and embrace his "inner entrepreneur." After working with him for several months, he took the plunge and opened up his business, eventually leaving his full-time job. Not only is he satisfied with his decision, he is also thriving and healthier because he is focusing on and using his strengths and talents.

Building a coaching practice is similar to creating a successful psychology practice. Developing your reputation as a talented, progressive, and ethical coach is imperative to your credibility in the field and to receiving steady and viable referrals. You also need to be a smart and creative networker and marketer of your services. This includes having a high-quality, optimized website; attending networking events; engaging in social networking; developing speaking opportunities; and writing articles or books about coaching in human resources, management, and business online and print publications. For example, I recently completed writing a book titled *Y in the Workplace: Managing the "Me First" Generation* (Career Press) about Generation Y in the workplace. Authoring a book like this will produce opportunities to offer workshops and seminars on the topic and will undoubtedly trigger viable referrals. Marketing also means that every time you step out your door, the potential of meeting someone who could benefit from your services or knows someone who can is right there. Be prepared to talk about how you can help and how, given your unique skill set, you are best equipped to help organizations and leaders accomplish their goals.

There are several steps you should consider if you are interested in pursuing a career in executive and leadership coaching. First, I recommend interviewing psychologists and nonpsychologist coaches who are active in this field about their professional experiences and experiences building a practice. Second, obtain education and training experiences to develop coaching skills. Numerous programs are available that can help build the foundation. There is a list of programs available on the International Coaching Federation's website that can provide the training necessary to earn certification in this field or provide continuing education. In addition, several organizations are available to enhance networking and education opportunities. These include APA Division 14 (Society for Industrial and Organizational Psychology), American Society for Training and Development (ASTD), International Coaching Federation (ICF), and other local organizations may provide connections in one's community to begin building a presence as an executive coach.

Finally, because coaching is such a booming industry, numerous books are available describing the coaching process, various coaching theories and styles, and how to go about building a coaching practice. Three books that I have found to be especially helpful are *Personal and Executive Coaching: The Complete Guide for Mental Health Professionals* by Jeffrey E. Auerbach; *The Psychology of Executive Coaching: Theory and*

Application by Bruce Peltier; and *Co-Active Coaching* by Laura Kimsey-House, Karen Kimsey-House, Henry Sandahl, and Phillip Whitworth. Interested psychologists should make it a point to begin educating themselves about business. I suggest making it a habit to read business periodicals, such as the *Wall Street Journal*, the *Harvard Business Review*, and other business resources to become knowledgeable of changes and terminology in the business world that could affect clients.

In my experience, pursuing a practice in executive coaching and leadership development has been highly rewarding. The income from my group practice allows me to build my coaching practice at a pace with which I'm comfortable. I'm surrounded by high-functioning, talented individuals within an "industry" that allows for a flexible lifestyle, free from the arms of managed care.

Elizabeth K. Carll

Responding to Trauma in the Workplace

17

Although virtually unheard of until the 1980s, trauma intervention services have increasingly become a necessary component in dealing with the aftermath of violence in the workplace. Workplace violence is often thought of in terms of homicide and suicide. However, it may also include a variety of incidents, such as threats, vandalism, equipment sabotage, personal conflicts among employees and supervisors, and hostage taking.

Trauma psychologists and consulting psychologists with a focus on stress management are in a unique position to develop workplace violence intervention services as a specialty within their practices or as a separate business entity. Specialized training is required to offer appropriate services and also to distinguish between psychological first aid following a violent incident and psychotherapy. In addition, psychologists who have had experience in the treatment of domestic and intimate partner violence will find their experience helpful because a significant number of workplace violence incidents involve situations in which a partner follows a worker to his or her place of employment. These confrontations are especially dangerous situations because it is not unusual that they result in homicide and suicide.

In the 1980s, specialized graduate school programs in trauma, violence, and disaster did not exist, and training workshops were conducted by experts. With the increasing reports of accidents and violence in the community, the need for crisis intervention following disaster and violence became apparent. As a result, in 1990, I established the first statewide volunteer disaster mental health network in the nation for the New York State Psychological Association and coordinated it for 10 years. The network also provided training. In addition, in 1991, I proposed the formation of a national network to the American Psychological Association to respond to the emerging need and served on its National Disaster Response Advisory Task Force for 7 years.

Since then, state and national disaster response networks have become commonplace and especially helpful in the wake of large-scale incidents such as the September 11 attacks. The visibility of psychologists onsite in the aftermath of crises has also demonstrated the value of psychological intervention. Having experience with large-scale community disasters, as well as my prior consulting experience with smaller workplace violence incidents and organizational stress, has been helpful in the evolution of onsite services.

Following a workplace violence incident, psychological first aid is needed to stabilize the workplace and identify individuals needing additional services. Providing crisis intervention services onsite for a company requires different skills than providing psychotherapy in one's office. In addition, follow-up psychotherapy for those requiring more intensive services may be provided by the consultant(s), or referrals can be made to appropriate practitioners. In larger organizations, this responsibility may be provided by the company's employee assistance program (EAP).

Typically, crisis response specialists will negotiate a written agreement with a company as to the types of services that will be provided, including fees, the specified number of days for the intervention, and any follow-up. In addition, follow-up services may be provided after 3 or 6 months to evaluate the aftermath. From my perspective, a violence prevention plan should be developed for a company following an incident, if one does not already exist. However, smaller companies often view the likelihood of a subsequent violent incident as unlikely and may not recognize the need. A summary report is provided for the company about the services provided and needs met.

Referrals in the aftermath of workplace violence may come from a variety of sources, including by word of mouth, referral by EAPs, publications a CEO may have read, or through human resources associations. I have been contacted through a variety of sources, including through the recommendation of a previous client I had seen for individual psychotherapy who was an executive with a company that had experienced violence in the workplace.

Some managed care organizations (MCOs) have attempted to provide onsite crisis response services. However, it is difficult to expect providers who have not met to be able to operate as a team, and therefore, the services may not be as effective. Because my practice is fee-for-service, I have not provided crisis-response services through an MCO.

One of the main difficulties in developing a workplace violence specialty is the need to be able to respond with minimal or no notice, usually within a day or two. Ideally, such a specialty works best if one has a part-time practice and can devote additional days responding to emergencies. Eventually, as referrals increase for onsite crisis intervention, a decision will need to be made whether to go in that direction full time or expand to a group practice or limit it and maintain a clinical practice. In my practice and consulting, I have been providing crisis intervention services as an adjunct service for 20 years because I decided to maintain a clinical practice.

Unlike other types of business consulting, workplace violence is a sensitive issue for companies, which typically expect confidentiality for services rendered and may go to great lengths to prevent incidents from being reported in the news. Hence, consultants should not list the companies for which they have provided services in a marketing brochure as is commonly done for other services, unless they have obtained permission to do so. As a result, marketing of workplace violence intervention services is somewhat different from other organizational consulting in which corporate client lists may be included to highlight experience.

Although crisis intervention work can be exciting and rewarding, it requires flexibility, availability, the ability to work well in an unstructured and sometimes tumultuous environment, and a calm, reassuring demeanor. Training is essential and can be obtained through workshops, conferences, and institutes. The resources that follow are included for those interested in learning more about responding to workplace violence.

Resources

Carll, E. K. (1999). *Violence in our lives: Impact on workplace, home, and community.* Boston, MA: Allyn and Bacon.

Carll, E. K. (Ed.). (2007). *Trauma psychology: Issues in violence, disaster, health, and illness: Vol. 1. Violence and disaster; Vol. 2: Health, and illness.* Westport, CT: Praeger.

Denenberg, R. V., & Braverman, M. (2001). *The violence-prone workplace: A new approach to dealing with hostile, threatening, and uncivil behavior.* Ithaca, NY: Cornell University Press.

Federal Bureau of Investigation. (2004). *Violence in the workplace.* Retrieved from http://www.fbi.gov/page2/march04/violence030104.htm

Kelloway, E. K., Barling, J., & Hurrell, J. (Eds.). (2006). *Handbook of workplace violence.* Thousand Oaks, CA: Sage.

David R. Starr

18 | Employee Assistance Programs

I am a psychologist in independent practice. My training is in counseling psychology, and my background is in community mental health and general rural psychology practice. I practiced in rural eastern Oregon for 22 years before moving to southwestern Idaho. The practice had been successful, and the kids were grown. My wife and I agreed that a new adventure in work and locale might be fun. I am licensed in both states and maintain offices in Nampa, Idaho, and Ontario, Oregon. My practice consists of assessment, consultation, relationship coaching, and employee–family assistance programming.

The employee–family assistance program stems from a contract with a large local employer. It is a confidential information, referral, and short-term counseling program that is available to all company employees and their dependants at no charge to them. I also conduct substance abuse assessments as part of a random screening program and provide management consultation and supervisor training. From time to time, I am requested to complete fitness for duty assessments as well. Overall, the activity represents about 15% to 20% of my clinical practice.

I was initially recruited in 1986 by a nationally known employee assistance program (EAP) provider to represent it within an industry local to my area. I had a background in counseling psychology, including vocational services. My dissertation was in occupational stress and burnout. I had extensive training in group dynamics and organizational consultation, including specific training with National Training Laboratories. It was a good fit for me, the company, and the EAP.

Originally, I was paid a retainer to make sure the services were regularly and competently administered. In 1991, the EAP provider decided to go into the managed care business and abruptly changed the method by which it compensated me from a reasonable retainer to a paltry hourly rate. I was familiar with what the local industry paid for the service, and I figured I could provide the service independently and save the client money. After all, I was doing all the work, and I was maintaining the community liaisons. I paid the "no compete" fee to the original EAP that was part of my contract with them and offered the local industry a direct contract, which was accepted.

Much of my activity over the years has been maintaining relationships with the industry managers. My practice was in a small town, and many of my contacts occurred while attending kids' ballgames, waiting in line at the supermarket, and attending other community events. The usual considerations for dual relationships in small towns were always in consideration. The industry was one with which I was personally familiar. I had worked in the wood products industry in many capacities for years while I was in high school and college. I understood many of the ins and outs of the work issues, family issues, and community issues, and I think that was appreciated by my client.

Most referrals begin with a phone call from an employee, an employee dependent, or a manager or supervisor. Individual and family referrals usually involve psychotherapeutic intervention related to stress, depression, anxiety, relationship or family problems, or substance abuse. Supervisors and managers make referrals for fitness of duty evaluations generally involving substance abuse or threat of violence issues.

Over the years, this part of my practice has mostly been fun. It has offered me the opportunity to participate in applied psychology practice without having to always orient my thinking by the medical–mental illness model that pervades most clinical and counseling psychology practice. Many consultations consist of social support and sharing of information, often without the need for or use of clinical diagnosis. Occasionally, I have been confronted with a referral in the frozen foods section or by a phone call late at night, but that has been rare and not particularly unpleasant. There really has never been a downside to my doing this type of work.

I maintain local and toll-free telephone lines. I have two local associates who subcontract with me to provide some of the services. Referrals arrive usually by self-referral by employees and their dependents, who are regularly educated by the employer about the availability of the program. Managers and supervisors also make formal and informal referrals. Formal referrals are most often an outgrowth of potential discipline at work—that is, the employee's work performance has deteriorated to the point that the supervisor has decided that behavior change will be necessary for the employee's continued relationship with the company. The informal referral is when the supervisor refers the employee to the EAP out of concern for the employee's general wellbeing. I am paid quarterly in advance by automatic deposit from the company. The contracted fee is based on the number of employees on site times so much money per month. There is no billing for individual contacts. Some quarters have higher or lower utilization rates than others, which I suppose affects how I'm paid per hour. This issue is regularly and openly discussed with the client managers. The rate of utilization has always fallen within expected rates published in the literature for rural manufacturing settings. I list the client company and subcontractors as also-insureds on my liability policy. I provide the company with simple two-page quarterly reports emphasizing current utilization and projected annual utilization. The reports are clear and simple to prepare.

My recommendation for developing this type of practice activity would begin with identifying community boundaries and the industries that function within them. It has been a real plus to know the people personally who manage the company. Of course, this is easier in a rural environment. Second, I would focus on industries with which I was personally familiar. I think that improves the credibility of the psychologist with the decision makers when negotiating contracts. It is important to learn the going rate large companies on the national scene are charging for this service. Over the years, I have been involved with managed care organizations that have openly shared this information during contract negotiations. I have also informally discussed this issue with friends and associates in human resource roles in other companies. Once the going rate is known, it is fairly easy to offer a better, more personable service at a much lower cost. It helps to be visible in your community with managers, supervisors, and employees. If the psychologist is seen as a more or less regular person, then people really become more comfortable using the service.

The core services of an EAP are part of all psychologists' training. It is important to be able to communicate verbally and in writing. I have observed the highest utilization factors to involve relationship, marital, and family issues. Training in these areas is certainly helpful. Training and competence in chemical dependency issues are helpful as well. Most general practice psychologists have the skills to do this work. Specific training or continuing education may be necessary in the areas in which one does not feel adequately skilled. For those interested in learning more about EAP work, consider browsing the website of the Employee Assistance Professionals Association (http://www.eapassn.org/public/pages/index.cfm?pageid=1), read articles from the *Journal of Employee Assistance* and the *Journal of Workplace Behavioral Health* or read *EAPs: Wellness/Enhancement Programming* by Michael Richard, William Emener, and William Hutchison (2009, published by Charles C Thomas).

Daniela E. Schreier

19 | Stress Management for Corporations

I am a licensed clinical psychologist, licensed clinical professional counselor, and certified stress management consultant. I obtained my doctorate in clinical psychology with specialization in multicultural and forensic psychology at the Illinois School of Professional Psychology in Chicago. I am the lead psychologist of S.M.A.R.T. Living, LLC, a psychological cooperative focusing on individual and organizational stress and life management and forensic and clinical evaluation and interventions. I have held a core faculty position in the Department of Counseling at the Chicago School of Professional Psychology since 2008.

Approximately 50% of my practice is spent consulting and providing stress and life management skills to corporations. My activities consist of presenting to, and talking and consulting with, upper management. Once contracted, I provide a needs assessment and then create a customized program based on these data. Training and implementation follow, with emphasis on stress management workshops, wellness talks, and prevention-oriented activities. Other programs and services that I provide include group and individual coaching and seminars on how to deal with difficult work situations. A primary goal is to offer healthy means of dealing with stress, especially providing an alternative to substance abuse as a means of coping.

My first career was in international marketing. My background is international, having worked for 10 years in South America, Southeast Asia, Europe, and, finally, the United States. I am quite familiar with the stressors in diverse industries and businesses, including the ever-increasing demands on management and employees. I have experience with how individuals worldwide avoid dealing with work-related stressors and how companies often ignore the importance of prevention and mental well-being. Personal issues can severely affect the quality of work performance and vice versa. The work environment (e.g., the architecture of workspace and flextime) is an additional influence that affects the ability to focus. My interest in these issues grew out of my own work experience.

I enjoy all aspects of these activities. My services are customized according to the need of each company. At times, this is a great challenge, but a rewarding one. For example, it can be difficult blending the various concerns of the human resources department, management, and the workforce. It is these varied concerns that are addressed by my customized approach.

Many of my clients contact me via the Internet; others approach me following lectures. In addition, I launched an active marketing campaign. Recently, many referrals have come by word of mouth. I work on a retainer basis or develop other payment options (usually 70% up front, 30% postintervention). A company on retainer is billed every 3 months; otherwise, a portion of the fee is billed before rendering services.

Most important is the development of a marketing strategy. It is vital to view our work as a business. Become comfortable with preparing proposals, customizing packages for corporations, giving talks, and being informed about the business world, particularly those institutions that might become potential customers. Start by finding out about the business setup and potential employees' and employers' needs. What's going on in the industry at the time you approach them? How is the company doing in the market? Then contact the human resources department and offer your potential services. Follow up with a customized marketing package to introduce yourself and your services. Follow up again with a phone call, and try to set up a personal appointment or a "free talk." Act like a businessperson. If you are unfamiliar with the demands of selling your services, there is no harm in taking some business classes at a local university. The business environment is a fast-paced one, and any reluctance to deal smoothly with businesspeople must be overcome. Become familiar with coaching techniques and stress management techniques. It is a different mind-set—a different game plan—and you must understand it if you want to play. It is not a place for the shy or withdrawn; relating well to others and self-confidence are requirements. Being multilingual is a plus, especially if you work with multinational corporations. Familiarize yourself with the culture of the industry in which you wish to work. Do not be too broad in your endeavors. Learn about one sector first—and try to choose an area that interests you. Having product knowledge is a must and helps in making connections.

Most of my resources are European; preventative treatment programs in the workplace and treatment for burnout are well established in Europe. Helpful books and articles include literature on relaxation and stress reduction, autogenic training, positive psychology, meditation, and emotional intelligence and how they apply to different business cultures. Websites such as The Stress Management Society (http://www.stress.org.uk) and International Stress Management Association US (http://www.isma.org.uk/site/isma/content-folder/home) can be useful in developing ideas, exploring resources, and finding applications for this work. The *International Journal of Stress Management* (http://www.apa.org/journals/str/) may help to generate ideas for interventions in various aspects of the business world.

Kathleen V. Shea

Consulting to Family-Owned Businesses

20

All experiences shape us, and one of the wonderful educational experiences of my life occurred during my freshman and sophomore years in high school. I was the president of a Junior Achievement Club named the Porky Pig Step-Up Company. We made a stepping stool pig out of wood with plump sides, a flat back for the step, leathers ears, and a leather tail. We painted on the eyes and nose. The purpose of this product was to help small children reach the sink as they were brushing their teeth and washing their faces. The other purpose of this little manufacturing company was, of course, to keep many young teenagers busy and learning the art of manufacturing, sales, marketing, and teamwork.

Our Porky Pig Step-Up Company was sponsored by a local business that was family-owned. On occasion, the family members would stop by the Junior Achievement Building and help us make these strange little creatures. We were a successful company and won some awards. As a reward for our successes, we were invited to lunch and to visit the sponsor's manufacturing company. We were driven in a Rolls Royce to this huge facility and toured the premises from the board room to the manufacturing floors. Our guides were the actual family members sponsoring our Junior Achievement Club. It was the Wacker family of Chicago who sponsored this activity.

What was most impressive, both then and now, is how many different people can work together in achieving one goal to make a product in demand. The experience was the backdrop for my lifelong fascination, intrigue, and admiration of family-owned and family-run businesses. I have consulted to more than 50 such businesses and have sat as an advisor to the executive boards of more than 10.

Family-owned businesses (FOBs) make up 40% of all businesses in the United States. They include manufacturing and service businesses such as law offices, medical offices, service stations, entertainment and recreational entities, and now Internet businesses. Family dynamics are familiar territory for psychologists. The exercise of power, authority, and competency in a family emotional system is often similar to the dynamics found in an FOB.

Some familiar family conflicts are acted out in these organizations, and the ramifications can be devastating. Some of the issues are conflicts around the preferred son or daughter or the least preferred son or daughter, sibling rivalry, the family scapegoat system (e.g., an obviously dysfunctional member tolerated by all other members, with the dysfunctional member carrying the psychological burden of all family members), and entitlement issues around using family business resources for personal use. Birth-order dynamics are often present regarding the firstborn and first, second, and third generations of the FOB. All have different issues such as, "How can our original little family business support all of these people?" Finally, family members earning more compensation than nonfamily members while doing less work is an issue that often has to be addressed and repeatedly confronted.

These are only a few of the conflicts that require intervention from a skilled clinician. Other areas are succession planning, separating the family use of resources from the business resources, and establishing agreed-on policies and procedures such as job descriptions and retirements. Another dynamic found in FOBs is the direct lineage members pressured to outperform nonfamily member hired professionals.

A well-trained psychologist can bring skilled interventions to create an atmosphere of problem solving, team building, and a sense of objectivity to the FOB. Some of the interventions are personality assessment and feedback, examining basic assumptions about entitlements, and conflict management and training in "win–win" outcomes. Other effective interventions of skill building include assertiveness training, anger management, and assigning memberships in outside networking organizations with image-building tasks.

I received front page notoriety from the *Wall Street Journal* because of my research on the psychological health of high-achieving people. From this, I was appointed by the president of the United States, Ronald Reagan, to the Volunteer Advisory Board of the American Red Cross at National Red Cross Headquarters in Washington, DC. I served for

15 years on the board and worked on leadership and Equal Employment Opportunity affirmative action committees. This board-level experience serving a public not-for-profit national institution gave me insight and an opportunity to refine my skills in group work, process management of projects, and influencing change through consultancy processes. Other volunteers were owners of FOBs, and we discussed their generational and managerial approaches to running businesses. Throughout the 15-year experience with the American Red Cross, I focused on decision-making processes in groups. This was a foundational experience for developing one of my skill sets. Psychologist skills in observation, self-neutrality, and research lend well to volunteer experiences in community organizations, boards, and charitable groups.

Consulting in FOBs offers a broad range of challenges. It is different from consulting in businesses where employees are fired for poor performance or nonattendance because these family members are known as "members of the lucky sperm club" by the regular, nonfamily employees. They will never be fired because they are the organization's future leaders. The consulting process is the creative and constructive vehicle in which the consultant brings the family members into the journey of full performance and participation in the legacy building of the founder's dream of his or her original family business.

Resources

Family Business Magazine: http://www.familybusinessmagazine.com

Fleming, Q. (2000). *Keeping the family baggage out of the family business.* New York, NY: Simon & Schuster.

Lansberg, I. (1999). *Succeeding generations: Realizing the dream in families in business.* Cambridge, MA: Harvard University Business School Press.

Ward, J. L. (1990). *Keeping the family business healthy.* San Francisco, CA: Jossey-Bass.

SERVICES TO GOVERNMENT | V

David Lutz

Vocational Rehabilitation Assessments

21

have been in private practice for 28 years. I have always been in an office that housed from 5 to 15 practitioners. Initially, I shared staff with the other practitioners, but 7 years ago, I took over my practice completely, and I now do my own scheduling, billing, and all other duties associated with my practice. In addition, 10 years ago, two colleagues and I built the 7,800-square-foot office building in which we reside. We rent out 2,500 square feet to a dentist, another 1,900 square feet to accountants, and we inhabit the remaining space.

I built my practice initially on conducting individual and family psychotherapy. Although this practice developed nicely in a 5-year period, I moved in 1987 from Southern California to southwestern Missouri and needed to start over. Shortly after the move 21 years ago, I began doing evaluations for the Disability Determinations (DD) office of Social Security in a role as a consultative examiner (CE). This activity began through the good graces of another psychologist, one who worked at DD as a psychological reviewer and who asked if I would be interested in working as a CE.

My DD work continued steadily until 7 years ago, when DD in our area reduced the use of CEs drastically. I lost from 50% to 70% of this business, which was a major blow because DD work comprised 70% of my private practice income. At that point, I looked for other opportunities, which led me to start working with vocational rehabilitation (VR). I knew one person within the agency who was highly supportive of VR who had used me as a CE. VR also has a close relationship with DD, and the people at DD recommended me. It was a process that included several fits and starts but eventually developed into a consistent component of my practice mix.

Learning the VR work did not take any special clinical training experiences. Instead, this work built on my strengths, especially from my pre-doctoral internship, which had a heavy assessment component. I would have started earlier with this type of work, but I did not know that the agency contracted with psychologists. Once I did start working with VR, I learned the necessity of working quickly in all aspects of my interactions with the agency. This means scheduling claimants ideally within 10 to 14 days and no longer than 21 days. After the individual is evaluated, the report needs to be returned to the agency within 2 to 3 days and no later than 1 week. If I can give them overnight service, I do so. This entailed my developing a system that involved a speedy turnaround, a process not typically taught in our academic training. Thus, although I had been trained clinically, I needed to learn the business side of maintaining a relationship with my referral sources. That is, quality service delivered in a timely manner is what is important to them; therefore, it is important to me.

The referral and billing processes are straightforward. VR looks for CEs within certain areas. I work in a metro area of about 400,000 but could likely have more work if I were willing to travel a couple of hours to rural areas. If VR values the report and you can get the information back to them quickly, they are likely to use your services with greater frequency. I was told early not to write a report with many intrapsychic references and numerous qualifiers and hedges but instead to write a clear, behavioral report that answered the referral question directly. For VR, it meant, "What psychological and/or learning difficulties hamper the individual from obtaining employment?" After the report is completed, it is sent to the agency. The billing is included, and reimbursement is received 3 to 6 weeks later.

Doing the assessments suits me well. They are focused with a clear purpose and are behavioral in nature. I can compartmentalize them much more than I can psychotherapy sessions. Once the report is sent, I do not need to think about that claimant again unless VR asks further questions. This rarely happens because I attempt to tailor the report to their needs. On the negative side, I rarely have all of the information, especially background information that I would like in completing the evaluation. To do this kind of work, you need to be comfortable making judgments and decisions without having sometimes important, even crucial information. I make my best estimate and make it clear to the referral source the limitations of my judgments. If I do not feel confident in my conclusions, then I make that clear. Another negative is that these evaluations do not pay full fee. The fees are set on an annual basis by the agency, often at fees that are 35% to 90% of full fee. Psychologists who pursue this work must find a way to make the evaluations work for them financially. For me, this means that rather than writing notes, I type my reports on my computer as I interview the claimants. Claimants have accepted this style and some even seem to like this style because they perceive that I am recording the information more accurately than if I took written notes. Other psychologists might use dictation software. The point is to try to minimize the use of staff, which is expensive. My style allows me to generate a 5- to 10-page report in 50% to 75% of the time that other psychologists tell me that they spend on similar reports.

Psychologists who want to develop this niche might consider the following. First, look at the website for the VR offices in your state. Second, make contact with someone at VR who works with practitioners. This person can let you know whether the agency is looking for more contractors and what is required of them. Although these programs are largely funded at the federal level, they are run at the state level, which means that guidelines and fees are different across the states. If the agency does not want to use you immediately, persist. Ask the agency for an example of a good report that you can use as a model for structuring and generating your reports. Third, if you are chosen to work with VR, become highly skilled with all of the assessment tools that are required. The agency might want you to use some tools with which you may not be familiar. Fourth, develop a system that you can use consistently, remembering that you need to develop good content in a timely manner. Finally, become increasingly familiar with the literature on topics that you are likely to face, including malingering and learning disabilities. Understand that the impact of psychological disorders on work behaviors is not nearly as straightforward as one might think. In addition to completing assessments, in some states, VR will pay for psychologists to do psychotherapy with individuals whose emotional difficulties impair their ability to return to work. This work is considered to be targeted and focused and not work that examines general life issues or family of origin issues or attempts to change personality structure.

Molly C. McKenna

22 Completing Social Security Disability Assessments

I am a licensed psychologist in Oregon specializing in assessment and evaluation. I work in a solo private practice where I perform psychological, neuropsychological, developmental disability, and learning disability evaluations. I complete consultative examinations for the Disability Determination Services (DDS) branch of the State of Oregon Department of Human Services, otherwise known as Social Security Disability. Approximately 30% of my practice time is spent doing this type of work.

I became interested in disability assessments during my internship at a VA Hospital and postdoctoral residency. At the VA hospital, I completed compensation and pension evaluations, which determined whether any disabling conditions were linked to a veteran's military service. I found these examinations interesting primarily because I have always enjoyed diagnostic interviews and the "detective" nature of evaluating new clients.

Social Security evaluations became a focus of my evaluation during my postdoctoral residency. My supervisor performed a large number of these evaluations, and I spent a great deal of time administering intellectual and memory instruments to disability applicants. I found the diversity of clients fascinating. When I entered private practice on my own, I contacted Disability Determination to become a consultative examination provider.

Disability Determination consultative examinations are conducted at the request of the Office of Disability Determination to provide them with additional information regarding an applicant for disability benefits. Individuals are eligible for Social Security income if they are disabled. *Disability* is defined as having a condition that results in the inability to do substantial gainful activity and can be expected to result in death or has lasted or can be expected to last for a continuous period of not less than 12 months.

The majority of necessary information to determine disability eligibility comes from a claimant's treating providers, who provide documentation of conditions and treatment to DDS. If this information is insufficient to make a determination, DDS sometimes requests additional information from independent evaluators. These consultative examinations help provide additional information to the Social Security Administration (SSA).

For psychologists, consultative examinations have three forms. The first is a psychodiagnostic evaluation, generally consisting of a comprehensive diagnostic interview and brief records review. The second is an intellectual evaluation, consisting of a comprehensive diagnostic interview and the administration of psychometric tests to determine intellectual capabilities. The third is a neuropsychological evaluation, consisting of a comprehensive diagnostic interview, intellectual testing, and brief neuropsychological testing, typically to assess basic memory and executive function in addition to domains tapped by a general ability measure. In my state, SSA asks for specific testing instruments to be used and at times will ask for additional procedures or specific evaluations. It sometimes requests a comprehensive records review and forwards more complete medical records than in other cases. It has requested administration of the Minnesota Multiphasic Personality Inventory—2 (MMPI–2) or validity testing with several cases as well.

A typical referral from SSA is scheduled by phone 2 to 3 weeks before the appointment date; the scheduling person informs me of the type of evaluation and any scheduling requirements. Communication with the claimant is done by SSA, which gives the individual the necessary information about the date, time, and location of the appointment. SSA then forwards me an authorization form for the evaluation, along with any important records pertaining to the claimant. The number of referrals depends on the number of SSI claimants in the area. In my state, consultative examination providers can make arrangements to block out regular time to be filled by SSA, and they make an attempt to fill that time regularly. Some consultative examination providers contract with SSA, under an agreement in which they agree to accept a reduced rate for evaluations in exchange for a more regular flow of referrals. On the date of the appointment, I meet with the claimant and conduct the necessary procedures, including all testing. Some examiners do use testing technicians to administer their intellectual and neuro-psychological tests.

SSA has a preferred format for its evaluations, but most psychologists have their own template to cover the requested information. SSA specifically requests information about the history of the alleged disabling condition, the extent to which it affects the claimant's regular function, and the prognosis. Additional information to be included is the claimant's ability to perform activities of daily living, impairment in social functioning, and episodes of decompensation. SSA also wants to know testing results, as well as the credibility of the claimant's self-report and supporting evidence.

After I have finished the evaluation, I am responsible for writing up my findings and submitting them to SSA within 7 to 10 days. Reports can be as brief as 4 or 5 pages for a psychodiagnostic evaluation or as long as 11 or 12 pages for a more complex neuropsychological evaluation with records review. SSA pays a flat rate for each type of evaluation, with additional amounts for specially requested procedures, such as a records review or MMPI–2. Once SSA has received my information, they pay me promptly (usually within 2 weeks) via electronic transfer.

I enjoy the wide range of clients who present with disabling conditions. Clients of all ages apply for SSI, from young children to senior citizens. I also see a wide range of impairments and disorders. One challenge of this type of work is evaluating for malingering. Disability payments are a clear external incentive that motivates some people either to fabricate or exaggerate their symptoms, and an astute evaluator must always keep an eye out for contradictions, signs of suspect effort or motivation, or indicators of outright faking. However, the vast majority of clients are cooperative and motivated to be open and honest. Additionally, clients referred by SSA have a moderate no-show or no-confirmation rate. SSA attempts to contact me in advance to cancel appointments if a claimant has not confirmed, but sometimes these cancellations are only 1 or 2 days in advance of the appointment, making it difficult to fill that time with another client. Sometimes claimants simply don't show up for their appointments. In many states, SSA compensates these providers for these no-shows, either at a percentage of the consultative examination fee or a flat no-show rate. In other states, or under some SSA arrangements, providers are not paid for no-shows.

The training that has prepared me most specifically for this type of work is developing good diagnostic interviewing skills, having familiarity with a wide range of *DSM–IV* conditions, and experience in both intellectual and neuropsychological testing. Good clinical interviewing skills are a must, because some clients have long and complex histories. Differential diagnosis is important, but perhaps more important is conducting an interview that helps provide SSA with specific information about what activities a claimant can and cannot perform given his or her impairments.

The primary direct source for information regarding disability examinations is the Blue Book, published by the SSA. It can be ordered from the SSA or found online at http://www.ssa.gov/disability/professionals/ bluebook/index.htm. Also, the American Psychological Association (APA) provides a workbook and video produced in conjunction with the SSA regarding the Mental Impairments program of the SSA disability program. These materials can be ordered free of charge through APA's Independent Study programs at http://www.apa.org/ce. Articles pertaining to disability consultative examinations are also sometimes published in journals such as *The Clinical Neuropsychologist* and the *Journal of Consulting and Clinical Psychology.*

To begin working toward adding Social Security disability determination examinations to your practice, contact your state's Disability Determination office. The national Social Security office or website (http://www.ssa.gov) can help you locate an appropriate contact.

Douglas C. Haldeman

Evaluating Pilots and Air Traffic Controllers

Psychologists and the Federal Aviation Administration

23

am known primarily for my clinical work and guideline and policy authorship relative to the ethical and competent treatment of lesbian, gay, bisexual, and transgender individuals in psychotherapy. It may, therefore, surprise some to learn that for 25 years, a mainstay element of my independent practice has been aviation psychology. At any given time, 10% to 25% of my clinical work can be devoted to the assessment of those pilots and air traffic controllers who keep the skies safe for flight of all types—commercial airlines, air cargo, as well as private planes. This is an element of my practice that I enjoy tremendously for a number of reasons: It is an excellent way to maintain my interest in testing and assessment in a non-forensic setting, it offers me a distinct variation from the types of cases I typically see in my psychotherapy practice, and—dare I say it?—it is lucrative.

My initiation into the world of the Federal Aviation Administration (FAA) as a psychologist evaluator took place in 1985. At that time, I was in a group practice with a psychiatrist, a marriage and family therapist, and a social worker who specialized in treating addictions. I mentioned one day at lunch that I had always loved psychological assessment during graduate training and internship and that I missed testing. The psychiatrist, it so happened, was a regional evaluator for the FAA and asked me whether I might be interested in working with the assessment team in the Pacific Northwest. He explained that pilot and air traffic controller (ATC) evaluations were conducted by teams of three: a physician, a psychiatrist, and a psychologist. He went on to explain who was involved as clients, what kinds of tests were required as part of the evaluation, and how it all worked from a business standpoint.

Most commonly, the client pilots or ATCs identified or self-reported as alcoholic or drug-addicted and had lost their medical clearance to fly. The clients typically had been through some form of inpatient treatment, followed by a period (usually a year) of outpatient recovery. Before being cleared to return to work, the pilot would need to establish his or her medical readiness for flight duty. In addition to being examined by a physician and a psychiatrist, the pilot would need an evaluation by a psychologist, including an interview and a battery of tests. At issue is whether or not the pilot's chemical dependency has had a lasting effect on his or her cognitive and psychological abilities and whether the pilot's recovery appears to be stable, as demonstrated by participation in 12-step or other recovery programs. If the team agreed, the pilot's medical clearance could be reinstated, and he or she would return to work; if not, an additional period of recovery would be required.

Not all of my clients have been grappling with alcoholism, however. A good number of them have had issues with on-the-job stress, particularly the ATCs. There have been cases of anger management in which the client must demonstrate his or her ability to work collegially in the pressure-cooker environment that is aviation, a male-dominated profession. Other cases involve individuals whose histories are such that they must first undergo a "P&P" (psychological and psychiatric) evaluation before receiving a medical certificate from the FAA. Most often, these are individuals with histories of depression or anxiety who have needed to be on medications that are disallowed by the FAA for pilots. These would include all psychoactive medications used to treat depression or anxiety or stabilize mood. Those evaluations address the question: Can this person fly or direct air traffic without using certain medications?

Another crucial question is this: Given certain individuals' backgrounds, is there any reason to believe that the person might represent a danger to the flying public? I remember the case of one young man who had applied to ATC training school but had 10 years earlier, in what he described as a foolish postadolescent "phase," joined a neo-Nazi White supremacist group in Idaho. The FAA provided a statement that he had signed at the time filled with racist invective and wanted to know his current status. This provided an interesting evaluation question: Was this indeed a rehabilitated young man? Or would I be the psychologist mentioned as the one who had given the ATC a pass when, some years hence, he directed the El Al and Air Namibia flights approaching JFK to collide? I declined the evaluation, following my philosophy that it is better, in this type of work, to err on the side of caution. I explained that I wished him all success in life, but that there were some jobs for which his history would be a deal breaker, and ATC was one of them.

Actual experience as a pilot is not a prerequisite for this work, although it is certainly helpful. Expertise in psychometrics and a strong background in chemical dependency treatment, however, are the fundamental requirements of the job. Before meeting with the client, it is important to review the relevant documents carefully (treatment records, personnel records). The interview itself is critical for obtaining the client's history, as well as for observing his or her behavior. The FAA requires a battery of tests, always including the Wechsler Adult Intelligence Scale (WAIS), the Minnesota Multiphasic Personality Inventory (MMPI), and the Rorschach. Additionally, a neuropsychological screening test is required: I generally use the Trail-Making Tests and the Booklet Categories Test. If there appears to be any sign of neuropsychological dysfunction, I refer the subject for a complete workup by a neuropsychologist. Other tests (Sentence Completion, Millon Clinical Multiaxial Inventory, Thematic Apperception Test) may be used according to the psychologist's discretion.

Pilots in general have higher than average WAIS scores, flat MMPI profiles, and constricted Rorschach responses. The strong defenses against affect are actually a desirable characteristic in aviation, for obvious reasons. Finally, collateral contacts, such as current psychotherapists or sponsors, must be contacted after the client is interviewed. Most pilots are eager to return to work; nevertheless, the evaluator must be as confident as possible that the individual's chemical dependency recovery is stable. It is, in my experience, unusual for a pilot to emerge from alcohol or drug treatment psychologically or cognitively impaired, and after a year's sobriety, most are engaged in solid recovery programs. In most locales, there are special 12-step meetings for pilots. After evaluation and consultation with the physician and the psychiatrist, the vast majority of pilots are returned to work.

The business aspects of aviation evaluation are different from those of my typical psychotherapy practice. Insurance coverage for psychological evaluation can be quite variable; as a result, instead of billing the pilot's insurance directly, I ask for payment at the time of service. I make other arrangements only in the event that the pilot's company is covering the cost of the evaluation, as is the case, for example, with Federal Express. Most commercial airlines require the pilot to pay for the evaluation, sometimes with partial reimbursement from his or her health insurance. The evaluations typically require about 10 to 12 hours of my time, considering document evaluation, interview and testing, data analysis and report preparation, all of which is billed at my hourly rate. In the end, I always ask myself: Would I put myself and my family on a plane being flown by this person?

The FAA is a bureaucratic organization, and as such, has been slow to replace psychologists who have retired or discontinued their aviation evaluation practices. There are opportunities in this field, particularly in certain geographic areas, for psychologists interested in aviation evaluation. I recommend it highly, and those interested in learning whether psychologists are needed for this service in their area should contact the chief of aeromedical services at the FAA in Oklahoma City.

Stephen F. Curran

24 Public Safety Services

P olice and public safety services, occupational risk management, and forensic services have been the core of my professional practice for the past 15 years. I consider myself, first
and foremost, a police psychologist. My success is based on
hard work, having positive customer relations, and providing
prompt response to requests for services.

My beginning was not unlike that of many psychologists. I had been in solo practice for about 2 years, during
which discussions with other psychologists about forming a
practice began. After a year of these discussions, a traditional
mental health practice was formed in 1986. Several psychologists and social workers provided services to children, families, and adults with billing to insurance carriers through the
corporation. Within 10 years, the business model, fueled
by the increasing aggravation of managed care intrusions,
evolved to spin off any work associated with managed mental health care.

My professional background was primarily in the areas of
substance abuse research and treatment of criminal offenders
and related areas of violence. I was directing prison mental
health services while starting out in a part-time solo clinical
practice when a serendipitous opportunity fell in my lap
through membership in a fraternal organization. A large police
agency had experienced two events that would determine

my professional career path. First, a police officer murdered all family members and then committed suicide. Next, a recruit in training committed suicide while on a weekend pass from the residential academy. A recently appointed superintendent of the agency wanted to develop confidential psychological services that would reduce the occurrence of such events. Through my fraternal organization acquaintance and an officer in the agency, I was asked to start a confidential counseling program to officers and their families. As part of the groundwork, I was asked to conduct a postmortem psychological assessment of the deceased recruit. I was stunned to learn that the agency was administering a psychological test but that no psychologist was involved in scoring, interpreting, or interviewing prospective recruits! The answer sheet was simply placed in a file without further evaluation. Since then, my career has been spent completing preemployment psychological evaluations of police and other public safety applicants. More than 70% of my professional activities are delivered to law enforcement agencies at the local, state, and federal levels. These services include applicant selection, training, organization consultation, traumatic stress interventions following critical incidents, and coordinating a national confidential counseling program for a federal law enforcement agency. These areas require extensive knowledge of employment law ranging from Equal Employment Opportunity Commission regulations to worker compensation requirements.

All professional services provided through my business have one element in common—an area of the law. These include occupational assessments such as independent medical examinations (IME) in which findings of causality and impairment ratings are opined and court-related evaluations of offenders before or after sentencing. Another area for my practice is "expert" services, which includes conducting workshops for Pearson Assessments and testimony in civil cases such as wrongful death claims and professional malpractice.

I love what I do! No 2 weeks are the same. My day can start with an IME, have two or three crises reduction sessions with a recently injured worker, and conclude by conducting a preemployment evaluation. I am rarely in the office 5 consecutive days because I have a training segment to conduct at a federal law enforcement academy, travel to a city to conduct preemployment evaluations, or, perhaps, at a detention center conducting a presentence psychological evaluation for the court. How great is that! Sure, there is report writing, but with computer technology, time management, and balance, the work does not lose its allure. There are frustrations, of course, often associated with the management within organizations, both private and public, that resist change in organizational practices. However, I have learned not to sweat the small stuff.

The growth of a business has two concerns: how to find business and how to get paid promptly at an acceptable rate for professional services. The stability for getting referrals is twofold: contracts awarded through competitive bid and referrals because of quality of service, including providing a prompt response. The latter needs elaboration because many psychologists seem to be behind the curve when an exchange of information is involved. When I get a referral on a traumatic case, the referral source has evaluated the employee for physical injuries and then referred for crisis reduction. An appointment is sought within 48 hours, and a report (a consultation note) to the referring source is required to be delivered within 24 hours. This is because the employee will typically return to the workplace within 7 days, if not sooner. Submitting reports days, even weeks, later will result in the cessation of referrals.

Payment for my services is from the organization requesting a service, not the individual I have seen for services. The referral is accompanied by a clear understanding about who is responsible for payment. Typically, payment is received within 2 weeks of billing and, rarely, beyond 6 weeks; thus, cash flow is predictable—a cornerstone of managing a business.

There are a number of approaches to becoming involved in a practice area not bound to managed care. First, hard work! I believe many of my successes are rooted in the practice early in my career of spending hundreds of hours doing ride-alongs with police officers, responding to call-outs of the tactical teams and responding to the scene of officer-involved shootings, no matter what time of night. My current police-related contracts have resulted in relying on up to 12 psychologists around the country to do work for me in the area of preemployment psychological evaluations of public safety applicants. Each psychologist has his or her own story about about how he or she became involved in police-related services. One recent example was a newly licensed psychologist who called a police department to ask who its psychologist was. When provided with my name, the psychologist then called me to express her interest, which led to meeting for lunch, and we then formed a working relationship. Within months, she achieved an alternative income stream, in addition to growing her own practice.

Among the best advice I ever received early in my career was from a major of a police agency who introduced me to the International Association of Chiefs of Police (http://www.theiacp.org)—the premier organization of police chiefs and law enforcement executives. I learned that IACP had a Police Psychological Services Section. My first meeting was among fewer than 10 like-minded psychologists engaged in direct services to police officers. The section has grown to more than 130 members with high numbers attending each annual meeting. Another organization to consider is American Psychological Association Division 18 (Psychologists in Public Service), which has had mostly low-level activity since the late 1980s, but recent leadership points to exciting growth. The third organization for its educational value is the Society of Police and Criminal Psychology (http://www.policepsychology.org). With respect to occupational health matters ranging from IMEs, workability and fitness for duty assessments, and traumatic stress interventions, I encourage a solid foundation in conducting forensic assessments, including psychological testing expertise. Your opinions will be scrutinized for scientific accuracy; therefore, you must be confident in your ability to assess and communicate your opinions in writing. There are few organizations specifically related to this specialty area, but a relatively new group might be considered: the Association for Scientific Advancement in Psychological Injury and Law (http://www.asapil.org).

Marla W. Deibler

25 | Psychological Evaluations for State Agencies

A s a clinical psychologist, wife, and mother of two young children, I have found myself faced with the challenge of building a successful, fulfilling career without sacrificing the joys of family life. My challenge has been to establish a professional life that allows me to spend quality time with my family while also being fulfilled and profitable. After 5 years in the stressful world of academia, I decided to venture outside of the medical and dental school world and into the clinical practice realm—to enter the challenge of professional fulfillment and success in a world of mental health disparity and managed care.

Upon leaving my faculty post, I accepted a subcontracting position with Delaware Valley Psychological Services (DVPS), a practice directed by Meryl E. Udell, PsyD. This position met my goals—it involved interesting clinical work that could be done on-site 2 days per week, with reports written on my own time (at home in the evenings and, often, well into the night, a sacrifice I was certainly willing to make to spend my days with my children). The compensation also exceeded that of my full-time academic position.

Currently, approximately 35% of my professional time is spent providing assessment services for DVPS. As a psychologist with DVPS, I provide psychological, neuropsychological, and psychosexual evaluations in contractual agreements with state agencies and private nonprofit organizations. These contracts have been acquired over the course of 20 years as a result of the movement toward the privatization of state agencies that ensure the safety and stability of children and their families. Each year, these organizations are provided with a budget for behavioral health services by the state, and, in turn, the organizations contract with clinicians such as DVPS to provide behavioral health services, including assessment and treatment. Referral sources are caseworkers and other coordinators employed by these organizations that require such services for their clients. This may be due to a court order or behavioral health concerns, including questions of capacity. These caseworkers and coordinators schedule appointments for their clients with DVPS, and we provide the services requested. Reports are then written and submitted to the referring professional. Typically, billing for services provided for clients of a particular referral source is processed monthly. Invoices are submitted to the organization, which issues payment from its behavioral health care budget. The size of this budget is determined by the state.

Having attended a practitioner–scholar model clinical psychology doctoral program with a concentration in health and neuropsychology, my training involved a substantial emphasis on completing psychological evaluations. Naturally, my practicum and internship experiences further developed these skills; accordingly, providing such evaluative and consultative services was a comfortable outgrowth of my training. I have found such consultative work enjoyable because it affords me the experience of seeing a wide range of clients, challenges me to further hone my diagnostic skills, and provides me the opportunity to generate recommendations that ensure the safety and stability of children and their families.

Such contractual work offers a number of advantages for psychologists. Contractual agreements allow clinicians the freedom to provide services without the tedium and complications of having to request preauthorization for services or justify one's assessment and treatment plans. There is also certainty that the clinician will receive payment for services rendered, without rejection or requests for further information. Fees are also paid as determined by the contract; regular fees as well as no-show fees are set by the clinician and agreed on before contract finalization. In addition, referral sources are motivated by their employers, court systems, and the contracts themselves to ensure that the client attends the appointment; therefore, no-shows are rarely a concern. In fact, many such organizations provide transportation for clients to and from appointments. Furthermore, such work could be completed without the need for an office funded by the clinician. Many organizations are willing to include the use of their office space in the contractual agreements. Evaluative work also offers flexibility in that testing is done onsite, and report writing can be done elsewhere at one's own availability.

There are also potential disadvantages to such contractual agreements. For example, clinicians who do not enjoy testing or report writing may find this work laborious and unpleasant. One must also have the ability to organize data and generate evaluative reports in a timely manner. There are typically relatively short deadlines for completing such documentation as set by courts and the organizations themselves. Although payment is guaranteed for services, it is not immediate, and there are times when funding from the state is delayed for various reasons, which results in a delay of payment delivery. Moreover, the abundance of referrals is largely dependent on state budgets and responsive to budget deficits. Therefore, in lean economic times, state funding for behavioral health services to these organizations can be limited, which often results in a decrease in referrals.

When considering adding contractual agreements with state agencies and private nonprofit organizations to one's scope of practice, it is important to investigate the organization of state systems to determine the viability of such arrangements. Contacting agencies of this nature in one's area and asking with whom their behavioral health services are contracted is one way to identify practices such as DVPS. The clinician may then choose to contact such practices directly and inquire about subcontracting opportunities. Networking with other local professionals and organizations is also critical to developing and maintaining such relationships. Knowing basic business models and procedures is advantageous, as is identifying consultants such as financial advisors, accountants, and attorneys. Developing assessment skills, using dictation software, and becoming proficient in dictating and developing organized templates for report writing are also helpful to increase efficiency.

My work with DVPS has provided me with the flexibility to establish my own private practice, The Center for Emotional Health of Greater Philadelphia, where I provide specialized psychotherapy and psychological assessment services outside of managed care. Providing specialized services to meet the needs of the community has afforded me success as well as an interesting, enjoyable, and truly rewarding career. Independent practice coupled with subcontracting my clinical services with DVPS has freed me of the limitations imposed by managed care. I have saved time and money and have shielded myself from the frustrations and stress long associated with managed care networks. I am in control of my career, the clinical care I provide to others, and my schedule. Most important, I have established a professionally and financially rewarding career without sacrificing my role as mother and time available to family.

SERVICES TO ORGANIZATIONS VI

Frank Froman

Working With Developmentally Disabled Adults

26

had been a private practitioner for about 20 years in a small Illinois community when we received word that a 15-bed home for mentally challenged adults was opening. These homes for residents formerly warehoused in larger state facilities were opening across Illinois and would provide a comprehensive total living structure. The home needed a psychologist who would provide assessments, mainly IQ testing, to certify that each resident met criteria for admission. They also needed a psychologist to be in attendance at a quarterly staff meeting to evaluate residents' behavior and adjustment to the facility, as well as to deal with any significant behavioral challenges that the residents or the facility faced.

Providing the assessments was the easy part. Desired tests included the Stanford–Binet, 4th edition, used in preference to Wechsler testing because it did a better job of identifying lower functioning adults. The Vineland Social Maturity Scale was used, when needed, to assist us in measuring a client's social competence and adaptive behavior. Other tests included simple skill tests such as the Wide Range Achievement Tests and Berry Visual Motor Integration Tests to find hidden skill areas or deficits and to assist in educational programming.

The work has evolved over the years of my consultation. Our community now has two such facilities that house 30 residents. Three adjacent communities each have one facility, resulting in 75 clients under my wing who need periodic evaluations and four staffings per year. Other facilities, called CILAs (community integrated living arrangements), have also come on line to provide housing and programs to another 25 or more residents, thus giving me approximately 100 clients for whom I have psychological responsibility in the community.

Each resident is carefully evaluated on entry to a facility and then reevaluated once every 5 years. Thus, there are about 20 evaluations performed per year overall. Each resident is staffed in quarterly meetings, held at their respective facilities. This accounts for approximately 1% to 2% of my practice. Invoices for these services are given to the facilities, which pay for services rendered. We contract an amount to cover testing and consultation services. These amounts are easily renegotiated annually.

Working with residents, testing them, visiting with them, and attending summer outings and holiday parties with them have provided an extraordinary gateway into how effective these programs are and can be. Residents bond with those of us who see them, and we bond with them as well. Warm and hearty handshakes, lots of hugs, and delightful smiles of recognition have punctuated the work that has become an important part of not just my practice but my life. As we solve problems attendant to living, deal with intrusive behaviors and frank psychoses, and create life plans that enrich otherwise meaningless lives, the rewards of such a practice are found to be inestimable.

I have never found any annoyances in working with these clients or these homes. Long staffings can be a bit of a problem at times, but ours are made enjoyable by lunches provided and colleagues who know and trust each other after years of working together. Written reports are often remarkably brief, averaging about two pages. Mostly, they want to see a diagnosis and an IQ score, because both are needed to keep residents in their programs. Other content is written in plain English to enable readers at any educational level to understand. Some of the staff at our facilities have high school diplomas, and others are college educated.

I had the advantage of being a school psychologist for 5 years before going into clinical psychology. Those years gave me experience in assessing and consulting with children, teachers, and parents of youngsters who would eventually become this population. The testing was second nature, although finding ways to truly assess intelligence was sometimes tricky. Some residents were used to giving up before they tried. Others gave one-word answers. Lots of coaxing, reframing, and modification in test questions sometimes brought out capabilities where testing showed that none existed.

For one contemplating working with persons who have developmental disabilities (DDs), several things should be helpful:

- Become familiar with the tests that your facility requires. Know the items, and get comfortable asking questions in ways that give you answers.
- Study behavior modification techniques with adult DD populations. Note that you cannot do things that might be viewed as exclusionary or punishing. You will find that simple things occasionally work well (e.g., giving a Tic-Tac once an hour for pro-social behaviors). Complex solutions usually fail in these facilities because staff members are not able to administer them.
- Don't feel that every behavior has to be modified. Learn to identify what you can and cannot change in people. For example, we've had a person who loves to talk to her dolls and has a wonderful exchange with them. It's harmless and does not require modification. Avoid feeling that you must always change someone as part of your work with them.
- Be yourself. These clients love warmth, hugs, genuine affection, and interest. They don't like formality and distancing. Some will applaud themselves when they believe they did well on a test. It's not a bad thing to join them in the applause.
- Carry some candy with you. They'll remember you for it, and it'll help cement bonds.
- Visit other facilities where seasoned clinicians have worked. No sense in reinventing the wheel.
- Have a friendly consultant who can coach you when you've got a tough or thorny problem.
- Read whatever you can on working with DD clients and their families. Family members can be either helpful or problematic. Many promise to visit and then don't show up, creating a powerful hurt that is acted out by the client. Others never visit, while others overindulge their family members and keep them obese with snacks.
- Understand that low-functioning citizens have feelings and often feel things most intensely. They may have a lot of trouble expressing those feelings in words, but they are very much a part of them. Ignoring or minimizing those feelings is easy to do but nonproductive.
- Realize that you are helping to take people from lives of nothingness, in some cases, to lives where they can actually live. They can attend classes, work, make some money, party, have fun, ride bikes, take walks, go to Disney World and do well as a group, and have the dignity of a door that they can shut when they go to bed. You are helping them to achieve a real sense of being.

For more information about working with this population, the Association for Mental Retardation (http://www.aamr.org) has a website with a good deal of helpful information, as does the American Psychological Association's Division 33 on Intellectual and Developmental Disabilities. To develop a practice in this area, visiting local homes for persons with DDs is often the best way to start. Registering your interest and letting it be known that you have expertise in this area of practice can help open doors when clinical consultant vacancies occur. Offering to assist when their clinical staff might not be available or taking a referral for psychotherapy from the facility is also often helpful and appreciated. If you can help clients who have problems with aggression, self-management, or sexual acting-out behaviors, you will be valued.

Working with adults with DDs can be a great practice niche that, in addition to being financially rewarding, can also become a true labor of love. You'll be forming relationships that can last for years and be tremendously important to a group of people whose lives will be demonstrably better for your participation.

Thomas G. Plante

Assessment of Men and Women Entering Religious Life

27

I am a full-time psychology professor at Santa Clara University as well as an adjunct clinical associate professor in psychiatry and behavioral sciences at Stanford University. For the past 20 years, I have also maintained a small, generally one-day-per-week private practice in Menlo Park, California. My part-time practice is managed care free, and approximately 90% of my clinical work involves working with the Roman Catholic and Episcopal churches. I conduct psychological evaluations for applicants to religious life, such as priests, nuns, deacons, and so forth, and I provide evaluation, consultation, and psychological treatment for clergy members who experience a wide range of troubles. These difficulties have included anxiety, depression, stress management, conflicts with religious superiors and congregations, sex offending, Internet and other pornography use, crises in vocation. Furthermore, I serve on sensitive incident and diocesan review boards for several religious orders and dioceses to consult with the Church when their clergy or other employees sexually violate children or vulnerable others. Finally, I serve on the national review board for the United States Council of Catholic Bishops, assisting the bishops in policy on managing the sexual abuse crisis that has troubled the Catholic Church in recent years.

I am fond of saying that this clinical specialty came to me and I didn't seek it out. When I began my part-time clinical practice 2 decades ago, I focused primarily on behavioral medicine (child and adult cases), as well as the assessment of children and adults for learning disabilities, giftedness, and other matters. As an active, practicing, and engaged Roman Catholic for my entire life, clergy friends and colleagues began sending me referrals basically stating, "You're a psychologist and a Catholic, perhaps you can help us with this problem". Over time, more and more referrals came, and once I had established trusting and ongoing collaborative relationships with various religious superiors and Church officials, there was no going back.

In the meantime, there has been little training available for those interested in integrating religion and psychology in general, and this is certainly true with specific religious groups such as Roman Catholics. I consulted with a number of colleagues who acted as clergy and psychologists as well as lay professionals working in this area. I also read everything that was published in peer-reviewed professional outlets to determine the state-of-the-art science and practice available. Finally, I obtained ongoing consultation from a priest and psychologist whom I knew well and trusted. Over time, I began conducting research in this area, which resulted in a number of published books and articles. For those interested in developing this area of practice, a growing literature is now available for review. Develop high-quality psychological assessment and report-writing skills, and seek out supervision from someone who has previously done this type of work.

In terms of a typical evaluation process, I administer the Minnesota Multiphasic Personality Inventory—2, Millon Clinical Multiaxial Inventory—III, Sixteen Personality Factor Questionnaire, and Forer Sentence Completion tests to applicants to ordained ministry and ask them also to submit their autobiographical statement and resume. Then, a 90-minute interview is conducted that includes feedback on the testing results. A written report of approximately four single-spaced pages is completed and submitted to the religious superior. I make clear to all applicants that I don't tell the Church what to do or not to do but provide information about that candidate's psychological and personality functioning and highlight any potential risk factors that should be considered in the evaluation and potential formation process. Thus, the Church, not I, decides who to accept and reject.

I feel that my work with the Church is highly gratifying. It blends my interests in both psychology and religion, and I feel that it allows me to use my gifts as an academic, teacher, and clinician to help care for the needs of clergy and the Church. I would say that it has become a vocation for me and a specialty that can have an impact on many people in important ways. The primary challenge is keeping up with the demand and writing so many psychological testing reports. Over the past 20 years, I have conducted approximately 500 psychological evaluations on clergy applicants with close to 100 in the past year alone as more and more religious groups have contacted me to work with them. It is difficult to keep up with the demand, especially when I have a separate full-time job as a professor and must limit my practice to 1 day per week. It can make for a very long day indeed and may require writing reports on weekends.

In terms of billing, an invoice for services is sent to the religious organization and paid in a regular and punctual manner. No insurance is used, with the exception of ongoing psychotherapy with clergy members, but in general, the religious organizations manage those details and simply pay my invoice upon receipt.

Working with clergy and religious organizations is satisfying and avoids the stress and hassles of managed care. It is an excellent way for psychologists and other mental health professionals to conduct their professional practices. However, I tend to think that being an active and engaged member of a religious tradition helps one do this work with integrity, understanding, compassion, and mutual trust. So many clergy and religious superiors feel comfortable and at ease knowing that I not only respect and support what they do in ministry but also am an active member of the Church.

There are a variety of books and articles that professionals interested in this type of practice may wish to review. A selected list of my work in this area that focuses on working with the Roman Catholic Church follows. In addition, please visit my website to download pdfs of other articles I have published in this interesting area.

References

Plante, T. G. (1999). A collaborative relationship between professional psychology and the Roman Catholic Church: A case example and suggested principles for success. *Professional Psychology: Research and Practice, 30,* 541–546.

Plante, T. G. (Ed.). (1999). *Bless me father for I have sinned: Perspectives on sexual abuse committed by Roman Catholic priests.* Westport, CT: Praeger/Greenwood.

Plante, T. G. (Ed.). (2004). *Sin against the innocents: Sexual abuse by priests and the role of the Catholic Church.* Westport, CT: Praeger/Greenwood.

Plante, T. G. (2007). Ethical considerations for psychologists screening applicants for the priesthood in the Catholic Church: Implications of the Vatican instruction on homosexuality. *Ethics and Behavior, 17,* 131–136.

Plante, T. G. (2009). *Spiritual practices in psychotherapy: Thirteen tools for enhancing psychological health.* Washington, DC: American Psychological Association.

Plante, T. G., & Boccaccini, M. (1998). A proposed psychological assessment protocol for applicants to religious life in the Roman Catholic Church. *Pastoral Psychology, 46,* 363–372.

Edward A. Wise

28 | Consulting With Health Care Organizations

My practice has evolved over the years from a sole private practitioner, to a partnership agreement with several other mental health professionals, to the managing partner of that group, to the president of Mental Health Resources (MHR). MHR is a multidisciplinary private practice. My practice activities have also changed as our service delivery model has evolved. Initially, I spent approximately 90% of my time in direct service and generated the majority of the practice income. I now spend less than 20% of my time in direct service activities. The consultations described here were not contemporaneous with one another but reflect endeavors over a period of years and represent possible opportunities for non–managed care revenue.

For the first 20 years of my practice, I provided inpatient and outpatient services. My inpatient practice was initially limited to freestanding psychiatric hospitals, and later I worked in a large private nonprofit medical hospital system. It would be fair to say that working in the psychiatric hospital settings allowed me to learn the ropes of inpatient practice, the medical hierarchy, and the physician's style of practice. In the large medical hospital system, there were many opportunities for clinical work, but there was limited recognition or acceptance of psychologists. I spent some time going to various department meetings and committees, trying to learn my way around and gain exposure. It was frequently the case that department or unit administrators recognized the value of psychological services, but there were numerous obstacles to implementing referrals. It became clear that psychology needed an organized voice, and I was one of the founding members of the Division of Psychology within this hospital. In my role as chair of the division, I started providing lectures to the internal medicine residents on relevant, topic-specific disorders (e.g., comorbid depression with chronic pain, heart disease and psychological factors), which served to increase my visibility and professional credibility. One of the internal medicine professors had an interest in pain management and began to refer his patients to me for assessment and treatment. We had consistently favorable results and presented some case studies to the residents.

Later, I was invited to serve as a consultant to the physician hospital organization preferred provider organization (PPO). As PPOs and managed care organizations (MCOs) were proliferating, they realized a need to better understand and work with mental health professionals. I had the opportunity to meet with and speak to the chief executive officer of the PPO, who requested that I serve as a consultant with them to develop a set of credentialing criteria for psychologists and master's level providers. As our credentialing criteria navigated its way through their bureaucracy, I was afforded numerous opportunities to speak about the value of mental health services to primary care physicians. As this task was winding up, I became involved in a series of discussions that resulted in doing some research for the PPO on its physician referral patterns (Wise, 2001). This project involved an extensive survey of primary care physicians' views of their PPO's mental health utilization and network.

Meanwhile, in the hospital setting, there was a large demand for pain management services, but limited lengths of stay in an acute inpatient setting, to address the multitude of issues adequately. The Comprehensive Pain Management Clinic was developed as an outpatient program to identify and address the needs of these complex medical patients. The physicians involved had read some of my psychological evaluations and believed it would be helpful to develop a similar workup for their pain patients. We all knew that managed care would not authorize psychological evaluations on the majority of patients, that most patients did not need a complete evaluation, but that a psychological evaluation could help identify new patients with comorbid psychological problems and serve a triage function. A brief psychological screening battery was developed, with appropriate caveats, that was administered to every new patient seen at the clinic, and this was paid for by the clinic. Over the course of our 8-year relationship, many of these patients were referred for more in-depth evaluations, others for individual psychotherapy, and eventually we were seeing many of their patients for mental health services.

Similarly, there was an extended care hospital within the larger hospital. An extended care hospital is designed to serve acutely ill patients who require longer care but who can be stepped down from acute care. This 40-bed unit provided cardiac rehabilitation, physical rehabilitation, wound care, and a ventilation weaning program; the average length of stay was approximately 30 days. I had known the administrator of this program from her work in the parent hospital, where she was in charge of one of the medical units. She called me to discuss possible models of intervention for patients and family members. However, upon meeting, it was discovered that it was neither the patients nor the family members who were distressed, but the multidisciplinary medical team providing care. It became clear that what was needed was a way to help educate and support the staff, because they dealt with death, family conflicts, noncompliance, and the spectrum of problems that could be expected to arise from such stressful and prolonged circumstances. As part of developing a plan, I suggested that I sit on a few team staff meetings, where the patient's medical and psychosocial problems were discussed. These meetings helped clarify what type of help and support the staff needed. I reported back to the administrator with a plan to address some specific, ongoing clinical issues (e.g., dying, noncompliance, addiction) and to discuss management strategies for particular patients that the staff identified as problematic. This very satisfying consultative arrangement afforded me contact with the entire medical team in a way that allowed me to help other caregivers manage their patients. This arrangement spanned approximately 4 years, during which I spent approximately 2 hours per week consulting with the medical team. However, after the administrator received a promotion, and when a new administrator took over, the agreement was unfortunately terminated.

My interest in consultation grew out of my need for diversification and a desire to interact with other health care team members and understand their culture and how we could work together. These consultative relationships involved productive, bright, fellow professionals, who provided a needed balance to my client caseload. The billing arrangement in such consultations is straightforward. Typically, an hourly rate is agreed on, billed directly on a monthly basis, and paid accordingly. Building a medical organization and practice consultation service requires ongoing contact with these organizations. It requires recognition, credibility, and networking. One must be willing to do some volunteer work, such as lecturing to residents, attending meetings, and serving on committees, to make the necessary contacts. A systems orientation is also necessary, and my training as a community systems psychologist aided me in navigating the medical health care system. Keeping current with the interface of medical and mental health practice–related issues is important. Readings that address the interface of medical and psychological issues are also required (e.g., journals such as *Hospital and Community Psychiatry, Clinical*

Psychology in Medical Settings, Psychosomatics: The Journal of Consultation and Liaison Psychiatry). Consultative relationships with other mental health providers practicing in medical settings are invaluable, particularly when entering new settings or specialty areas. Belonging to organizations (and attending conferences) such as the Society of Psychologists in Management and Society of Consulting Psychology, as well as multidisciplinary conferences and workshops, such as those sponsored by the American Academy of Pain Management and the Society for Behavioral Medicine, can be helpful in developing skills in this area.

Reference

Wise, E. A. (2001). PPO primary care physician survey on mental health utilization. *Journal of Psychotherapy in Independent Practice, 2*(4), 57–72.

FINANCE VII

Steven J. Hendlin

Coaching Traders and Investors

29

L icensed as both a psychologist and marriage and family therapist, I have been in independent practice for over 33 years, all of it in Orange County, California. My main professional activity has been doing psychotherapy and counseling with adult individuals, couples, and families in a traditional office setting. Except for the company of my psychologist wife, who has her own separate office in our suite, I've always been in solo practice. In addition to my clinical practice, over the years I've developed specialties as a sport psychologist working primarily with amateur and professional golfers and as a coach for online traders and investors.

Coaching those who specifically come to me wanting help with their investing is now about 10% of my practice. The bull market of the late 1990s and again in middle of this decade, along with the rise in computer technology, led to the popularity of online trading and all of the pressure that accompanies this activity. In 2001–2002, I was writing a highly visible weekly column for TheStreet.com on the psychology of trading and had just published a book on the same topic. During this period, approximately 25% of my practice was related to coaching professional traders. However, with the more recent market crash and severe recession, large numbers of traders and investors have soured on the markets and online trading. With this change, the nature of my coaching has also changed to be more inclusive of all the issues related to coping with a poor economy. These include dealing with investment losses and job insecurity, managing mortgage and credit card debt, and the various family stresses related to money and inheritance issues.

Because of this economic climate (and the fact that they know of my specialty in this area), perhaps up to 80% of those who now enter psychotherapy with me at some point want to talk about finances and their personal investments. Some come in specifically to deal with the stresses of investment losses and job fears, which create a spiral of worry, anxiety, rumination, family arguments, psychosomatic symptoms, insomnia, catastrophic thinking, and depression.

So, although the focus has changed somewhat from direct online trading issues (for example, "How can I handle the fast-paced pressures of trading?") to dealing with market losses and economic and job insecurity, I still consider this, in a more inclusive sense, part of my coaching practice. Because they know of my expertise in the area of investing, some may also ask for direct advice on what to do with their savings and investments. I will usually point them to resources to help them make informed decisions. Sometimes, with patients with whom I have long-term relationships and who directly ask, I offer advice as to how to protect themselves and preserve their capital. I also help them deal with the psychology of inheritance issues and estate planning, having published a book on this topic.

My interest in coaching investors began with my desire to learn the new technology of online investing during the mid-1990s for my own retirement portfolio. I became fascinated with all the psychological issues specifically related to online investing and realized there was no good book available to help those dealing with them. These issues included how a trader could feel in control of sorting out the welter of information flashing on the monitor, how to balance fear and opportunity, how to discriminate in taking in news, and dealing with the pressure to exercise discipline in decision making with significant amounts of money on the line. So I did research and then wrote a book focusing on these topics. My research involved interviewing traders at a trading academy, taking seminars on the techniques of short- and intermediate-term trading, and practicing on the speedy trading computers, which, at the time, were superior to home computers. I also read a sampling of the literature on the psychology of investing. I directly pitched my proposal to an editor at McGraw-Hill and, after acceptance, found an agent to help me work out the contract details. The publication of this book led to some national publicity and an invitation to write a weekly column at the TheStreet.com.

To do this work, you need to have a strong and sustained interest in learning about investing—which includes the fundamental and technical aspects of stocks and companies, as well as the psychology of trading. Related areas of knowledge include understanding business cycles, macroeconomics, political news that affects the market, and the use of online trading technology. This work requires a good deal of study, especially if you are to appreciate what is going on in the minds of those who are not just occasional investors but do more frequent online trading. Taking hands-on workshops on trading would be highly desirable, as would reading business and market-related news.

I like coaching investors because they are usually grateful for what they gain. And what they gain is quantifiable in real dollars and good sense. Unlike the more subjective changes often brought on by the lengthy process of psychotherapy, which may not always be translated into observable behavior, coaching investors usually has an immediate and tangible effect that validates the help I provide. I also like the aspect of working by phone with investors located in other geographic areas. Because we are subject to the vagaries of the economy and stock market, it wouldn't be wise or realistic to see coaching as more than a subspecialty activity rather than as an area for full-time concentration.

Referrals come from those who have read my book and column, as well as other articles related to dealing with money issues. All coaching done by phone is charged up front. After making initial phone contact and obtaining an agreement for services, I ask that a "retainer" be sent to me before we begin the coaching process. I do not offer services by phone without being paid up front. For those who come to my office, my fee is paid at the time of service. Insurance does not cover this type of service because we are not addressing a diagnosable health or mental health condition in this work.

Psychologists interested in incorporating this kind of coaching into their practice should start by evaluating whether the financial wealth in their geographic area is high enough to warrant this type of specialty practice. If it isn't, it won't matter how qualified one is, because there simply won't be sufficient interest for this type of coaching service. Then, psychologists should learn everything they can about the psychological issues related to the stock market. The books listed in the Resources section are a good place to begin. Also, interested psychologists should do some online investing, so they know what it feels like, and attend seminars offered by market experts to increase their knowledge. Finally, they should focus on making contact with local traders, investor groups, and financial institutions and planners in the community who may be able to make referrals. To make contact, I suggest speaking to local investor groups and writing articles for local publications related to investing. E-mail (via websites), phone calls, and in-person contact are the best ways to make contact.

Resources

Cramer, J. J. (2009). *Jim Cramer's real money: Sane investing in an insane world.* New York, NY: Simon & Schuster.

Douglas, M. (2001) *Trading in the zone: Master the market with confidence, discipline and a winning attitude.* New York, NY: Prentice Hall Press.

Hendlin, S. J. (2000). *The disciplined online investor.* New York, NY: McGraw-Hill.

Hendlin, S. J. (2004). *Overcoming the inheritance taboo.* New York, NY: Penguin/Plume.

Schwager, J. D. (1992). *Market wizards: interviews with top traders.* New York, NY: Collins Business.

Tharp, V. (2006). *Trade your way to financial freedom.* New York, NY: McGraw-Hill.

Brad Klontz

Consulting With Financial Planners | 30

My interest in the psychology of money and personal finance sprung from the ashes of my own financial mess. After racking up a six-figure debt after a decade of higher education, I decided to make a quick fortune trading stocks. With little more than a modicum of financial acumen, I plunged head first into the life of a day trader. I sold everything of value that I had and invested all of my money in technology stocks. I drove a $400 car and lived in a house with no furniture. It didn't matter, though, because like millions of other Americans, I was making some easy money. When the technology bubble burst, and the dust finally settled, I ended up with less than half of what I had invested. The pain from this experience, and my curiosity about how I came about having it, started me on a journey of self-discovery that has also driven my professional passions for the past decade.

Since then, I have not only transformed my own relationship with money, turning my six-figure debt into a six-figure retirement savings, but I have been able to help thousands of others do the same through my program development, research, columns, media interviews, trade and professional books, and consulting in the areas of financial psychology and the treatment of disordered money behaviors. I also found a financial service profession with individuals who were hungry for knowledge and skills to improve their effectiveness in helping their clients stop self-destructive financial patterns, improve family relationships, identify their core values and life goals, and develop a healthy relationship with money. In addition to working directly with clients, The Klontz Consulting Group (http://www.klontzconsulting.com), which I founded with my business partner, coauthor, and father Ted Klontz, PhD, frequently consults with financial planners and financial planning firms.

Many of our financial services industry consulting philosophies and tools are highlighted in our book *Facilitating Financial Health: Tools for Financial Planners, Coaches, and Therapists* (Klontz, Kahler, & Klontz, 2008). Some of our more frequent consulting topics include the following:

- *Building a trusting relationship.* Establishing effective relationships based on honesty, appropriate boundaries (e.g., recognizing the boundaries among financial planning, coaching, and psychotherapy), respect for a client's right for self-determination, and knowing when and how to refer to other professionals.

- *Listening skills.* Teaching "exquisite" listening techniques, including the effective use of strategic reflection, summarization, open-ended questions, and interacting through invitation versus coercion. With a mastery of these skills, financial planners can be much more effective in their interactions with clients, making sure to honor and respect their clients' needs.

- *Change technology.* Understanding the stages of change, elements of change, techniques for facilitating change, and strategies for honoring and working with client resistance to healthy financial behaviors, such as limiting or eliminating the use of credit cards, holding to their budgets, or maxing out their 401(k) contributions. Like all change agents, financial planners often have clients who have difficulty following through on advice and recommendations. An understanding of the concept of ambivalence toward change and honing techniques for noticing and dealing with such resistance can be invaluable.

- *Identifying money scripts and disordered money behaviors.* Helping financial professionals identify self-limiting financial beliefs, recognize the signs and symptoms of money disorders (e.g., pathological gambling, compulsive buying disorder, financial enabling), understand how and when to refer a client to coaching or psychotherapy and how to collaborate with mental health professionals in the service of their clients.

- *Working with couples.* Money is the number one source of disagreement in the early years of marriage and a common area of conflict for couples. Financial planners often find themselves in the crossfire. Financial planners who frequently work with couples can benefit from learning techniques to defuse heated conflicts in their office, strategies for encouraging couples to have healthy money dialogues, and when and how to refer to couples therapy.

Psychology as a profession has generally stayed away from these issues. Psychologists who are interested in consulting with financial planners may first need to explore their own relationships with money. It is also beneficial to gain a mastery of basic financial planning concepts, including the importance of budgeting; the differences between stocks, bonds, and mutual funds; and the basic types of insurance. Although we won't be providing financial advice, it helps to know some of the language. Financial planners are accustomed to working with other professionals, including accountants and attorneys, but not mental health professionals. A study of financial planners showed that although they were aware of the close link between financial health and psychological health, they didn't refer to psychologists because (a) they didn't know a psychologist, (b) they did not have a relationship with a psychologist, (c) they fear a negative reaction from their clients, (d) they did not know what psychologists do, and (e) were not able to pick up on psychological issues that could be referred (Taylor, Bernes, Gunn, & Nixon, 2005). The most efficient way to get involved in financial psychology is by bridging this gap and getting to know financial planners in your area. Take them out to lunch. They will recognize the value of a free meal. Ask them about their most difficult client. Within a few moments, your potential value to them will be apparent.

The vast majority of financial planners are hardworking, ethical, conscientious, and caring professionals who are dedicated to the financial and emotional well-being of their clients and their clients' families. Whether it involves direct services to clients of financial planners, consultation with financial planners and financial advising firms, or collaboration with financial planners in direct service, psychologists' knowledge and skill can be of tremendous benefit to the financial planning community.

Resources

Klontz, B. T., Bivens, A., Klontz, P. T., Wada, J., & Kahler, R. (2008). The treatment of disordered money behaviors: Results of an open clinical trial. *Psychological Services, 5,* 295–308.

Klontz, B., Klontz, T., & Kahler, R. (2008). *Wired for wealth: Change the money mindsets and unleash your wealth potential.* Deerfield Beach, FL: Health Communications.

Klontz, B., Kahler, R., & Klontz, T. (2008). *Facilitating financial health: Tools for financial planners, coaches, and therapists.* Cincinnati, OH: The National Underwriter Company.

Klontz, T., Kahler, R., & Klontz, B. (2008). *The financial wisdom of Ebenezer Scrooge: 5 principles to transforming your relationship with money.* Deerfield Beach, FL: Health Communications.

Taylor, T. D., Bernes, K. B., Gunn, T. M., & Nixon, G. (2005, April). How financial planners can collaborate with professional counselors. *The Journal of Financial Planning.* Retrieved November 18, 2009, from http://hdl.handle.net/10133/393

Your Mental Wealth website of Dr. Ted Klontz and Dr. Brad Klontz: http://www.yourmentalwealth.com

TEACHING AND SUPERVISION | VIII

T. J. Price

Supervision of Psychotherapy Providers | 31

I am a licensed psychologist in Lakewood, Colorado, in private practice. I am neither in a solo practice nor a group practice, by traditional definitions. I started a solo practice in 1996 and have progressed to where I have two licensed psychologist associates and a doctoral graduate student working with me in a suite. I have strived to develop a progressive, client-centered agency in which ethical, creative, and motivated professionals want to learn from each other, as well as teach and assist people to reach their highest potential.

I supervise graduate or doctoral students (in bona fide human services programs) or graduates needing supervision before licensure. I incorporate clinical and some business supervision into the work, depending on what the supervisee needs or what we have contracted for. I have found that, in some agencies, a large portion of supervision can be paperwork or concern other matters that the supervisee has no interest in or need for once he or she leaves that agency. Approximately one tenth to one quarter of my time is usually spent supervising others.

I have learned that I need variety and different kinds of challenges in my work. My relevant history includes training positions in a previous profession, a cooperative learning experience in college, guest speaking, teaching college courses, and field placement in graduate school. It has been said, "Those who can, do, and those who can't, teach." However, I have found that to train people well, you must not only be able to do the job but also have developed mastery and a deeper understanding of various aspects of that job. I was fortunate in that I was able to experience teaching and supervision by several psychologists, each of whom had different ways of supervising and of seeing the world.

Supervision requires more than therapeutic skills and more than teaching ability; it requires role-specific skills. The American Psychological Association (APA) and Colorado State Psychological Association (CPA) have sponsored training regarding supervision. The Erickson Foundation has included seminars in supervision at many of its conferences. Being a psychology staff member in an APA-approved community mental health center has been important to me in developing this skill area. There were usually monthly meetings and special trainings around supervision of interns. Nonstructured meetings with other supervisors are helpful because we all face some similar but also unique supervision challenges.

For me, providing supervision has several positive aspects. It entails working with someone who has positive energy and hope for clients and themselves. Good supervision results in learning (i.e., progress) for everyone involved. It is a powerful way to give back to a university and the field.

Supervision quarterly evaluations can be unpleasant, but with preparation they can be a good tool and integrated into a useful supervision process. Different people learn different things at different speeds. Some supervisees will not get what you are trying to teach or model the first, second, or third time around. Crisis or urgent calls sometimes come at inconvenient times. Supervisee mistakes or errors can be upsetting. I recommend learning to accept mistakes and to use them for learning; it is also worthwhile to screen potential supervisees well, including how they have handled crises, their moral reasoning, their ability to admit faults and mistakes. It can be annoying when supervisees do not submit paperwork on time or do not finish paperwork when they move on from your supervision (and the supervisor is called upon to do it).

Referrals for supervision are often made by the University of Denver (with whom I have developed an ongoing relationship), past supervisees, people with whom I have worked, and via the Internet. I often do volunteer supervision of doctoral students from the University of Denver while they are in graduate training. They sometimes refer others or return for supervision for licensure. My website is becoming more important to help people find me. Being a part of various networking and professional groups and letting them know that I do supervision as part of my practice are also helpful. When the topic of supervision comes up, being able to answer questions and hand out a business card makes for effective connections.

For those people I charge for supervision, I charge a little less than I do for a full hour of psychotherapy. Some may consider this fairly low pay, but I find you can still charge more than most managed care companies will reimburse. I bill the supervisee directly. I specify my standard rate, interview him or her, and make sure we both believe the supervision experience will be helpful. When people pay consistently at the time of supervision, I give them a slightly discounted rate.

To develop supervision skills, pursue a wide variety of experiences and training, from performing specific techniques to conceptualizing cases from multiple perspectives, from team behind the mirror work to crisis work. Be as open to and familiar with the language of different psychological orientations as possible. There are more aspects of becoming proficient at supervising than there are of providing direct psychotherapy. Use audio and videotaping, live supervision, and coleading. Be clear with the supervisee about whether the session and process of supervision is to be mostly clinical, paperwork, business, pragmatic, or theoretical; make the implicit explicit. Although it can seem that psychologists are being inundated by paperwork, there is a need for a clear contract or agreement spelling out needs, processes, responsibilities, evaluation, and outcome measures. Keep your eyes open for training opportunities, and read as much as you can about supervision. Be open to learning and maintain a "beginner's mind" (from Eastern philosophy); develop a habit of striving to see things from different perspectives; and learn about research findings, individual differences, and the power of synergistic work when psychotherapeutic relationships develop. There is wisdom in various psychological orientations; I recommend developing a meta-theoretical orientation to supervision.

Resources

Aten, J. D., Strain, J. D., & Gillespie, R. E. (2008). A transtheoretical model of clinical supervision. *Training and Education in Professional Psychology, 2,* 1–9.

Falender, C. A., & Shafranske, E. P. (2004). *Clinical supervision: A competency-based approach.* Washington, DC: American Psychological Association.

Falender, C. A., & Shafranske, E. P. (2008). *Casebook for clinical supervision: A competency-based approach.* Washington, DC: American Psychological Association.

Oraker, J. (1998). *The slippery slope of supervision. Colorado Psychological Association Bulletin, 31,* No. 8.

Williams, A. (1995). *Visual and active supervision.* New York, NY: Norton.

Valerie L. Shebroe

32

Integrating University Teaching Into Independent Clinical Practice

O ver the past 25 years, I have had a number of different practice and professional activity time arrangements in university positions as well as being in independent practice. In teaching and consulting with the Michigan State University (MSU) Psychology Department, my academic appointments have ranged from being an adjunct faculty member and clinical supervisor for 2 hours a week, to teaching one course a semester, to holding a 50% time assistant professor appointment. The following is a description of my experience initially as a volunteer clinical supervisor, which then expanded into a paid position as an assistant professor serving as the community outreach coordinator for the MSU Psychological Clinic, the clinical psychology graduate training site.

In full-time independent practice, I felt that I was missing the opportunity for broader impact through teaching and training developing professionals. During an informal conversation with the director of the Psychology Graduate Training Clinic at a professional meeting, I inquired about opportunities to supervise graduate students. There was a need, and I was invited to become a clinical supervisor. The position of clinical supervisor was unpaid, although one was granted an adjunct faculty title and issued a university library card. Being a volunteer clinical supervisor led to being invited to teach a number of graduate-level practicum classes, for which I was paid.

After a number of years of supervising students and teaching graduate-level courses, I had the opportunity to meet with the director of clinical training to discuss some of the challenges of clinical training in terms of a lack of child, adolescent, and family referrals. As a practicing psychologist in the community, I was aware of the lack of referral resources for children and families who needed low-cost mental health treatment. I suggested that a perfect solution would be to market the psychology training clinic and expand services to the community. As a result of this suggestion, I was invited to write a proposal for how to increase referrals for the training clinic, which was in essence writing my own job description. This paved the way for an exciting, paid 50% time appointment in the Psychology Department as the community outreach coordinator for the Psychological Clinic.

My proposal included having a team of graduate students (paid) to function as the community outreach team. We conducted a needs assessment of preschool, primary, and secondary schools; physicians; religious organizations; and community organizations. The needs assessment aided the clinic in designing training opportunities that met the needs of the community, and the process of collecting this data immediately increased referrals.

Aside from developing on-site clinical services to meet community needs, such as children of divorce and social skills groups for children, other collaborative activities were also developed with public schools and community organizations. One example was a preschool trauma and loss group at a local Head Start preschool (Huth-Bocks, Schettini, & Shebroe, 2001) that provided graduate students hands-on application of their research in domestic violence and other trauma, provided a valuable clinical service for a high-needs population, and yielded a publication for me and the graduate students involved.

In addition to supervising the community outreach team, I attended all community meetings with students, supervised all community presentations, and also provided clinical supervision in group and individual formats. These activities not only were energizing but gave me communitywide exposure as a psychologist. Although I attended meetings as a representative of the Psychology Department, I was also recognized as an independent psychologist and a potential referral resource.

Despite the advantages, working with a university psychology department can have several drawbacks. First is the issue of funding, which is not an uncommon problem in universities. I was hired for a 50% time contract, and I often exceeded this time agreement. Second was the need to evaluate constantly how my time was spent and prioritizing the use of my time. It is also important when working contractually and off campus to maintain some amount of visibility with faculty and staff. Aside from attending meetings on campus, I also maintained visibility in the department by sending monthly activity reports to faculty and graduate students.

Supervising, teaching, and working as the community outreach coordinator was a perfect complement to my independent practice. It was helpful in terms of diversifying my day-to-day professional life, updating myself through teaching various classes, and learning more about my community; community organizations and leaders also learned more about what services I had to offer.

There are many opportunities to work in university settings that include formal and informal teaching opportunities. I have described working in a psychology department setting, but no matter in which department one works, the following concepts apply. First, and foremost, think about your own professional interests and needs. What drives you? What excites you professionally? Consider how your current interests and needs may intersect with needs of a program or department and what you specifically and uniquely have to offer. Second, look for needs and be willing to write your own job description in a way that will satisfy a university or community need, as well as enhance or complement your own practice. Third, be willing to volunteer. As I described in my own experience, I initially started out as a volunteer clinical supervisor. Volunteering then led to getting paid for teaching opportunities. Fourth, consider the synergy between your practice and other professional opportunities. Will the professional opportunity enhance or detract from your practice? Fifth, think about how much the activity will "cost" you. For example, teaching a class for the first time not only involves class time, travel time, and time outside of class to communicate with students; it also takes an enormous amount of time to prepare for teaching. There is no such thing as adequate compensation for teaching from a monetary perspective as far as I'm concerned. However, the "cost" of teaching decreases every time you teach the same class again because one still needs to revise and update, but those activities are not as labor intensive as an initial preparation.

In addition to monetary compensation for a position, consider other benefits, such as free publicity, opportunities to market oneself, and the value and or prestige of being associated with a university and holding a faculty appointment. Teaching and consulting part time has certainly helped to enhance my independent practice.

Reference

Huth-Bocks, A., Schettini, A., & Shebroe, V. (2001). Group play therapy for preschoolers exposed to domestic violence. *Journal of Child and Adolescent Group Therapy, 11*, 19–34.

Mitchell W. Hicks

Teaching Online 33

am a licensed clinical psychologist in the Chicago area practicing primarily psychotherapy with adults and older adults, with special interest in working with men's issues, relational problems, sexual compulsivity, and religious and spiritual issues. In addition to my private practice, I am a full-time faculty member in the School of Psychology at Walden University.

Through my affiliation with the clinical psychology doctoral program, I currently teach three courses per quarter, serve as chair or committee member for doctoral dissertations, and have modest committee responsibilities. In addition, I attend three face-to-face residencies each year. As a full-time member of the faculty, I spend approximately 60% of my professional time engaged in activities related to this commitment. Part-time faculty members are afforded far more flexibility in the amount of time spent in various activities. For example, some of our part-time faculty teach one course per term, whereas others may teach two or three, mentor dissertations, and attend residencies.

Upon entering graduate school, I was not interested in working in academia full time. However, I did serve as both a teaching assistant and instructor under supervision during my graduate studies. After spending a few years working in correctional environments, I transitioned to a full-time faculty position at a traditional brick-and-mortar university. This afforded me the opportunity to develop further the basic pedagogical skills first learned in graduate school while becoming skilled at connecting all course activities to the learning objectives for the course.

Like many professionals entering distance education, I was relatively unfamiliar with how a quality education could be provided through this delivery model. Fortunately, most online universities provide significant training before assignment of one's first course. To date, I have participated in well over 10 weeks of training related to use of the online classroom environment, best practices for teaching in an online environment, mentoring theses and dissertations, and the research review processes.

Teaching in an online environment provides both unique opportunities and challenges. The most important reason that I chose to resign a tenure-track faculty position to work for Walden University is that the online environment provides me the ability to reasonably balance multiple professional and personal endeavors. In addition to these responsibilities, I am able to maintain an active clinical practice and spend ample time with family while providing a steady income and health benefits (as a full-time faculty member). I also appreciate the opportunity to work with students from all over the country and throughout the world who do not have ready access to a traditional clinical psychology training program, such as those students from rural areas. Those interested in teaching part-time would have the flexibility to choose their own level of commitment.

All of the readings, assignments, and discussion questions are predetermined in the classroom. I find this to be a mixed blessing. On the one hand, I do not like having limited input from term to term regarding how I conduct a particular class. On the other hand, I am able to devote my energy to activities other than course preparation. I do assert my creativity and academic freedom by adding what I believe to be important information into the course discussions. I also miss the face-to-face interaction of the traditional classroom. Attendance at residencies also tends to be very demanding and takes me away from my clinical practice. Although these are not optional for me as a full-time faculty member, those teaching part-time are able to choose whether to participate in residencies.

A psychologist wishing to seek employment teaching online has at least two options. A number of universities operate exclusively or almost exclusively online, and position openings can be readily accessed through their websites. The largest of these are Walden University and Capella University; and Fielding Graduate University is the only American Psychological Association–accredited clinical psychology distance preparation program available online at this time. In general, these institutions allow the faculty member to live anywhere. The second option is to connect with a traditional brick-and-mortar institution that has expanded its offerings into the online environment. Often these positions are advertised in the *Chronicle of Higher Education* (http://www.chronicle.com). If one has a particular area of expertise that is unusual or cutting edge, contacting department heads, program directors, or other administrators can help get oneself noticed. Regardless of which type of institution one chooses to align with, it is imperative that research be done to make certain it is accredited by one of the bodies recognized by the Higher Learning Commission (http://www.ncahlc.org).

To learn more about online teaching, I suggest that the reader consult the following resources.

Resources

Keeton, M. T. (2004). Best online instructional practices: Report of Phase I of an ongoing study. *Journal of Asynchronous Learning Networks, 8,* 75–100.

Ko, S., & Rossen, S. (2001). *Teaching online: A practical guide.* Boston, MA: Houghton Mifflin.

Lazarus, B. D. (2003). Teaching courses online: How much time does it take? *Journal of Asynchronous Learning Networks, 7,* 47–54.

Palloff, R. M., & Pratt, K. (2003). *The virtual student.* San Francisco, CA: Jossey-Bass.

Task Force on Distance Education and Training in Professional Psychology. (2002). *Principles of good practice in distance education and their application to professional education and training in psychology.* Retrieved from http://www.apa.org/ed/graduate/distance_ed.pdf

Tish Taylor

34 Conducting Workshops for Teachers and Educators

I began the process of leaving a job with a steady income and benefits and ventured into business for myself in 2007. When I did so, I conceptualized a dual role that included conducting psychological evaluations and psychotherapy with children and adolescents and being an educational consultant. I have spent the majority of my time developing the direct service side of my business but have also managed to engage in aspects of the educational consultant role. I have felt comfortable incorporating this role because I spent 14 years working in the public school system before opening my practice. Within this time, I have gained experience as a school psychologist, coordinating mental health services at a district level, planning and conducting trainings for educators, working in and supervising a school-based day treatment program for children with significant mental health issues, and problem-solving difficult and multidimensional cases for the school district. In addition, I have taught graduate and undergraduate courses for 7 years in the areas of child development, life-span development, educational psychology, and general psychology.

I believe that my current abilities in these areas are the direct result of my willingness and commitment to develop my skills and knowledge base consistently. I have always sought out new information and research within the fields of educational psychology, school psychology, and child clinical psychology through activities such as pursuing continuing education, coediting a book on classroom management, and seeking specific experiences in my doctoral training. I have always dived into new projects, and by engaging in challenging efforts, a tremendous amount of learning took place; consequently, my skills developed.

A second consideration I had when developing my role is the needs I perceived of children and adolescents and the current services available to them, the needs within families, and the needs within educational systems. As a businessperson and entrepreneur, I believe it is essential to maintain a business mind, which means making keen observations about how the market will bear my skill set. Continually evaluating this allows me to adjust my focus and direct my marketing efforts.

One area of need I have noticed is training for educators. Teachers, school counselors, principals, school psychologists, paraeducators, and other support staff are continually interacting with children and adolescents with emotional and behavioral needs. These needs are exhibited within the school setting and affect learning and the learning environment. Specific information on how to intervene and apply research-based information within an educational setting is valuable for educators. For example, an understanding of oppositional defiant disorder, its effective interventions and treatments, as well as examples of how these interventions can be implemented within the confines of a school is knowledge that educators need and want. In addition, continuing education hours are needed for educational licensure. Because of these needs, I developed a full-day training seminar that addresses children's behavioral, emotional, and psychological health and how to manage it within a school setting.

What I find enjoyable about conducting seminars for educators is that I have developed and created something all my own. There is satisfaction in defining a need, fulfilling it in a creative and individualized way, and being paid to do so. Developing a full-day seminar takes a tremendous amount of work in the beginning. It requires continued work over time as components are updated and adjusted. However, this becomes easier the more often the seminars are conducted. It is also enjoyable interacting with the participants, hearing their experiences, and then offering my experiences and knowledge to help them come to new realizations and take new ideas back with them to their schools. An amazing aspect of conducting these seminars is that when they are allowed an opportunity to share specific examples and pose questions for in-the-moment problem solving, it adds to everyone's knowledge base, including my own. This allows me to modify my seminar content to ensure that I am meeting the content needs of the participants.

There are aspects of conducting seminars that I find less desirable. The first is developing the seminar invitation list and sending the invitations.

I engaged in the tedious task of looking up schools within state education directories as well as on district websites to develop my invitee list. However, to target the right market, I believe it was worth the effort. The second difficult aspect for me is managing the degree of anxiety associated with standing in front of many people whom you do not know and hoping to meet their expectations. To manage anxiety, I focus on my preparation, rely on my skills of delivery from past experiences, and remind myself to have fun with the presentation. By doing these things, it becomes easier to allow for a natural flow, and aspects of my personality emerge, which makes presentations more engaging.

In terms of collecting payment, the seminar flyer I created includes a registration component. Within the registration component, individuals indicate their form of payment, which includes check, debit or credit card, or purchase order. I allow these methods because some individuals pay out of pocket and some school buildings or districts pay for the seminar. Therefore, as most participants register, I receive payment with the registration forms because they paid out of pocket or with a school credit card. As I receive purchase orders, I immediately send a bill to the accounts receivable department indicated on the purchase order. Most purchase orders are paid within 2 to 4 weeks. I have had to follow up with a few districts regarding payment but have always been paid within 5 weeks of the seminar.

My suggestions for developing seminars for educators are to evaluate your particular skill set, know how that knowledge would be useful to educators, and know how to apply it to an educational setting. Considering these aspects will assist you in developing a targeted and effective seminar. It will also assist in determining which particular individuals to target when sending out invitations and registration forms.

Finally, I believe it is important to stay abreast of current issues and topics within the field of education or the field you may be addressing. Many pertinent issues are found within national organization websites. Websites that I find helpful include the National Association of School Psychologists (http://www.nasponline.org), the American Psychological Association's Divisions 15 (Educational Psychology) and 16 (School Psychology), and the U.S. Department of Education (http://www.ed. gov/index.jhtml). I believe it is also important to stay aware of what is occurring at the state and local levels. It provides more credibility when the issues or challenges that are occurring locally are acknowledged. This information can generally be found within newspapers and state board of education websites.

Educators are a population of professionals who find the knowledge and skills of psychologists useful, especially when these skills are directly applicable to their current challenges. They are also consistently pursuing training opportunities. Therefore, with a directed vision and determination to provide a helpful seminar, psychologists can be well on their way to a successful endeavor.

Mark Gilson

Combining Treatment and Professional Training Within a Private Practice Model

35

I am a clinical psychologist and founder of the Atlanta Center for Cognitive Therapy (ACCT) Treatment and Training program. Our center began in 1985. The group consists of psychologists, psychiatrists, counselors, and social workers. We have two levels of affiliation within the group. There are the owner and managers who essentially contract with each other to maintain the group by being on the lease, owning equipment and furnishings, and coordinating office staff and services. The second level involves subleases for professionals who contract on at least a year-to-year basis with the option to buy into the first level. We are basically an overhead-sharing group where no one profits from the other's practice. It is a communal effort, but business decisions are made by those at the first level with input from those who sublease. We can reasonably state that this structure has endured the test of time. However, in no small part, compatibility of practice colleagues has played a major role in our success.

Our referrals come from many long-established relationships in the community and as a result of a positive profile that our Training and Certification Program in Cognitive Therapy has provided. Several of us are adjunct faculty at either or both Emory University and Georgia State University. Members of the practice each have their areas of expertise but are also generalists in their practice. My focus is treatment of anxiety and depression.

In 1979, I began to develop a dissertation idea based on perceptual selection in vision as it relates to mood. At that time, a book by Aaron T. Beck, MD, and his colleagues, *Cognitive Therapy of Depression*, was creating quite a stir. I thought the concepts of bias in visual selection and report paralleled Dr. Beck's contention that there is distortion in thinking and information processing that occurs in depression. To organize my research, I wrote Dr. Beck a letter outlining my ideas. I did not expect anything more than a polite acknowledgment in return. Instead, I received a lengthy letter that concluded by inviting me to do my research at his center. His response changed the direction of my career. I later found that Dr. Beck enjoyed doing similar things for many other people when he saw potential. I worked and trained at the center and participating in research projects that were seminal in the establishment of cognitive behavior therapy (CBT). After almost 3 years as a fellow and faculty at University of Pennsylvania's Center for Cognitive Therapy, I came back to the place where I finished my degree, Atlanta, to create the ACCT in 1985.

My supervisor at the University of Pennsylvania was Arthur Freeman. Art was (and still is) offering training all around the world and has authored a large catalog of professional books. My intent in returning to Atlanta was to start my private practice. It was Art and I who developed a structured Cognitive Therapy Training Program that includes four parts. The first is level 100, the Fundamentals of the model, which I teach. It involves two all-day classes, readings, and an exam at the end. Level 200, Applications of Cognitive Behavior Therapy, includes three all-day classes with guest faculty. We present workshops with our contacts from organizations such as the Academy of Cognitive Therapy and the Association for Behavior and Cognitive Therapy. These workshops are open for registration individually and are also part of the total sequence, allowing the center to collect tuition that was sufficient to cover expenses, pay our guest lecturers, and earn some profit. Over the past 23 years, our guest faculty has included professionals such as David Barlow, Aaron T. Beck, David Burns, Don Meichenbaum, and Jeff Young. Topics have ranged from treating anxiety, depression, and obsessive–compulsive disorder, managing anger, impulse control, and even how to produce a treatment manual. Level 300 of the program involves writing a paper on an application of CBT. Level 400 focuses on case consultation and case conceptualization. There is a total of 70 continuing education hours awarded for completion of the program.

Providing credible training and the association with so many luminaries in mental health treatment have had advantages in establishing our center as a mainstay in the Atlanta community. In the late 1980s, credentials for the training program were sought. The first step was to become approved as a continuing education provider by the American Psychological Association (APA). Rigorous standards were met to achieve this distinction. This includes the required statement that ACCT maintains responsibility for our program and its content anytime we mention APA approval. We also obtained approval from the National Board for Certified Counselors. The program branched into home study where videos of the programs were provided, now on DVD. This has allowed registering professionals in the Certification Program from around the world.

Training has also been provided for separate groups, such as hospitals and university programs, both nationally and internationally. Contracts with an organization would either be spread out over a year or sometimes concentrated into a version of the program presented over a period of 5 days. An advanced certification is also offered that involves intense case consultation for those who have been certified by our program or another credentialed establishment.

The training arm of our center has been an enhancement to our group and has built our reputation and credibility. In the beginning, promotion of the program involved writing a brief outline of its content and mailing it to professionals in the Atlanta area. Now the Internet provides a means for most communication, both local and long distance. I never thought the program would continue this long. Now I have to consider who will take it over when I retire. It has been a pleasure to establish a self-employed teaching position as part of my practice.

Personally, I truly enjoy being a psychotherapist, and that is the major part of my schedule. The training program obligations are shared with my colleagues, and most recently, collaboration with Institute for the Advancement of Human Behavior (IAHB) has allowed us to continue to work with well-established guest faculty and an organization that produces professional workshop tours for training experts.

Other practitioners can establish programs and training at a variety of levels. With the advent of the Internet, e-mail, craigslist, and listservs, it is possible to produce training for professional audiences; don't forget old-fashioned snail mail, either. Credibility is essential. My route was to become trained and certified by the father of CBT, Aaron Beck. One does not obtain credibility overnight. The advice would be to gain a particular empirically validated skill as a psychotherapist and master it. However, audacity does play a role. Art Freeman worked on me for awhile before I was convinced to take on the task of creating a program. It is good to have a mentor. For those considering creating their own training program, I know of no books that offers a map for such an endeavor. What psychologists can do is look at what other successful programs are doing. Consider looking at websites such as ACCT (http://www.cognitive

atlanta.com) and IAHB (http://www.IAHB.org); review what is being offered in professional newsletters such as APA's *Monitor on Psychology*. It also helps to develop a reputation as an expert in one's area by presenting at national conventions or writing in professional publications. Our treatment manual for overcoming depression is now in its second edition (Gilson, Freeman, Yates, & Freeman, 2009).

There are many good ideas out there, and it is not necessary to reinvent the wheel. Just like the process of developing a research idea for a dissertation or study, see what others have done, and ask yourself if you could take it to the next level.

Reference

Gilson, M., Freeman, A., Yates, J., & Freeman, S. (2009). *Overcoming depression: A cognitive therapy approach*. New York, NY: Oxford University Press.

SPECIALTY GROUPS

Gina Hassan

Pregnancy Support Groups | 36

As a clinical psychologist, my interest in working with pregnant and postpartum women has developed over the past several years. After finding this transition through pregnancy to motherhood in my own life to be one of such profound meaning and deep transformation, I began to explore possibilities of how to incorporate this work into my private practice.

Initially, I joined a peer consultation group that focused on perinatal psychology, attended trainings in this area, and read books on the topic. After about a year of participating in the consultation group, a couple of colleagues and I decided to form a collaborative relationship, and together we founded Perinatal Psychotherapy Services (http://www.perinatal psychotherapy.com), a collective of therapists providing services to women during the childbearing years. As a group, we have taught, written, and provided consultation to various professional groups. Individually, we each have a private practice in which we see individual psychotherapy clients and couples, as well as lead groups. The groups I have led include new mothers' groups, and pregnancy support groups. The group I focus on in this chapter is the pregnancy support group.

The purpose of this group is for women to gain support through the emotional adjustment of pregnancy and the transition to motherhood. The group is designed to be a place of support, information, insight, and connection-building.

It has a psychoeducational component through which women are taught the importance of making room for and respecting the emotional changes that occur during this period. Information is provided about the kinds of things that can help one's emotional adjustment during and after pregnancy, and the distinction is clarified between pregnancy and postpartum blues on the one hand versus clinical depression or anxiety on the other.

These pregnancy support groups vary in size. They are generally ongoing groups with some degree of shifting membership. Women are asked to commit to a group for at least four sessions and to then recommit for 4 weeks at a time. (Exceptions are made for women close to their due date.) The groups meet one evening per week for 90 minutes. Topics of discussion in the groups vary depending on the particular interests of group members.

Groups begin with a check-in and then proceed to focus on a particular topic. Topics may include hopes and fears around labor and delivery; identity changes during pregnancy; sexuality during pregnancy and the early postpartum period; changes in one's relationship with partner, family, and friends; shifts in body image; the emotional roller-coaster of pregnancy; the role of hormones; feelings of loss; the impact of your own childhood and the kind of parent one wants to become; planning for the weeks after the baby arrives; returning to work; how to deal with unwanted advice; and worries about bonding with one's newborn.

Members sign a group agreement that outlines issues of confidentiality and stresses the importance of maintaining a nonjudgmental stance. It reads as follows:

> Everyone deals with this transition in their own unique way and there is no right way to "do pregnancy" or "parenthood" but a myriad of choices are available. This group is designed to help you figure out what is right for you and your family and to provide you with support and information in thinking about the choices and decisions that are before you.

In general terms, although it may be useful for clinicians to have personal experience to run such groups, therapists can also gain knowledge on the topic through reading and professional training. Because many women who choose to join this kind of group are struggling with emotional issues during their pregnancy, such as anxiety or depression, it is important to have some background in perinatal mood disorders. Postpartum Support International (http://www.postpartum.net) offers an excellent 2-day training on perinatal mood disorders, as does the Postpartum Stress Center (http://www.postpartumstress.com). Another organization that offers conferences on related topics is the North American Society for Psychosocial Obstetrics and Gynecology (http://www.naspog.org).

Referrals can be generated by advertising in the community (for example, newsletters of local birth-related organizations, obstetric and family practice clinics). Contacting local midwifery organizations may also be helpful in generating referrals or writing a piece for a local parenting newsletter. Billing can be done on a fee-for-service basis, or insurance can sometimes be billed depending on the individual's health plan. In my practice, most of the women prepay for the group in 4-week installments.

In thinking about what I have found most enjoyable about running these groups, the rewards have included feeling that I am helping to set the stage for a smoother postpartum transition by helping members build a support network, providing them with a more realistic picture of early motherhood, and giving them the information and tools that might help reduce the likelihood of postpartum depression and other such disorders. What I have found most frustrating is that the population is one with a rather small window of time during which members are appropriate for the group. This has meant that it has at times been difficult to reach a critical mass for the formation of the group. A minimum of four members seems important to generate the feeling of there being a group. Furthermore, this can be a population in whom not feeling well or being overly tired can cause irregular attendance; it can be difficult at times to weather this irregularity. With persistence, however, there will be periods of committed membership and group cohesiveness such that some of the women will continue their bond and friendship well beyond the period of attending the groups.

The following brief list of books may be helpful in learning more about some of the issues related to pregnancy and motherhood. For a more complete list, feel free to contact me at ghassanphd@aol.com.

Resources

Bing, W., & Coleman, L. (1997). *Laughter and tears: The emotional life of new mothers*. New York, NY: Holt Paperbacks.

Coleman, L., & Coleman, A. (1991). *Pregnancy: The psychological experience*. New York, NY: Farrar, Strauss & Giroux.

Leonhardt-Lup, M. (1995). *A mother is born: Preparing for motherhood during pregnancy*. Westport, CT: Bergin & Garvey.

Louden, J. (2005). *The pregnant woman's comfort book: Self-nurturing guide to your emotional well being during pregnancy and early motherhood*. New York, NY: Harper One.

Plaskin, S. (2000). *Mothering the new mother: Women's feelings and needs after childbirth*. New York, NY: Newmarket Press.

Laurie Little

37 Assertiveness Skills Training Groups

I am a licensed clinical psychologist and co-owner of Little Psychological Services, PLLC. My husband and I founded the practice in 2002. Since that time, we have expanded our staff to include four full-time psychologists, a full-time billing coordinator, and a full-time receptionist. Our practice is a general psychology practice in which patients of all ages are seen for diagnostic assessment, psychotherapy, group psychotherapy, and neurotherapy.

One of the more enjoyable aspects of my practice is leading a psychoeducational group called Assertiveness Skills Training. This group meets for 90 minutes once per week for 8 weeks. A maximum of eight participants all agree to make their best effort to attend all sessions. No participants join midway through the group because each class builds on the information from the prior class.

In the first class, a great deal of emphasis is placed on defining the psychoeducational group. Participants are reminded that although emotional material may be discussed while in the group, it is within the context of learning new social skills. Discussing emotional material is not for the purpose of processing or "working through," as is often the case during psychotherapy groups such as those patients may have attended in the past.

A review of confidentiality and other group guidelines is also completed in the first class. Participants receive their syllabus outlining what they will be learning over the course of the 8 weeks, along with their homework assignments. The following topics are reviewed: definition of assertiveness, passivity, and aggression; boundaries; asking for what you want; saying no; self-esteem and self-respect; and the importance of maintaining healthy interpersonal relationships. Handouts are provided for each new area. The typical format for each class thereafter has one half of group devoted to reviewing homework, with the second half devoted to learning the next skill.

This is one of the most rewarding and enjoyable aspects of my work, and I feel very fortunate to have had the opportunity to do this group for the past 13 years. I became interested in doing this type of work while in graduate school working as a practicum student. Through my training in dialectical behavior therapy (DBT), I came to understand the tremendous value of the skills training group. Marsha Linehan (1993), researcher and developer of DBT, posited that individuals suffer not because they choose to but because they often lack the skills that are necessary to be assertive, to soothe themselves, or to tolerate emotional pain. Linehan suggests that when taught how to ask for want they want, how to say no, how to self-soothe, how to manage emotions, and how to become more mindful, patients will learn how to accept their emotions rather than fight them and eventually reduce emotional suffering.

After my practicum, I attended a 2-year predoctoral internship specializing in DBT. During my internship, I co-led DBT skills training groups, conducted individual DBT therapy, and was a member of the DBT consultation team. I also attended two 1-week intensive training courses in DBT taught by leaders who were themselves trained by Dr. Linehan. Although skills training groups is just one aspect of DBT, it was through this experience that I became best prepared for leading all kinds of psychoeducational groups. I went on to lead assertiveness groups after seeing such a great need for it among patients in our practice.

This work allows me to use my skills as a teacher. It is a skill set different from that of a psychotherapist and a change in pace from the other parts of my day. The patients thoroughly enjoy this experience as well. They love learning useful, practical skills that they can immediately put into practice in their daily lives. The skills are concrete, tangible, and effective. These qualities are highly rewarding to the patient, and the groups have an energy that can be a welcome change from seeing a depressed or hopeless client in individual psychotherapy.

Once the group is developed, it is relatively easy to maintain. Because I have done each group many times, I have the content of the material memorized, so there is little preparation needed prior to each group.

Yet each group is different because the participants are unique individuals, so the sessions themselves do not get boring or predictable. In fact, I have experienced some of my most surprising, delightful, and most meaningful therapeutic exchanges while in one of these psychoeducational groups.

On the downside, it does take much preparation to develop the content of the group as well as the syllabus, handouts, and homework assignments. Marketing the group, organizing the group's membership, and maintaining the group all take time. However, it has clearly been worth the effort because it has become a stable part of my practice for many years now.

In addition to getting the appropriate training in assertiveness skills training, it is also essential to put the extra effort into the development of the group. Although it is additional work up front, it saves time in the end. When the syllabus, handouts, and homework are all organized and filed chronologically in a binder, it makes things smoother and more efficient for the group process.

Because this is not a psychotherapy group, it is not covered under health insurance. Patients are charged a flat fee per session and are offered a discount if they pay for the entire series in advance. Payments are expected at the beginning of each group meeting.

Marketing to the community is essential. Sending out letters to all referral sources is a necessary component. It is helpful to include color flyers that referral sources can post in their waiting rooms. I post a color flyer in my waiting room to let current patients know that a new group is forming. An ad in a local newspaper can also generate additional referrals. Sending notifications out to other psychologists in the community is also essential. Because it is a time-limited skills training group, many mental health professionals are willing to refer their patients because they do not see it as competition but as an additional resource for their patients.

For additional information on DBT or leading assertiveness skills training or other psychoeducational groups, see Behavioral Tech at http://www.behavioraltech.org/index.cfm.

Resources

Linehan, M. (1993). *Cognitive behavioral treatment of borderline personality disorder.* New York, NY: Guilford Press.

Linehan, M. (1993). *Skills training manual for treating borderline personality disorder.* New York, NY: Guilford Press.

McKay, M., Wood, J., & Brantley, J. (2007). *Dialectical behavior therapy workbook: Practical DBT exercises for learning mindfulness, interpersonal effectiveness, emotion regulation, & distress tolerance.* Oakland, CA: New Harbinger Press.

David O. Aspenson

Mind–Body Skills Training Groups | 38

I am a solo practitioner who has been training and practicing in my community since the early 1980s. I have been in full-time private practice since 1998. My professional experience is primarily related to health psychology, and I have an enduring interest in what could be called *mind–body interventions,* such as hypnosis, biofeedback, and meditation. While working in a family medicine department and seeing patients in this setting, I became interested in models for teaching self-regulation tools and mind–body medicine. That experience and interest eventually led me to the training programs offered by the Center for Mind–Body Medicine (CMBM) in Washington, D.C. This center was founded by James Gordon, MD. I conducted my first mind–body skills group while still in the family medicine department. Since then, I have incorporated that training in a variety of ways in my own private practice.

The Mind–Body Skills Group (MBSG) is a 10- to 12-week program that serves as a self-regulation intensive training experience. The groups could probably be done with up to 10 to 12 participants, but I prefer a smaller number because I use my regular office, where about seven participants is more comfortable. The meetings generally last 2 hours and include didactic and experiential components. Participants are introduced to skills such as biofeedback, meditation, autogenics, guided imagery, self-hypnosis, and the use of drawing and movement. Some more unusual active meditations are also introduced, such as shaking or chaotic breathing. We cover some basic information on the physiology of stress as well.

The groups do not function as a traditional psychotherapy group in which there is considerable focus on the interaction between group members. In the MBSG, members are encouraged to work on their own self and are free to determine their comfort level of self-disclosure. The activities vary from brief explanations of a particular skill, time to practice in the group, and opportunities to share how the skills are being used in the participants' lives, along with any struggles they may be having. Part of the clinician's job is to keep things focused and create a supportive environment. Without abdicating my responsibilities as the leader, I like to foster the sense that we are all fellow travelers rather than maintaining a posture of the psychotherapist as somehow different or more evolved then the participants. Even though the groups have some structure, part of the skill (and fun) in leading them is to be open and flexible to the more organic components of the process. Each group and each group meeting has its own particular rhythm and flow.

The mind–body skills training has infused and enriched both my practice and my life in a number of ways. Part of the personal benefit is the ongoing attention to the ever-present needs of self-care. One of the organizing principles of both the training and the intervention model is taking active responsibility for your own health and effective self-care. Personally, I have always found it easier to talk that game then actually live it. Consequently, this work is a reminder to be more congruent in this arena, and I am consistently challenged to practice more of what I preach.

In my practice, I draw on the mind–body perspective in a number of ways, including individual work in which I integrate skills training with general psychotherapy. I also might offer a short workshop focusing on stress in which I draw on this approach. Recently, I taught a few short classes at a local retirement center where the format was more of a lecture on stress, but the participants also practiced some the same mind–body skills. I organize an MBSG "whenever I feel like it" or when I have a good collection of candidates in my practice.

Clients are more typically referred to me individually, as opposed to being referred for a specific intervention or format. The groups then evolve out of these referrals. When I start a new group I advertise to colleagues, physicians, former clients, and the local integrative medicine programs. I make hard-copy brochures and am increasingly using e-mail as a marketing tool. For those who might not be ready to commit to the intensive 10-week group, I also offer shorter 3-hour workshops on mind–body stress relief as a way to provide some exposure to me and the work. I am also beginning to experiment with marketing the groups more specifically to both the medical and alternative medicine communities such as acupuncturists, naturopathic physicians, and massage therapists.

When I was doing my clinical practice in a large academic family practice center, my referrals included many demanding medical presentations. It was while working with this multifaceted array of challenging referrals that I became invested in learning and teaching self-regulation tools. This dovetailed with the growing interest in what is typically referred to as complementary or alternative medicine. I was originally interested in the training offered by the CMBM because it was directed by one of the visible leaders in the field. The training was extremely engaging, evocative, useful, and enriching. My fellow trainees came from a wide variety of physical locations and disciplines. The other participants ranged from psychologists, psychiatrists, family physicians, acupuncturists, massage therapists, and even high-level hospital administrators.

There is a growing body of evidence on the efficacy of mind–body skills in helping to manage and treat a variety of conditions. There is also an abundance of resources available to psychologists who wish to integrate mind–body resources into their practice. Herbert Benson, one of the pioneer investigators of the benefits of meditation, offers mind–body orienting training programs that are affiliated with Harvard Medical School. The National Institute for Clinical Application of Behavioral Medicine (NICABM) also offers relevant training including an online distance learning program and "master practitioner" certification focused on mind–body practices. I do not have firsthand experience with these programs, but a colleague who has completed some of the NICABM online courses reports they are excellent. As mentioned, my training has primarily been with the CMBM. That has included attending the 5-day Professional Training, receiving some supervision for the group work with their faculty, and twice attending the 4-day Advanced Training Program. The CMBM also offers a certification program and an extensive community network.

To move one's practice in this direction, I would recommend fostering contacts in the community with alternative and other like-minded practitioners. For example, I often collaborate with acupuncturists, and we exchange referrals (I also have treatments myself). Programs that are commonly referred to as *integrative* in nearby hospitals or medical schools are also good places to make connections.

James Gordon, the CMBM director, has published some excellent resources. In *Manifesto for a New Medicine: Your Guide to Healing Partnerships and the Wise Use of Alternative Therapies,* he draws on his own personal experience as well as interesting case studies to provide a broad and creative framework for the place of mind–body practices. His more recent book, *Unstuck: Your Guide to the Seven Stage Journey Out of Depression,* describes most of the components of the training model. Gordon and the CMBM also developed an audio program that basically contains all the features of the group training called *Best of Stress Management,* which is available on their website (http://www.cmbm.org). One could use these resources to build the content of a 10- to 12-week MBSG. However, I think it much more faithfully captures the spirit of the work to go through the professional training, have the experience as a participant in the group, and begin with working on self. As our old friend Ram Dass has said, "I help people as a work on myself and I work on myself to help people."

FORENSIC PSYCHOLOGY

Steven N. Shapse

Serving as a Guardian Ad Litem 39

n recent years, the role of child custody evaluator (CCE) or guardian ad litem (GAL) is increasingly being filled by psychologists, social workers, and other mental health professionals. Even in jurisdictions where lawyers continue to be appointed in this role, there is an emphasis in working in tandem with mental health professionals. Those interested in pursuing such work should be warned that child custody evaluations are complex, challenging, and potentially risky because CCEs are subject to professional ethics complaints, more so than in any other mental health professional role.

Psychologists working as GALs are considered forensic practitioners. Such psychologists find themselves spending as much time interacting with attorneys, judges, probation officers, and other legal professionals as with patients. In the forensic world, the client is more often the attorney, court, or company, not the individual. In the case of the GAL, the client is the court, generally the juvenile, probate, and family courts, not the parents or the child, even though work is conducted under the "best interest" (of the child) standard.

The role of GAL is relatively new to the mental health field. Although states have traditionally appointed only attorneys to serve in this capacity, more and more states, such as Massachusetts and New Hampshire, are seeking mental health professionals to conduct the comprehensive family investigations required by the courts when deciding on child custody matters. Serving as a GAL requires extensive knowledge of child development, family systems, parenting, psychopathology, and divorce from a psychological perspective. In addition, involved mental health professionals require familiarity with family law, court procedures, and court-room etiquette. Psychologists need to be comfortable interacting with attorneys and the law. They must have the ability to provide depositions and testify in open court with the ability to remain neutral, calm, and focused in the face of cross-examination, which at times can be grueling. The GAL psychologist needs a good working knowledge of legal procedures, the rules of evidence (including a knowledge of the Frye and Daubert rulings regarding the admissibility of evidence), and be comfortable with the court's style of viewing information as black or white, true or false, without the subtle nuance often employed by psychologists in clinical settings. The practitioner needs to be at ease with being challenged at every turn. The GAL needs to take for granted that one or both parties will be dissatisfied with the work performed and scrutinize every detail.

Those who perform GAL services have found themselves intellectually challenged to bring to bear all of their knowledge, training, education, and experience in an integrated manner. They find themselves pushed to be lifelong, continual learners, often researching not only the applicable mental health literature pertinent to the matter but legal case law as well. Serving as a GAL challenges one to be continually on top of emerging research, psychological and legal, as well as psychosocial and legal trends. Services are funded by either the parties or the state. Serving as a GAL requires the professional to be flexible in scheduling and in the length of appointments with clients. GALs are frequently called to appear at depositions and to testify in court. Although the GAL generally knows well in advance as to when a deposition or trial is scheduled, sometimes the command to appear, or subpoena, allows only for a 1-week notice. Testimony takes time, and often a GAL will be required to allot a half or full day for these processes, and sometimes more. The good news is that all time is billable. The bad news is that it can be disruptive to a regular practice schedule, especially if one is providing both treatment (psychotherapy) and forensic services.

The psychologist acting as GAL will be challenged in ways that a clinical practitioner might not. The GAL requires honed communication skills, both oral and written, because one of the key duties is to write extensive reports and testify in court about findings and recommendations. The psychologist needs to present findings in clear, concise, unambiguous language. Practitioners will be required to make definitive statements about their findings and opinions that relate primarily to psycholegal issues such as the ability to be a fit parent, judgment, dangerousness and executive functioning. They may find themselves in adversarial roles because trials are adversarial processes. Although the GAL psychologist starts the process as a neutral evaluator, once findings are issued, the GAL has likely taken a position, which is no longer neutral.

Although many professional schools of psychology include courses on the interface between psychology and law, GAL psychologists generally become trained on the job or, in other words, through trial by fire. The following is a checklist of recommended skills for success: (a) specialized knowledge of the legal system and relevant laws, (b) specific knowledge of the different courts in which GALs serve, (c) excellent communications skills specific to the courtroom including the ability to answer questions as yes or no, (d) quality teaching skills and the ability to translate and apply behavioral science into legal findings and to case specifics so as to aid the court in reaching its determinations, (e) good listening skills including the ability to ask the questioning attorney for clarification, (f) comprehension and acceptance of the difference between a neutral role as the court's expert witness and the therapeutic role, (g) and patience and anxiety-reduction skills (being on the stand is stressful and anxiety provoking.)

Resources

Ackerman, M. J. (2006). *Clinician's guide to child custody evaluations.* New York, NY: Wiley.

Fulero, S. M., & Wrightsman, L. S. (2008). *Forensic psychology.* Belmont, CA: Wadsworth Press.

Gould, J. W., & Martindale, D. A. (2009). *The art and science of child custody evaluations.* New York, NY: Guilford Press.

Melton, G. B., Petrila, J., Poythress, N., & Slobogin, C. (2007). *Psychological evaluations for the courts: A handbook for mental health professionals and lawyers* (3rd ed.). New York, NY: Guildford Press.

Rohrbaugh, J. B. (2007). *A comprehensive guide to child custody evaluations: Mental health and legal perspectives.* New York, NY: Springer Science and Business Media.

Jeffrey Zimmerman

40 | High-Conflict Divorce

The impact of high-conflict divorce on children and parents is legendary. Since the mid-1990s, I have been providing professional services to parents, specifically designed to help decrease the impact of conflict on the well-being of children while strengthening parental communication and the parents' ability to coparent successfully.

Currently, after spending more than 20 years as managing partner of a successful group, I am in full-time independent solo practice. Although my practice is a diverse one (individual and couple's therapy, organizational consulting, practice-management consultation), I also spend approximately one third of my billable time working with individuals, sets of parents, and lawyers in the arena of high-conflict divorce.

The bulk of this work involves consulting with divorcing or divorced parents using an intervention model I developed with a colleague (Elizabeth Thayer, PhD). This intervention teaches parents to focus narrowly on collaboratively coparenting, despite the hurt, anger, or animosity they feel toward each other. In this model, I do not conduct traditional psychotherapy. This intervention is directive and instructional, steering away from an exploration of feelings because the strength of parental emotion often interferes with or contaminates parents' ability to communicate effectively. Instead, this intervention is directly related to helping parents have effective dialogues about the children and their needs. It is heavily focused on improving parental communication and decision making, problem solving, and conflict resolution. I also consult with attorneys and work individually with divorcing parents to help them avoid getting encumbered by the conflict, which often results in their losing sight of the needs of the children.

This work developed out of the recognition that the legal and mental health systems' response to divorce was limited and frequently not able to protect children from the deleterious impact of parental conflict and poor parental communication. The system often (a) referred children to psychotherapy to help them deal with the significant stress, if not trauma, of their parents' high-conflict divorce and (b) referred parents (and also the children) for expensive and time-consuming child custody evaluations to help guide the court in determining what access schedule should be in place. Unfortunately, these interventions were not addressing the root of the problem for high-conflict families. They did not teach parents the skills necessary for postdivorce parenting in an attempt to promote a reduction in, or amelioration of, the high level of parental conflict and its consequent negative impact on children. In fact, these interventions (especially child custody evaluations, as each parent tried to "prove" the deficiencies and inadequacies of the other) often led to more prolonged and intensified conflict.

It became apparent that parents needed to be seen together, outside of the legal context, to help them refocus and shift their behavior to support the best interests of their children. The working assumption was that children needed their parents to be parents first and not divorcing spouses and litigants. In other words, divorcing parents should be taught how to parent together while living apart, thereby protecting their children from conflict and poor decision making.

To become more proficient with this population of parents, I read extensively (both research and self-help literature) to identify basic concepts and approaches offered to high-conflict divorcing parents. In addition, I attended workshops to learn more about high-conflict divorcing families and approaches used to address the needs of these families and especially the children.

This work can be immensely gratifying, when one observes parents (who have been described as "impossible," "the worst," "both have severe personality disorders," etc.) actually begin to communicate and make joint decisions on behalf of their children. For example, some parents sometimes arrive with restraining orders in place, not having even sat and spoken about their children for some time. They then learn to be civil, polite, and respectful to each other, enabling them to be present together at their children's activities without acrimony. As one child said to his parents who had completed a course of coparent counseling, "I'm so glad you guys are friends again." This child did not have to learn to cope with prolonged parental conflict. His parents were able to change their interactions in the right direction. There are wonderfully positive aspects of this work because it is preventive in nature, can lead to direct visible parental change, and may have a lasting positive impact on children.

Engaging in this work has led to additional applications in this population. For example, I now often serve as a facilitator in settlement conferences, as a consultant to children's attorneys (or guardians ad litem), and as a mental health professional in the collaborative divorce process (an alternative dispute resolution model in which the attorneys pledge to not litigate the divorce). I find these roles less demanding and extremely rewarding. One other benefit I have noted is that my other work (reducing conflict between executives in corporations and doing couples therapy) has been enhanced because some of the techniques and active strategies from working with high-conflict divorcing parents generalize to these other venues.

However, as a clinician, one can be affected by the chronic exposure to high conflict. One can repeatedly experience parents totally disregarding the needs of the children to make a point to the other parent (or the clinician). One can be verbally assaulted by parents as they vociferously complain (in the office and by voicemail, e-mail, and fax, as well as through their attorneys) about the clinician's approach and lack of understanding about the flaws of the other parent, while at the same time having little awareness of their own contribution to the dysfunctional coparenting relationship.

Referrals for this work generally come through attorneys (for either parent or the children) and the court. Many attorneys who hear about these services are eager to get help with these challenging and difficult cases. They are looking for reasonable solutions and to help parents and children get through the divorce in as healthy and productive a fashion as possible. Some parents attend voluntarily and by agreement, whereas others are court-ordered to attend. Parents pay on a fee-for-service basis (at the time of the visit) and are seen for a full hour at a higher fee than for psychotherapy. Insurance reimbursement is not applicable, because diagnosis and treatment of a mental disorder is not being provided in the course of this work.

Clinicians considering working with this population should be experienced in working with children and families. This work requires a high level of skill at simultaneously managing relationships with warring parents, while also managing the content (often related to child development and the likely impact of parental actions on children) and process of each session. Additionally, one should not do this work in a vacuum but find mentors and peers with whom to consult on approach, intervention, and the countertransference that can easily develop and affect the clinician's effectiveness.

For additional and related information, contact the Association of Family and Conciliation Courts (http://www.afccnet.org). They publish *The Family Court Review,* which has many pertinent articles. The American Psychological Association (http://www.apa.org) is another resource; its focus on parent coordination is related to this work. One can also seek training in mediation and collaborative divorce (often useful training, even if the clients in those venues may not routinely have quite as high a level of conflict on the average). I have also coauthored two books with Elizabeth Thayer (*The Co-parenting Survival Guide: Letting Go of Conflict After a Difficult Divorce* and *Adult Children of Divorce: How to Overcome the Legacy of Your Parents' Breakup and Enjoy Love, Trust, and Intimacy*), which further describe the concepts and principles related to helping families of a high-conflict divorce.

Eric G. Mart

41 | Assessment of Competency

am a forensic psychologist in private practice based in Manchester, New Hampshire. I am also licensed in Massachusetts and Vermont and do considerable work in those states. I am basically in solo practice, although I have recently hired postdoctoral trainees to assist me in my work. Forensic psychology constitutes approximately 80% of my practice. This consists almost entirely of assessment and expert testimony, although I also provide some consultation services to organizations and private attorneys. I began my forensic work evaluating juvenile delinquents for the state of New Hampshire because this was a natural outgrowth of my experience working with children and adolescents in the schools. Later, I began performing a wider range of assessments including competency to stand trial, mental state at time of offense, sentencing, child custody, and testamentary capacity. I received the diplomate in forensic psychology from the American Board of Forensic Psychology in 2001. The remaining 20% of my nonforensic practice is typically split among school psychology consultations, individual psychotherapy, and teaching.

For individuals wishing to expand the practice into forensic psychology, the assessment of competence to stand trial is an excellent area to choose as a jumping off point. Although it is clearly important to know what one is doing when performing such assessments, the legal standard that informs such evaluations is not difficult to understand, and the techniques involved are generally within the skill set of most doctoral-level psychologists. Although demand for such assessments varies from jurisdiction to jurisdiction, it has been my experience that in most areas of the country demand generally outstrips supply, and there is always room for a new evaluator.

To prepare for doing such evaluations, it is essential to become knowledgeable about the techniques involved in performing either adult or juvenile competence to stand trial assessments. I recommend a number of steps. First, read a number of important books that deal with this issue on a practical level. Thomas Grisso's (1988) *Competency to Stand Trial Evaluations: A Manual for Practice* is indispensable reading for assessing adults for competence to trial, and his more recent *Evaluating Juveniles' Adjudicative Competence: A Guide for Clinical Practice* (2005) is equally good. The latter book also contains forms and a structured interview to allow practitioners to perform the type of assessment that Grisso described in the book.

Second, I strongly recommend that those wishing to perform these types of assessments attend continuing education workshops that focus on the assessment of criminal competencies. Workshops sponsored by the American Academy of Forensic Psychology (http://www.abfp.com) are among the best and generally have presenters who are knowledgeable and respected in their field.

Finally, I think it is prudent to obtain the services of a consultant with experience in evaluating competence to stand trial to review one's first attempts and offer input into such issues as instrument choice, format, and report writing style. Such a consultant can also prepare practitioners to testify about their findings. The use of a consultant will help ensure that initial reports to the court and testimony are up to the standard that is expected in a given jurisdiction.

After preparing for performing such evaluations, it is necessary to have the proper tests and forms to provide the assessment. Instrument choice in competence to stand trial evaluations is, to some extent, a matter of personal choice and philosophy. Practitioners need several competence assessment instruments such as the MacArthur Competence Assessment Tool—Criminal Adjudication, the Evaluation of Competency to Stand Trial—Revised, and the Juvenile Adjudicative Competence Instrument to screen for competence to stand trial. Because incompetence is usually related to low intelligence and associated developmental disabilities, severe mental illness, or learning process deficits, practitioners will also need a reputable IQ test such as the Wechsler instruments or the Reynolds Intellectual Assessment Scales. For addressing learning process deficits, it is important to have some type of achievement test such as the Woodcock–Johnson III, the Wechsler Individual Achievement Test—2, or the Basic Achievement Skills Inventory (which is handy because it can be administered on a laptop). Some type of neuropsychological screening battery such as the Repeatable Battery for Assessment of Neuropsychological Status or the Kaufman Short Neuropsychological Assessment Procedure—2 are necessary, as is some type of personality test, such as the Minnesota Multiphasic Personality Inventory—2 (MMPI–2), MMPI–2 (Restructured Form), or the Personality Assessment Inventory. Finally, because underperformance and malingering are often issues in these types of cases, it is necessary to familiarize oneself with instruments and techniques designed to assess these issues such as the Test of Memory Malingering and the Structured Interview of Reported Symptoms.

Having a clear report writing style is important. It is essential for forensic psychologists to present their findings in a way that allows the court to understand the connection between the data elicited in the assessment and the conclusions that are drawn in the report. Testifying in court can be a daunting experience until one becomes used to it. A number of excellent books provide guidance about how to testify effectively, and books by Stanley Brodsky (1991, 1999) are among the best.

Finally, professionals interested in this work will have to market their services. Writing articles for local bar journals is effective, as is speaking before bar association sections. I have found print advertisements to be less effective, but others may have some success with this means; it will be necessary to experiment to find the right marketing mix. However, in my experience, once the legal community becomes aware that a practitioner performs these types of evaluations and does a good job, it is not necessary to do a great deal of marketing.

Resources

Brodsky, S. (1991). *Testifying in court: Guidelines and maxims for the expert witness* Washington, DC: American Psychological Association.

Brodsky, S. (1999). *The expert expert witness: More maxims and guidelines for testifying in court.* Washington, DC: American Psychological Associatioin.

Grisso, T. (1988). *Competency to stand trial evaluations: A manual for practice.* Sarasota, FL: Professional Resource Press.

Grisso, T. (2005). *Evaluating juveniles' adjudicative competence: A guide for clinical practice.* Sarasota, FL: Professional Resource Press.

Mart, E. (2005). *Getting started in forensic psychology practice: How to create a forensic specialty in your mental health practice.* New York, NY: Wiley.

Marcia Knight

Serving as an Expert Witness

42

am a New York State licensed psychologist with a PhD in clinical psychology and postdoctoral training in neuropsychology. I work in a private practice setting in which the mix of the types of cases I see has varied over the years. Currently, I spend about 70% of my time doing psychological and neuropsychological evaluations. Many of these consist of expert witness, mostly personal injury, cases. However, I also do competence assessments, both in criminal cases and custody disputes. In addition, I take private referrals to evaluate learning disabilities, workers' compensation cases, disability cases, and the like. The rest of my time is spent doing individual psychotherapy and supervision of a clinical psychology trainee.

I was introduced to conducting psychological evaluations as an expert witness soon after I started my private practice after working in a psychiatric outpatient clinic for 7 years. At that time, I was referred a case in which a man had lost his forearm in an industrial accident and (understandably) became depressed. I was asked to evaluate the emotional sequela of that injury and write a report. This initial work led to further referrals. The first time I testified as an expert in court was when I examined a woman who lost an eye because a prankster placed a firecracker in the peephole of her door.

At some point, an attorney asked me if I knew anyone who could evaluate the neuropsychological sequela in a head injury case. In those days, the task of differentiating *organic* from *functional* mental illnesses was a significant part of clinical psychology training. In fact, at the time, I was working as a consultant to a private hospital doing exactly those types of evaluations. I therefore readily offered to take the case in question. Also during that time, I was working part time at a developmental disabilities clinic under the direct supervision of a neuropsychologist. Given this background and expertise, I began getting expert witness referrals relating to adults with head injuries and children with learning disorders due to birth injures, head injuries, and lead poisoning. All this was occurring during the 1980s, a time when neuroscience and neuropsychology were beginning to boom. I began taking postdoctoral courses and even a course in brain dissection at a medical school.

Over the next few years, I spent about half my time doing psychotherapy and the rest doing evaluations as an expert witness. I also did evaluations privately and as a consultant to hospitals and the education system. During that time, managed care was becoming more and more of a force. As a result, my psychotherapy fees and the number of sessions I was allowed were being reduced. I had also had a child and was finding the late hours and other demands of being a psychotherapist more onerous than completing psychological and neuropsychological evaluations. The latter work usually involved seeing one or two patients over the course of a business day and writing the reports at my leisure. These could almost always be done wherever and whenever I pleased, including at home. I grew to truly like the work itself, finding the assessments of emotional trauma and neuropsychological issues fascinating. I therefore found myself spending more and more time doing these evaluations and spending less time doing psychotherapy. Another plus was that getting payments for those evaluations was usually more reliable and less labor-intensive than dealing with managed care.

A typical evaluation usually starts with a review of relevant records. Depending on the injury, these often come from hospitals and rehabilitation facilities. Sometimes police and accident reports are provided. School records are invaluable to assess premorbid functioning in any type of neurological case. With children, they are helpful to assess premorbid functioning following psychological trauma as well. When working with children who have neurological injuries, birth records are important.

At the examination, I interview the patient and, ideally, a significant other. In head injuries, especially, the patient often does not remember the injury. Therefore, getting input from someone close to the individual can be essential to get an impression of what happened to the patient and how he or she has changed. Examinations can take from about 3 hours for emotional injuries to, on average, 5 to 7 hours for neuropsychological cases. The report writing often takes as long as or longer than the evaluation.

For the most part, my referrals come by word of mouth from attorneys and other professionals, such as neurologists, psychologists, and medical doctors. In expert witness matters, I directly bill the person referring the case, but sometimes patients pay, depending on arrangements they have made with their lawyer. I usually ask to be paid a retainer before starting a case.

One negative aspect of expert witness work is the pressure and anxiety of actually going to court. More than 90% of personal injury cases settle before they come to trial, so I do not testify often. However, when I do, it always gives me the feeling of being in the midst of final examinations at college or graduate school, only worse. The preparation is similar in the sense of having to know the case and the psychological issues well, and being up to date on relevant research materials. Imparting that information during the direct part of my testimony can be satisfying. It gives me the feeling of being a teacher. The cross-examination, however, sometimes makes me wish I had never entered this field. I try to keep in mind that it is the opposing attorney's job to make me look bad, but knowing that does not make it easier. Although only a minority of opposing attorneys are outright abusive, occasionally some are, and they are within their rights to make a vigorous argument. The trick is to stay cool, know your material, and answer as best you can. The hardest cases are those in which the attorney does not really know the issues and asks provocative questions that can be impossible to answer (especially when he or she tries to limit you to responding with a yes or no).

Another aspect that can be difficult is that lawyers are often rushed to provide their experts' opinions within a certain time frame. Therefore, I sometimes do not have the option of writing the report at my leisure but have to complete it as soon as possible. Also, when cases come to trial, I have little say in choosing the date I will appear. This means canceling other appointments and sometimes changing my own plans. In those situations, the ability to manage my own schedule is overturned. Because making my own schedule was one of the things that attracted me to this kind of work in the first place, it is stressful. I have heard of cases in which experts were brought back from vacations, but fortunately this has not happened to me—*yet.*

In competence cases, there are situations in which one has to examine the patient in jail or on a jail ward in a hospital. These are obviously not ideal conditions, and being in those venues is stressful. In child custody cases, the family atmosphere is nearly always hostile, and the pull by the parties to take sides can be difficult. In fact, I found those cases so difficult that I stopped taking them and refer them to others.

Those interested in undertaking this work might visit with or send introductory letters to local attorneys. I belong to the National Academy of Neuropsychology, to American Psychological Association Divisions 40 (Clinical Neuropsychology) and 41 (American Psychological–Law Society), and other neuropsychological and clinical psychology associations. I also belong to the Society for Traumatic Stress Studies, now known as the National Center for Crisis Management. I subscribe to several journals in neuropsychology, as well as *Law and Human Behavior*.

Ray Kamoo

The Role of the Assessment Psychologist in Immigration Evaluations

43

am a Michigan-based licensed psychologist with a PhD in clinical psychology. I have an extensive background in community mental health and in working with individuals from various ethnic and cultural groups. I founded Immigration Psychology Associates (IPA) to focus on the evaluation individuals and their families who in the midst of the immigration process.

I graduated from a clinical psychology program that was fully accredited by the American Psychological Association and then began an internship in the Department of Psychiatry and Behavioral Neurosciences at Wayne State University and the Detroit Medical Center—Sinai Hospital, located in Detroit. Based in an urban setting, the program's emphasis was on neuropsychological testing, crisis stabilization, and psychotherapeutic treatment with inpatients and outpatients. The experience proved invaluable.

I had been working in community mental health at the time and began a small private practice right after graduation. Although my main office is in Bloomfield Hills, Michigan, I am also licensed to practice in Illinois and Virginia. In addition, I have practice privileges in other jurisdictions, meaning that I can evaluate individuals in other states after first receiving approval from that state's board of psychology. Currently, I work in private practice and devote approximately half of my time to psychological evaluations of various types. I also maintain a small number of psychotherapy clients whom I have been treating on a long-term basis.

My work in this highly specified and new field really came about by chance. I was introduced to conducting immigration evaluations several years ago when my cousin, a Detroit-area immigration attorney, asked whether I would be interested in evaluating a foreign scientist who had been working in the United States. Curious, I agreed simply because I had never heard the term *immigration evaluation,* nor did I understand what such an assessment involved. This initial evaluation and my subsequent curiosity led me to inquire of other immigration attorneys as to the role of such evaluations in immigration cases. After some time and reading as much as possible on the field (very little was available), I began to understand the potential value of a comprehensive psychological evaluation in describing and explaining immigrants' psychological and emotional functioning as they deal with the various stages of immigration proceedings.

Historically, individuals presenting with problems or psychiatric symptomatology would often be directed to visit their family doctors to ask for some type of letter attesting to their condition. If they wrote anything at all, physicians often provided terse comments that would be of little or no benefit to the immigration attorney. Psychologists can conduct comprehensive evaluations that fully assess their client's condition, be it depression, anxiety, psychosis, a developmental disability, or any other debilitating circumstance. IPA provides this service.

Immigration proceedings are often an intricate web that is best navigated with the assistance of an attorney. An immigration evaluation consists of a thorough clinical interview, a review of pertinent documentation, communication with the attorney, and the administration of a battery of standardized psychological tests. Testing is critical and necessary because government officials reading the report often view the psychologist as a hired gun, that is, an expert who will say whatever the paying client wants them to say. Naturally, this is not the case, and the use of empirically derived instruments will greatly assist in helping to discern the existence of any psychiatric symptoms. The tests also add credibility to the report and potentially offer the attorney more to advocate on behalf of their clients.

Psychological evaluations are used in four major areas in immigration cases. Extreme or exceptional hardship cases involve the assessment of a U.S. citizen or permanent legal resident. They are usually the child or spouse of someone who is in deportation proceedings or has already been deported. The evaluation seeks to assess the existence of any psychological difficulties that are beyond what is to be expected from such a separation.

Asylum cases involve individuals who have fled their home country and entered the United States, often after having been subjected to some form of abuse because of their political or religious beliefs or because of their gender. In these cases, the evaluation involves an assessment of their disorder (e.g., posttraumatic stress disorder), how they have fared in the United States, and what is the likely outcome if they were forced to return to their homeland.

The Violence Against Women Act involves the psychological and physical abuse of a foreign national or threat of deportation by a U.S. citizen or permanent legal resident spouse. The central issue in these cases is the assessment of the impact that such abuse has had on the foreign national. Male victims of abuse can also be assessed under this act.

The last form of evaluation involves individuals aiming for a waiver of the history and civics section of the U.S. Citizenship examination. These individuals are evaluated to assess whether their claims of varying degrees of cognitive inabilities are valid. The assertion is that said incapacities prevent them from learning information, even in their native tongue, to take the test.

The evaluation of individuals involved in immigration proceedings is as rewarding as it is heartbreaking. Often, families feel as if the government's only aim is to break them up. Children can potentially be separated from one or both parents and spouses from one another. Individuals come into the office distraught about the possibility of having to leave this country, even after many years of being a model and productive citizen.

Nonetheless, psychologists are needed to evaluate their symptoms and document their psychological status. A high percentage of these evaluations are referrals from immigration attorneys, although I do get inquiries from many who find out about my company from our website. Potential clients are told beforehand that these assessments are to be conducted with no particular result in mind and that an independent and professional judgment will be exercised on all aspects of this evaluation. They are also informed that my findings would be discussed with their attorney and that the evaluation is not psychological treatment. Finally, clients are informed of the fee and told that they are responsible for payment in full. Medical insurance companies almost never cover immigration evaluations.

Although there are benefits to this type of work, challenges also exist. Attorneys will call and indicate that deadlines are often only days away. That means evaluating the client on short notice and struggling to find time to write the report. This necessitates having a flexible schedule and possibly canceling other scheduled appointments. Additionally, an attorney may ask the psychologist to testify on behalf of the client. This also requires schedule flexibility, although these are typically scheduled months in advance. Government attorneys are often grounded in the belief that any feelings the person may have are to be expected and are not extraordinary in nature. Lastly, a challenge exists regarding conducting assessments with clients from a variety of cultures and countries where English is not the primary language. In such cases, a translator is needed.

Although these types of evaluations certainly involve pressure, they are also rewarding. Those wishing to embark on this type of work are encouraged to join professional organizations such as the Society for Personality Assessment and the American Psychology–Law Society, as well as to continue forming relationships with those in the field of assessment. Talking and networking with immigration attorneys is critical and provides a referral base. Reading the vast literature on forensic evaluations and the role of the examiner is also mandatory. The scant material that does exist concerning immigration evaluations is also required reading and gives the psychologist a greater understanding of the complexities of psychology and immigration law. The following resources are essential readings in this area.

Resources

Evans, F. B. (2000). Forensic psychology and immigration court: An introduction. In R. P. Auerbach (Ed.), *Immigration and nationality law, 2000–2001 annual handbook* (pp. 446–458). Washington, DC: American Immigration Lawyers Association.

Frumkin, I. B., & Friedland, J. D. (1995). Forensic evaluations in immigration cases: Evolving issues. *Behavioral Sciences and the Law, 13,* 477–489.

Lisa R. Grossman

Evaluations of Professionals and Professional Practice

44

I am a clinical and forensic psychologist and have been in independent practice for more than 22 years. Before that, I worked in the Chicago criminal courts evaluating defendants for fitness to stand trial and insanity claims. I left the court system because, back in the day, I could work half the hours in private practice and double my income. I also enjoyed being my own boss, controlling my own hours, and doing psychotherapy in addition to forensic evaluations.

Currently, I divide my time between clinical and forensic work. In the clinical arena, I see patients in individual and marital therapy and conduct psychological evaluations on children, adolescents, and adults. In the forensic field, I do consultations for attorneys as well as conduct a variety of evaluations, including those in custody, personal injury, criminal, and professional practices.

My work with professionals and professional practice primarily involves psychologists who have received complaints against them from my state licensing board. I get referrals from either attorneys who are defending psychologists or from the state licensing board. When the defense attorney contacts me, it will be because the attorney is representing the psychologist in this complaint to the licensing board. At the initial stage of a licensing board complaint, the defense attorney will usually ask me to evaluate the psychologist in terms of his or her professional practice and whether any ethical violations may have occurred pertaining to the complaint. If there is an ethical violation, the attorney might then ask me to develop a program to help rehabilitate the psychologist. The attorney might then choose to use this plan in negotiations with the board on behalf of the psychologist. If I determine that the psychologist's actions did not appear to reach the threshold of an ethical violation, the attorney uses this information in his or her strategies with the licensing board. I may then be asked to testify at a hearing as the psychologist's expert witness.

Should the Department of Professional and Financial Regulation (DPFR) contact me, it will usually send documents for review and consultation with respect to the presence of ethical violations. If the case goes to hearing, the DPFR often asks me to testify as its expert witness with respect to what conduct is considered unethical in our profession, to cite the statutes that corroborate my testimony, and to apply them to the case at hand. There are other situations during the middle of the complaint process when the state licensing board may ask me to conduct a psychological evaluation with the psychologist to determine whether he or she is suffering from any emotional problems and, if so, to make treatment recommendations. At times, the psychologist's attorney may request a similar psychological evaluation, obviously hoping to demonstrate a lack of impairment.

At the end of the complaint process, should the psychologist be found to have violated one or more ethical violations, part of the disposition often includes supervision of the psychologist for either a specified time period or until such time as I feel that he or she is able to return to practice without restrictions. When I conduct supervision, there is usually a specific issue I must address, whether it is to focus on certain ethical issues within the psychologist's practice; supervising an educational component comprising readings, conferences, and workshops; or supervising the psychologist's overall practice. Regardless of the focus of supervision, I am required to send monthly reports to the licensing board addressing progress, cooperation, and areas of focus. At the end of the supervision process, I am required to send a written report describing the course of supervision, progress made, areas of concern, and whether I believe that the psychologist may return to an unrestricted practice.

There are also instances in which a psychologist who has been on either probation or suspension from practice is requesting his or her license be reinstated to unrestricted status. In these situations, either the psychologist's attorney or the state licensing board may request that I conduct an independent evaluation to assess whether the psychologist is ready to return to independent practice.

My work in the area of professional practice is not reserved for only psychologists, unless I am asked to conduct supervision or apply psychology's ethics code to a particular situation. For example, when asked to conduct an evaluation for possible impairment, the professional may be a nurse, physician, or dentist.

Becoming interested in ethical issues was a natural extension of my legal background. In addition to my PhD in clinical psychology, I am also licensed to practice law. When various attorneys began to ask me to consult with them or to evaluate their clients, I became known in the community as a psychologist who does this type of work. When DPFR began seeing my name involved in these cases, it began to contact me either to consult or conduct psychological evaluations.

Certainly, my legal background has added immeasurably to my training for ethical evaluations because the type of analytical thinking is not dissimilar. However, a psychologist certainly does not have to be an attorney to enter this niche. My experience on the state psychological association ethics committee has also prepared me, as did many presentations on the ethical issues confronting psychologists. In addition, my pro bono work consulting with Illinois psychologists on psycholegal cases has further enriched my understanding of ethical issues. Of course, consultation with my colleagues has always proved invaluable to my work, and the area of ethics has been no different. To complement these experiences, reading various books, articles, and attending workshops have all contributed to my training.

I enjoy this type of work because I find it intellectually stimulating to grapple with the nuances of ethics, law, and professional practice. I also find it rewarding to help educate psychologists in ethical decision making and to improve risk management skills in their clinical practices. What I do not enjoy is when I have to testify against fellow psychologists, despite their potential wrongdoing. I also do not enjoy having to wait for payment from DPFR because it does not pay up front or provide retainers. However, when I am hired by the psychologist's attorney, I get paid by the client or the attorney and am usually paid up front.

For psychologists who would like to develop this strategy in their practices, I suggest that they contact attorneys in their community who represent psychologists who have received licensing board complaints. Introducing themselves and letting attorneys know of their expertise can help generate referrals. Also, letting other psychologists know of their interest in this area can promote referrals. Probably the most important suggestion I can make is for the psychologist to obtain as much experience in the area of ethics as possible, whether it be through classes, workshops, presentations, consultations, or reading. Joining one's state psychological association's ethics committee can be invaluable, as can prior experience on one's state licensing board. As far as reading, the single most important document is the American Psychological Association's Ethical Principles of Psychologists and Code of Conduct. Many books have been written on the topic, such as Donald N. Bersoff's (2008) *Ethical Conflicts in Psychology*, Patricia Keith-Spiegel and Gerald P. Koocher's (2008) *Ethics in Psychology and the Mental Health Professions*, Celia B. Fisher's (2008) *Decoding the Ethics Code: A Practical Guide for Psychologists*, and Kenneth S. Pope and Melba J. T. Vasquez's (2007) *Ethics in Psychotherapy and Counseling: A Practical Guide*. I further suggest attending the American Psychological Association Insurance Trust workshops on ethical decision making and risk management in clinical practice, which are frequently cosponsored with state psychological associations.

PRODUCTS | XI

Genie Skypek

Developing Software for Social Service Programs

45

think of myself as a sort of entrepreneurial psychologist. Throughout my professional lifetime, I have worked in several areas in behavioral health as opportunities presented themselves. I began my career doing clinical work—starting, running, or acting as a psychologist in drug treatment programs in South Carolina and then Florida. After I moved to Florida, I started a health psychology private practice and stayed in some form of part-time clinical work until 1992.

I started surveying for the Joint Commission (http://www.jointcommission.org/) a few years out of school. The experience of looking at how program after program was designed and actually operated ended any parochialism I might have had about how things had to be done. Through my work as a surveyor, it became clear to me that organizations had to learn how to use data to help determine which of the various approaches to care or to the performance of administrative tasks worked best. Along came the whole field of quality or performance improvement as a structured way of doing just that. At the same time, electronic medical records were coming on the scene as a potentially meaningful and easy way to collect the data that would help all these leaders and clinicians determine how best to operate.

My first foray into the electronic world for behavioral health was the development of automated data collection systems for a variety of data collection needs, including service tracking, attendance tracking, Medicaid service tracking to maximize billing, clinical record auditing, quality improvement data analysis, client intake, and more. I partnered with people who knew software and software design. In one instance, we developed software that used barcodes to track client attendance and receipt of program services. From those data, we could calculate how best to bill to maximize money received for that week. We helped one organization increase its billing by $100,000 the first year the system was implemented. Unfortunately, we were too far ahead for the times, and we didn't have the capital to mount the kind of marketing campaign that would be needed to move a significant portion of the field in this direction.

My next foray was into automating data collection for outcome evaluation in juvenile justice treatment programs. One of the software functionalities we developed was a process to scan point system data into a database and then use those data as a real-time measure of progress.

At this time, I also consulted with organizations in paper-based clinical record design and quality improvement. One of those organizations contracted with me and my brother, a software engineer who was a design specialist as well as a programmer, to develop processing and assessment software for Juvenile Assessment Centers in the state of Florida. We did this, developing a system that managed more than 5,000 children a year for many years.

The assessment software was designed to allow for data collection so that it could be used for process evaluation and improvement decision support, as well as clinical documentation. On the basis of the data collected, we were to generate a clinical narrative that looked and sounded like something a regular clinician would write.

My brother finally decided, after several failed attempts at programming based on my layout of the if this, then this, then this decision rules, that it would be easier to teach me to program than for him to learn to think like a clinician. So I had to learn to break the clinical interviewing process into concrete data and decision tree (if this, then this) elements. It was easier for me than it might be for some because I had training in Skinnerian, operant behavioral models and the kind of precise thinking required in applied behavior analysis. We succeeded—our employer proudly told us that recent state reviewers were unable to tell that the narratives they reviewed were computer-generated.

We developed program- and population-specific modifications to our first Juvenile Assessment Center system and sold a few of them to several different kinds of treatment programs. However, organizations were being pushed by state funding agencies to use standardized assessment tools—some of those claiming to produce clinical narratives—although none as clinical as ours. Once again, we didn't have the capital to mount a major marketing campaign or research effort to produce our own standardized product, and we weren't sure how big the market really was at the time.

After these development efforts, I started consulting to behavioral health software developers and to organizations searching for the right electronic medical record system. With my experience as a database designer, as a clinician, as an evaluator, and as an accrediter, I could help the information technology folks communicate with the clinical folks and vice versa—and perhaps improve the value-added quality of any electronic record system to both clinical and administrative functions. For example, instead of automating a paper record keeping system designed mostly to meet the needs of external auditors and payers, an electronic system should be designed to facilitate process and outcome evaluation and support effective clinical decision making, as well as meet the demands of payers and other reviewers.

My current work in the field of behavioral health and electronics is the writing of eLearning content. As I noted at the outset, I tend to follow the opportunities as they develop—and eLearning was the next opportunity that came along. ELearning is not an uncommon field for psychologists. However, I was always surprised to see so few psychologists involved in quality or performance improvement and in the design of clinical record systems, whether paper-based or electronic. Perhaps our clinical training doesn't prepare us to see the significant role that administrative processes play in the delivery of high-quality clinical services in organizations. Consulting in these areas would allow us to make significant contributions to clinical quality at a level bigger than the individual practitioner level.

Software development is a highly time-intensive activity. Although I performed other work (e.g., surveying for the Joint Commission, consulting), I easily spent three quarters of my time on software development projects. I was constantly teaching myself about other software products, to "think database," and to program, so if I wasn't doing work specific to a project, I was learning.

Mostly I learned by doing, by reading, through instruction from my various software engineer partners, and by looking at software products to see what was being done—and, perhaps, to see what wasn't being done. It's as important to see how a system fails as well as how it works.

Perhaps the two greatest difficulties in this work lay in the amount of nitpicking detail that programming requires and the fact seeing that the software was well used required organizational commitment.

I got into this business as a result of my experience and reputation as a general consultant in quality improvement and clinical record keeping. People knew me, liked how I thought about clinical and administrative processes, and invited me into projects on that basis. It is important to understand the administrative needs of human service organizations to design software to help meet these needs. Although it is not direct clinical work, those wanting to pursue this area can have a significant impact on how clinical services are provided, especially because so much clinical care is provided in agencies.

Barbara Becker Holstein

46

Developing a Brand Around a Theme
One's Own Enchanted Self

I am a positive psychologist. Trained in psychodynamic psychotherapy and related modalities such as cognitive and ego therapy, I undertook case study research in the late 1980s with women, ages 35 to 75, outside of my practice. I was looking to see how negative messages received in childhood influenced these women as they aged. My research confirmed the heavy price that women pay for messages that interrupt positive growth. Often blows to self-esteem at critical moments had limited these women educationally, vocationally, and emotionally.

However, something else emerged in analyzing the data. All of these women had, even with early emotional blows, maintained capacities for living relatively successful lives and experienced periods when they felt terrific. During these special times, they talked about feeling competent, talented, on target, full of life, excited, and in "flow." I decided to label these various states of well-being *The Enchanted Self.*

The Enchanted Self state of being confirmed to me as a psychologist that there is resiliency and a capacity for positive "Self" development that defies the circumstances of one's upbringing. A disenchanting beginning can still often lead to an Enchanted Self. Helping women access, recognize, and strengthen the often hidden tools behind what I believe to be a natural capacity became my mission as a practicing psychologist, in the treatment room and beyond. This passion came from a strong professional dedication to women's development combined with a host of other skills that I was yearning to use, including writing, teaching, and performing.

I developed some key working concepts that I teach to others. Psychologists can overlay my concepts onto their own training and traditions. The public can easily understand the concepts because they are nonclinical. Although my research had been with women, I found the principles I teach to be universal. Some of these are the following:

1. Every person has a repertoire of talents, strengths, coping skills, and hidden potential. The work is to make these explicit, useful, easily retrievable, and alive.
2. Every person has a memory bank of unique experiences and personal reactions. Teaching people to use their memory banks to rediscover their talents, strengths, coping skills, and untapped potential is a great way to tap into positive growth.
3. Helping people develop their sense of self-worth and their capacity for taking positive action in life is essential to bring about increased positive states of being. For lack of a more perfect word, these states are called "happiness."
4. The Seven Gateways to Happiness are useful to frame the ongoing and often circular work that is necessary to grow emotionally while also increasing one's capacities for happiness. The Seven Gateways are Building Self-Esteem, Building a Positive Narrative to One's Life, Meeting One's Emotional and Educational Needs, Replenishing, Belonging, Mentoring and Being Mentored, and Positive Action and/or Good Deeds.

Following is some wisdom I have learned while taking The Enchanted Self to the world. These may apply to taking your concept to the world.

Establish yourself as an expert in your field. Write a professional book or paper. I was writing a trade book but had the good fortune to meet an acquisitions editor for an academic press who encouraged me to write a professional level book for other psychotherapists. That book, *The Enchanted Self, A Positive Therapy,* was published in 1997 and is in its second printing and published by Brunner-Routledge. To my surprise, trade books easily followed. I cannot recommend a better way to become precise, focused, and totally immersed in your subject than to write a book or at least a white paper that can be offered on your website.

Present academic and professional information and research as often as possible. I used all of my connections including my local psychological association, professional organizations, and local associations to make presentations of my work. This will refine one's thinking and develop public speaking skills. You may get lucky and fall into some wonderful publicity. By sharing at an American Psychological Association media workshop, I met a psychologist who invited me onto her cable TV show in New York City. When she left the program, I had my own show, *The Enchanted Self*, on public access in Manhattan.

Start small (one's home town is a great place to start) while dreaming big as far as building a public reputation. I spoke anywhere I could, including the public library, the local community college, my college alumni group, and so forth. I had a big hit. *The Enchanted Self* opened a major Women's Day at Brookdale Community College with me speaking and a group of dancers presenting The Enchanted Self Dance. Speaking locally also led to many local newspaper articles. Keep a data bank of everyone you touch and keep them updated on your talks, press, and so forth.

Use publicists and other business experts judiciously. I learned by hard knocks that publicists are not always a good investment. They can be expensive, and for me, they ate most of my profits. They did help me get on radio shows. However, I learned how to do much of my own publicity as I paid them. I learned the hard way to keep a data bank of everyone you touch, particularly journalists and reporters. Send them updates, even call them once in a while. Of course, join the American Psychological Association media referral service for free publicity.

Start to develop your products. You have the potential for products you may not even be considering. You may have the makings of a book. If not, you certainly can generate a short e-book that details some of your material as an expert. You can have a website. You can have a blog. You can have promotional products. Everyone needs a coffee mug with your logo on it! You can give teleclasses and then offer the recording of the class for sale as a CD or download. You can have your own e-radio show with podcasts on Blog Talk Radio for free. The products are endless, and I have done most of them. I even sell Enchanted Self necklaces that combine the heart of a woman with the spiral energy of life. Right now I have seven books for sale, all of which are self-published, except for the first. Several I published on demand. This is a fast and easy way to bring a book out and not have a garage full of unsold books. My latest book, *The Truth (I'm a Girl, I'm Smart and I Know Everything)* was self-published but found a national distributor. This book has done well, being number 6 on Amazon for Being a Teen. It is even coming out in China! Networking led me to a Chinese professor, who translated the book. The Chinese edition is an example of a product I hadn't even dreamed of.

Keep moving with the times. Nothing stands still. Last year it was blogs, this year it's Twitter. Who knows what it will be next year. I have gone with the flow and now have three blogs, www.enchantedself.com, www.positivepsychologyforwomen.com, and www.thetruthforgirls.com. Pay for expert consultants; they are worth the cost. I've used virtual assistants again and again to help me design my website, set up blogs, get me started on Twitter, and so forth.

Remember that everything changes, and you may as well. What starts off as one form of an expertise may end up as another. I am now focusing on girls and their moms. This has been great. I'm writing fiction and loving it. My second book in The Truth series is in the hopper, and more translations of the first book are happening. Yes, it is a dream come true, and it is not just my dream. Within you, one is also waiting to emerge or is already emerging.

POSITIVE PSYCHOLOGY  XII

Stuart Dansinger

Assessing and Counseling Gifted Children and Adults 47

I am a licensed psychologist and a licensed school psychologist. My initial training was in school psychology at the University of Minnesota between 1960 and 1965. I worked in schools for about 35 years, until I retired, and since 1997 I have worked in private practice. Counseling and assessing gifted children and adults have been a part of my practice on a part-time basis for about 40 years. Most of my clients are elementary school–age children. A parent may request testing information so that the data can be used to obtain needed services for a child in the school he or she attends. For those gifted students who also have special needs, additional counseling services are provided. There are times when a parent requests that I also act as an advocate by going to the school to review test data, negotiate accelerated learning programs, and help the child adjust to the school environment. I discuss communication strategies with parents in their efforts to obtain the desired school programs and the necessary academic resources needed. There are also times when I go to the school to observe how well the child performs in class and to interview teachers and other school staff in regard to the child. Most assessments for gifted children and adults are done in my office, although I sometimes administer tests in the person's home.

The types of assessments I perform include intelligence, academic achievement, social skills and maturity levels, emotional status, adaptive behavior (communication, socialization, self care, and motor coordination), study habits and attitudes, executive functioning, prevocational and vocational interests and aptitudes, educational preferences and interests, learning styles, functional behavior, classroom observations, and school performance measures. Not all tests are used with each client, and the selection of the assessment tools depends on the referral needs. Both parents and teachers are also asked to provide information through various rating scales and other comments. Parents may bring in portfolios and samples of their child's work. When an appointment has been scheduled, the parents are usually sent a questionnaire to complete. At the time of the intake with the parents, additional information is obtained. We then have discussion of the kinds of assessment techniques to be used to answer the referral questions. In most cases, parents want to use test data to obtain a better program for their child or to improve their school performance. After the parents agree to the services, a testing session begins. When the testing is completed, the results are reviewed, and a discussion of how the information and test results can be best used to achieve the parents' goals follows. Parents often share test results with their child's school personnel in the hope that my recommendations will be implemented. For gifted children who have special needs, a treatment plan would be developed, often including individual or family psychotherapy (or both).

For gifted adults, there is usually less testing involved. However, mental status and personality assessments are often obtained. Gifted adults often request psychotherapy to achieve one of their goals—to be successful in using their abilities to their full potential. Of my current clients, approximately two thirds would be considered gifted or talented.

In my training, I did have some exposure to gifted children but had no particular interest in the field. However, while working as a school psychologist, I was asked to evaluate students applying for early entrance to kindergarten. I reviewed research in early entrance and found it intriguing; it sparked my interest in evaluating gifted children. I then offered to take on more gifted referrals and also found opportunities to take on some gifted referrals in a part-time private practice. As I worked with gifted children, I felt increasing interest and passion in continuing to work with this clientele. The following year, I took additional courses in gifted educational psychology. With additional knowledge, I was able to form a gifted education committee in my school district. I received a great deal of help from my administrative supervisor, who was also a school psychologist. After the gifted school committee was functioning well, parents of gifted students were invited to participate. Parents of gifted children also developed their own group and invited educators to participate in periodic meetings in which I became involved. The Minnesota Council for the Gifted and Talented, a statewide organization of parents and educators, had a local chapter in the school district where I worked.

I had a satisfying involvement in its activities for many years. Later, I also became a member of the Minnesota Educators of Gifted and Talented organization.

There is much to like about working with gifted clients. They are motivated to obtain and use information and take appropriate action to follow through. In most cases, fathers of gifted children are as involved as mothers and fully participate in the process. They are willing to pay for services because the needs of their child are of high priority. Most parents of gifted children are also gifted themselves and have experienced frustrations in their own educational history. Thus, they know what emotions and thoughts their child may be having and want to prevent further problems from occurring.

There are a few slightly unpleasant aspects to working with gifted clients. Writing long reports is almost always requested. Although most clients pay at the time of service, a few delay their payments or request a lower fee. For gifted children, educational response to meeting their needs may not be forthcoming and is a frustration.

Referrals come from various sources. I have a website with a focus on gifted services that generates many phone calls and e-mails. I also obtain referrals from members of the Minnesota Educators of Gifted and Talented who are familiar with my work. At the annual meetings of the Minnesota Council for the Gifted and Talented, I usually present two workshops related to some aspects of gifted education. I also place an ad in the Minnesota Council for the Gifted newsletter, *Outlook.* Other referrals may come from public, private, or parochial school staff; pediatricians; or other colleagues who know of my work in this field. There are also a few regional websites about gifted education that can link to my website.

Psychologists who hope to incorporate gifted and talented services into their practice need to learn about current issues in gifted services. They need to learn which are the preferred tests and how to administer and interpret them. Practitioners should also be willing and comfortable with going to a school to observe, interact, and meet with school staff. They may have to take on an advocate role for the child when necessary. Psychologists also need to research various recommended school options for accelerated learning, including desired teaching strategies and academic enrichment programs. Unfortunately, it is difficult to find a psychology workshop devoted to gifted services. Therefore, it is helpful to make contact with professionals who provide gifted services or teach about gifted education. The percentage of gifted children and adults is approximately equal to the percentage of children and adults with special needs or disabilities.

I have used a number of extremely helpful books to increase my knowledge base. For overall program discussions with an emphasis on matching the program to the child, *Re-forming Gifted Education* by Karen Rogers has been highly informative. Other books that have been helpful include *Alternative Assessments With Gifted Students* by Joyce van Tassel-Baska, *Misdiagnosis and Dual Diagnosis of Gifted Children and Adults* by James Webb and others, and *The Social and Emotional Development of Gifted Children—What Do We Know?* by Maureen Neihart, Sally Reis, Nancy Robinson, and Sidney Moon. Two books on executive functioning that have been helpful regarding the gifted are *Different Minds* by Deirdre Lovecky and *No Mind Left Behind* by Adam Cox. *Upside-Down Brilliance—The Visual-Spatial Learner* by Linda Silverman is excellent. Wendy Skinner writes about life with gifted children in her book *Infinity and Zebra Stripes*. I am a member of the National Association for Gifted Children, which publishes a journal titled *Gifted Child Quarterly* that includes professional articles. The Minnesota Council for the Gifted and Talented publication *Outlook* has excellent articles as well.

Mitchell A. Greene

Developing a Sport Psychology Practice

48

I am a clinical and sport psychologist located in the Western suburbs of Philadelphia. I have worked in private practice for close to 14 years. I realize, in retrospect, that my training in sport psychology started long before I ever formally chose to pursue this specialty area of interest. When I was a young psychologist—freshly licensed—my senior colleagues tutored me on the fundamentals of the business of psychology. For instance, they showed me how to establish (and keep) referral sources, set fees, work free of managed care, communicate with other professionals, market my services, create a niche practice, and ask for help when I needed it. To this day, their valuable business advice has served as the backbone of my entrepreneurial pursuits, including my eventual foray into the world of sport psychology.

The opportunity to pursue sport psychology actually arrived many years later. I was transitioning from being a co-owner of a midsize mental health practice, which was replete with administrative duties, to becoming a full-time private practice clinician. I used this transition time to take stock of how I imagined the rest of my career unfolding. As a serious recreational athlete, I had always paid casual attention to what the sport psychology field had to offer. After going for a long run to work out my thoughts, I decided one day that I would finally begin the process of learning more about sport psychology while also continuing to build my child and adolescent caseload.

One of the first steps I took was to seek out consultation from Temple University kinesiology professor Dr. Michael Sachs, who has been involved for many years in sport psychology. Dr. Sachs helped me understand the realities and myths of becoming a sport psychologist. For example, he explained that it is quite rare for clinicians to make their entire income practicing sport psychology and that I should expect the process of becoming an income-generating sport psychologist to take years, not months. Humbled but not defeated by this conversation, I began attending local and national sport psychology conferences, joined Division 47 (Exercise and Sport Psychology) of the American Psychological Association (APA), and started telling anyone I could that I was ready to take sport clients. Dr. Sachs offered to supervise my work. However, I knew that nothing was going to teach me more about applied sport psychology (the term used for people working directly with sport clients) than beginning to consult with athletes, coaches, and teams.

The application of my sport psychology skills has been extremely varied, ranging from applying sport psychology principles to kids on the autistic spectrum, to consulting with high school– and college-level competitors, as well as recreational, elite, and professional athletes. My office location in an affluent suburb of Philadelphia has allowed me to operate free of managed care. On average, 75% of my clinical time involves working with kids, adolescents, families, and couples on clinical matters, and 25% of my time is dedicated to my sport psychology interests.

Here are some examples of my work, which have run the gamut. I have run a 1-week summer "camp" for kids on the autistic spectrum (a large percentage of my clinical caseload includes kids with Asperger's disorder). These children were interested and knowledgeable of sports trivia and facts but physically uncoordinated and did not fit into traditional camp environments. We played modified games out on a field and drew on lessons from their sports idols having to do with managing pressure, dealing with a locker room environment, and how to be a good teammate. This helped the youngsters talk about their own issues with anxiety, communication difficulties, and frustration. For this camp, I charged a flat fee, and parents paid out-of-pocket for my services. I have also volunteered to captain a dragon boat (a long skinny vessel that seats 20) team full of kids on the autistic spectrum who were able to paddle in an annual festival in front of thousands of screaming fans. Our "Boys of Summer" team—where our participants were called athletes and no other labels—was of course about more than just paddling. We talked about how important it is for athletes to pay attention to others, work as a team, and cope well with winning and losing.

I spent a year volunteering as a consultant to a new basketball training facility, Apex Academies in Cherry Hill, New Jersey, which was a terrific opportunity for me to talk directly to a group of high-performing athletes (and coaches) on topics such as peak performance routines, increasing motivation, managing pressure, and goal setting. The Apex experience was valuable in many ways. I quickly learned that the sport psychology consulting model is significantly different from the clinical model. As obvious as this should have been, it took time for me to adjust to the brief and targeted interactions I generally had with the Apex athletes versus the extended weekly–hourly format of traditional psychotherapy.

Through my own participation in marathons, I volunteered to be one of a few sport psychologists at the 2007 New York City Marathon. I was available to talk with nervous athletes (one woman threw up repeatedly from nerves) or others who just needed reassurance. Being a runner myself put me in an advantageous position of being able to draw on my own experience. My participation in triathlons has led to my becoming the sport psychology consultant to the Philadelphia Insurance Triathlon and the Danskin SheRox Triathlon series. In this role, I have written newsletter articles on topics ranging from "Guilt-Free Triathlon Training" to "Mental Tips for Race Day." All of these opportunities have allowed me to market my services and reach an audience across the country. Finally, I am also a sport psychology consultant to the athletic department of a local college preparatory school. In this role, I work with select coaches who are looking to learn more about the mental side of sports. We have focused on topics such as team building, developing new practice rituals, and helping players manage frustration and disappointment. In this consulting role, I get paid a "coach's salary."

In my office, I meet with athletes and coaches individually regarding personal issues affecting them on and off the field and talk with them about performance issues. I enjoy the diversity and challenge of being a sport psychologist. I spend a lot of time with my head in sport psychology books or watching DVDs of other sport psychology professionals in action. I enjoy the opportunities I have to write articles, get out of the office to meet clients, and work with athletes who are generally already performing at a high level. As the reader can see, I have worked to find creative ways to enter the field of sport psychology and gain experience. I think my greatest strength is that I am willing to jump into situations and learn from my mistakes and that I am also open to asking for help from trusted colleagues, such as Dr. Sachs. The challenges are that one must remember that there generally are only a few opportunities to interact with an athlete or coach; in that sense, first impressions are important. I take the time prior to meeting an athlete or coach to learn as much as I can about their team culture and the expectations surrounding that athlete or team. In that sense, no team, school, or athlete is the same, and that extra homework pays off when it comes to making my specific recommendations for that client. The following resources are helpful to learn more about this field: APA Division 47, Exercise and Sport Psychology; Association for Applied Sport Psychology (http://www.appliedsportpsych.org); Exercise and Sport Psychology listserv (SPORTPSY@LISTSERV.TEMPLE.EDU); and J. Lesyk's *Developing Sport Psychology Within Your Clinical Practice: A Practical Guide for Mental Health Professionals* (1998).

Kathy Martone

Retreats for Personal Growth 49

I graduated with my doctorate in counselor education from the University of Arkansas in 1980. I was the director of a small mental health clinic until 1985, when I went to work for Southwestern Bell Telephone as a company psychologist. I am currently a licensed psychologist in private practice since 1986. I have a Jungian orientation and work with adults in individual psychotherapy and conduct a number of monthly dream groups, as well as women's spirituality and dream retreats. I also have started to market my own line of dream-based artwork.

Early in my college career, I was introduced to the work of Carl Jung and became fascinated with the power of symbol and metaphor. As I continued in graduate work toward a master's degree in psychology, I felt increasingly frustrated with the limited effectiveness of traditional psychotherapy. Carl Jung's idea of the marriage of psyche and spirit resonated with me, and I understood its potential for bringing about change.

My own professional and personal growth has been enhanced through experiential group activities such as a year-long Gestalt Group Therapy supervision group, 4 years of group Radix Body Work, frequent attendance at Journey Into Wholeness Retreats, and 10 years of training with Dr. Jean Houston. In 1988, I joined a weekly Jungian dream group and attended two annual 4-day retreats with a Jungian analyst. I came to realize the power of group engagement using techniques of visualization, body movement (including dance), music, ritual and ceremony, and other experiential processes. Sharing these experiences in a secluded setting with few distractions and no time constraints provides just the right container for people to lower their defenses and deepen their psychological work. I am continually amazed at the life-changing transformations that occur as a direct result of these experiences.

Over the years since I entered my solo practice, I have encountered clients (mostly women) who are eager to deepen their psychological and spiritual work with me. To meet this need, I frequently offer weekend and 4-day workshops and retreats in somewhat secluded locations away from the city. Because of the time-consuming nature of these venues, not to mention the energy drain, I usually offer a maximum of four per year. It is also a substantial out-of-pocket expense for my clients, some of whom have to monitor their budgets carefully.

In teaching others, we further our own education in ways that are not otherwise available to us. When people gather together in a place surrounded by natural beauty with the intention of calling forth their own inner wisdom, the energy that is aroused is exceedingly powerful and highly effective in creating change. I often find that my own life—inner as well as outer—benefits from these highly charged events. I love my work, and I love sharing what I know with people who awaken to their own potential in some amazingly profound ways. The excitement that surrounds these psychological and spiritual insights is electric as well as contagious.

Some workshops are designed to be both educational and experiential, whereas others are strictly experiential. For the dual workshops, I prepare a syllabus or outline for each participant, but the only preparation I do for the experiential workshops is to gather supplies for any ritual or ceremony we might plan. With workshops that involve art work, I will often supply some of the art materials.

A typical dream retreat weekend begins with a short ritual that involves lighting candles and a prayer to call in the four directions and define the sacred space for our work. Dream work begins with one person telling her dream and then the entire group asking questions. I then invite the dreamer into an experience with her dream. Often this involves a role-play of one of the dream characters or a group enactment of the dream, with each participant playing the role of one of the figures in the dream. At the end of the last day, after dinner, we perform a ritual to celebrate the dream wisdom gleaned from the work. This often involves sacred dance, poetry readings, prayers, and music. Each participant also speaks to the group about the meaning of her individual dream and what the weekend has meant to her.

Referrals are generated mostly from my practice and from friends or acquaintances of my clients. I also advertise via e-mail, my website, and computer networking lists. Sometimes I receive potential clients from a public talk or classes I have taught. I have published a newsletter in the past and I have also participated in several leads groups. (Leads groups are professional meetings designed specifically to generate business leads for the participants.) I conduct several ongoing dream groups, and these groups each plan an annual retreat. If there are enough of these self-generated retreats, I do not advertise or organize any additional events. As much as I enjoy these functions, they are quite tiring because I am the lead "performer" for the entire show, which often begins at 9:00 a.m. and continues until midnight.

For advertised workshops, I require a down payment 30 days before the event, with the remaining payment due at the time of arrival. I do not bill for these services because I expect to be paid in full. I do not accept credit cards for these services, and insurance will not reimburse for them. For the dream group self-generated retreats, I have a set fee that I charge for events, based on number of days.

Housing is arranged sometimes through local lodges or event centers, such as the YMCA, religious retreat centers, or vacation resorts. Often with my dream groups, one or more of the members offer the use of their family mountain cabin. In this case, there is no additional expense for housing. Each member of the workshop or retreat is expected to help plan, organize, and prepare meals for the entire time we are away. However, on occasion I have paid to have the facility provide the meals, passing on this cost to the participants.

The best way to learn how to conduct experiential retreats is to enroll in such a group and undergo your own personal experience. Unless you understand what it is like, it is nearly impossible to translate for your clients, nor will you be able to guide them effectively. However, the following books by Arnold Mindell and Jean Houston could be instructional for beginners.

Resources

Houston, J. (1997). *The possible human: A course in enhancing your physical, mental, & creative abilities.* Los Angeles, CA: Tancher.

Masters, R., & Houston, J. (1998). *Mind games: The guide to inner space.* New York, NY: Quest Books.

Mindell, A., & Mindell, A. (2001). *Riding the horse backwards.* Portland, OR: Lao Tse Press.

Mindell, A. (2001). *Working with the dreaming body.* Portland, OR: Lao Tse Press.

David Yarian

50 | Tantric Sexuality Education

After completing a strong graduate program in traditional psychodynamic approaches at the University of Michigan in 1982, I entered private practice in Nashville, Tennessee. At first seeing mostly individuals, I grew interested in family systems theory and came to specialize in working with couples and families.

In 1998, I enrolled in a course of training in tantric sexuality: Margo Anand's Love and Ecstasy Training, an intensive 2-week immersion in tantric theory and practice. Her approach is properly "neo-Tantra," an amalgam of teachings and practices based on ancient texts and modern humanistic psychology methods. A description of tantric practice may be found on my website. I found the tantric approach to sexuality quite powerful, with its emphasis on working with the breath, moving energy throughout the body, and focusing on sensory experience. In the year after the training, I began offering tantric educational workshops for individuals and couples.

These workshops were, frankly, a lot of work for little financial return. I advertised in the local alternative paper and worked hard to market them but could not find a sustainable model. I tried different formats: weekend, day-long, half-day, free 1 hour introductory sessions. I led intensive 3-day retreats in other cities where friends gathered a quorum.

Then one day, it came to me that my interest in teaching positive approaches to ecstatic sexuality might be similar to what sex therapists do in their practices. I investigated the field of sex therapy and learned that I could become a certified sex therapist with some additional training. I went to the annual conference of the American Association of Sexuality Educators, Counselors and Therapists (AASECT), signed up for continuing education courses in sex therapy, and arranged for supervision of my work. Within a year, I had successfully completed the AASECT certification process. At that point, I was the only certified sex therapist practicing in Nashville, so I quickly began getting referrals.

There is a greater market for, and understanding of, "sex therapy" than there is for "tantric sexuality education." So, whereas most sex therapy referrals are focused on problems for which treatment is desired, I try to expand the frame and offer people a larger vision of what is possible for them. I often describe a continuum of possible outcomes for clients seeking sex therapy. This is partly from the recognition that the practice of sex therapy has a large educational component, and partly from my desire to locate sex therapy within a larger positive psychology context, focusing on strengths and possibility, beyond symptom removal. In this view, health is not just the absence of adverse symptomatology but an experience of vitality, strength, and resilience.

The quality of sexual experience falls along a broad continuum that may be described as follows: "You may be having: No sex—Bad sex—Good sex—Great sex—Transcendent sex!" By the time I get to the end of this little description, many clients are interested in moving beyond solving the problem for which they initially sought help and exploring what may be possible for their enhanced sexual experience.

Today, half my practice is sex therapy or sexuality education. Most persons arrive knowing that it is unlikely their insurance will cover these services and are prepared to pay out-of-pocket for their treatment. These cases are often short term, resolving presenting complaints with a combination of support, education, and focused interventions.

An important (and surprising) element in the success of my practice has been my website. The site contains articles, resources, book reviews, and recommended links.

Currently more than half of my referrals (two to four per week) are people who found me on the Internet. Several factors contribute to this stream of referrals. There is a large perceived need for help in the sexuality arena, and it may be easier (and more private) to seek information via the Internet. My site offers a combination of educational resources as well as the invitation to seek help. Viewers get a glimpse of me and my approach through what I have written.

In an era of increased competition and tight constraints on insurance reimbursement, it is vital to find a specialty niche for practice. Personal growth and personal psychotherapy—even marital therapy or family therapy—are services that the majority of psychotherapists provide. But what about services that are, at best, only marginally covered by the generic provider list? Services such as sex therapy, treatment for eating disorders, coaching for success in business or athletics, and many others are often poorly represented in provider lists. It has been my experience that a clearly defined niche (about which the practitioner is passionate) that provides a needed service, and for which there is little competition, trumps the constraints of traditional managed care provider networks.

It also helps if the specialty niche for practice is something for which potential clients feel a strong need. My friends who treat troubled adolescents and children report that their practices are virtually recession-proof. Parents will prioritize purchasing needed services for their children over most things. Sexuality treatment and education is similar in that persons experiencing relationship crisis or distress are often willing to pay for the services they need. I received a call last week from a former client who had dropped out after two sessions. She rescheduled, saying, "I thought I couldn't afford to do it—now I think I can't afford not to do it."

I wish I could say that the success of my practice is the result of considered thought, market research, careful planning, and 5-year projections. It is not. I stumbled into a specialty area, which really developed out of my own personal interests. Optimal or healthy sexuality is something I am passionate about, and finding a way to express that interest through certification in sex therapy has proved to be both financially rewarding and deeply satisfying. In addition to my website (http://www.davidyarian.com), helpful resources for those wanting to learn more about this practice area may be found at http://www.spiritedloving.com, http://www.Books4selfhelp.com, http://www.AASECT.org, http://www.ecstaticliving.com, and http://www.tantra.com.

Steven Walfish

Epilogue

The contributors to this book have demonstrated that psychologists can provide services in scenarios that fall outside of the purview of managed care. These clinicians looked at their skill sets and found ways to create opportunities for themselves.

Walfish and Barnett (2008) urged private practitioners to think of themselves as small business owners: "The success of this business is dependent upon the clinician's ability to provide a service that people want and to make a profit while doing so" (p. 11). Walfish and Barnett cited the work of Baron and Shane (2008) on how entrepreneurial principles can be applied to help develop a financially successful practice. Baron and Shane viewed the process of entrepreneurship as one in which an idea is generated, resources are developed to help bring the opportunity to fruition, and the product or service is developed and grown. Characteristics common to successful entrepreneurs include having a high energy level, self-confidence both as a person and as a skilled professional, a passion about goals and vision, and a willingness to take a risk. Baron and Shane noted that those who actively seek opportunities are the ones who are likely to find them. Idea development, according to Baron and Shane, emerges from using, combining, or stretching previous knowledge into a new situation or opportunity.

These concepts can be seen in the work of the psychologists in this volume. Susan Gamble's husband worked in the wedding industry, and she noticed how much stress was involved in this blessed event. This led to her work conducting premarital workshops. Brad Rosenfield combined his knowledge about learning theory and family systems with his passion for animals to develop his pet training service. Jeff Jones noticed that his clients with social skills difficulties were having trouble with high-pressure interviews. He developed a specialized niche to help with this problem area. David Starr was a subcontractor to a company that ran employee assistance programs. After gaining this work experience, he realized he no longer had to be a subcontractor and could bid on the work himself. Kathleen Shea was appointed to a national advisory board by President Reagan. This placed her in contact with owners of family businesses, and she was able to identify the psychological skills that she could offer to theses companies. Elizabeth Carll expanded her previous work responding to natural disasters into responding to workplace crises. Steven Hendlin became fascinated with online trading and noted there was no psychological book available on the topic, so he wrote one; this became his niche. Tish Taylor spent 14 years working in the educational system before becoming a private practice psychologist. Naturally, she would know what psychological input teachers might need in improving their work. Similarly, Stuart Dansinger brings his experience in the school system to his work with gifted children. Laurie Little's interest in assertiveness training was an outgrowth of practicum experiences learning dialectical behavior therapy. She then followed up with specialized training. Barbara Holstein's passion for her positive psychology work grew out of her research in which she found women could flourish despite many negative life experiences. She has grown her concepts to include her clinical practice, teleclasses, professional books, audio programs, and now fiction writing.

Passion for a practice activity can be spurred on by personal life experiences. Nancy Sidun first became interested in the whole area of adoption when she adopted a child. After going through her own experience with infertility, Lucille Keenan decided that she would gain the necessary training to develop this as a specialty area. Brad Klontz capitalized on his own experience with student loan debt and trading stocks to focus on consulting with financial professionals. Gina Hassan found her own pregnancy to be so personally meaningful that she sought out ways to incorporate pregnancy issues into her practice. David Yarian had a powerful experience as a participant in a 2-week tantric sexuality course. He then became expert in this area and certified as a sex therapist to be able to develop a financially successful practice focusing on sexuality issues. Mitchell Greene was a serious recreational athlete. He decided to take the time to obtain training so he could develop sport psychology as a specialty area. Marc Lipton's father smoked three packs of cigarettes per day, and Lipton later found himself smoking the same amount, so he can certainly relate to the smokers that he treats in his practice. I have no doubt that clients sense the personal commitment these psychologists bring to their work, which is fueled by their own experiences.

Oddly enough, simply telling colleagues of an interest in expanding in a different direction can lead to new opportunities. Doug Haldeman told a colleague of his interest in doing more psychological testing. This conversation led to a niche that has lasted for 25 years. David Lutz used a contact at a state agency, which led to his being able to do consultative examinations for that agency. Valerie Shebroe mentioned to a director of clinical training that she was interested in supervising students. This led to many university-based activities for her. Although he was not seeking work, Mark Gilson wrote Aaron Beck a letter describing his research interest in cognitive therapy. This letter led to a job offer and experiences that would result in developing his own center and training program.

Being active in the community, both personally and professionally, creates visibility that can bring work to a psychologist when a need for services arises. Stephen Curran's career took a turn toward public safety psychology when a member of his fraternal organization approached him about starting a confidential counseling program for police officers and their family members. He then creatively expanded the services that he could offer. Frank Froman practices in a small community. When a new community-based group home opened and there was a need for psychological services, he was the person that they called. Thomas Plante was active in his church, and when a need developed for a psychologist, church administrators contacted him. Ray Kamoo had a cousin, an immigration attorney, who asked if he would be interested in working on a case. This led him to learn more about the area and develop this unique specialty.

Walfish and Barnett (2008) presented "Twenty Principles of Private Practice Success." Principle Number 18 refers specifically to managed care:

> Participation in a managed care plan is not a requirement for being in private practice. If you choose to participate, you must clearly understand, and emotionally accept all of the financial and clinical ramifications and limitations beforehand. If you do not, you will set yourself up for a great deal of frustration during your participation. (Walfish & Barnett, 2008, p. 190)

As noted earlier, most psychologists would like to earn their living as far away from managed care as possible to avoid its clinical and financial limitations. It is hoped that the psychologists in this book have provided a framework for how to practice at least partially, if not fully, outside of managed care in a way that is both clinically and financially fruitful.

References

Baron, R., & Shane, S. (2008). *Entrepreneurship: A process perspective.* New York, NY: Southwestern-Psychology.

Walfish, S., & Barnett, J. (2008). *Financial success in mental health practice: Essential tools and strategies for practitioners.* Washington, DC: American Psychological Association.

Index

A

AASECT (American Association of Sexuality Educators, Counselors and Therapists), 223
Abundance, 17–18
Academic readiness evaluations, 47–50
Accident reports, 188
ACCT. *See* Atlanta Center for Cognitive Therapy
Achievement tests, 185–186
Ackerman, D. J., 50
Ackley, D., 3
Acupuncturists, 173
ADD (attention-deficit disorder), 51
ADHD. *See* Attention-deficit/hyperactivity disorder
Adolescents
   services available to, 157
   substance abuse interventions for, 29
Adoption, 36–39
Adoptive triad, 38–39
Adult Children of Divorce (Jeffrey Zimmerman and Elizabeth Thayer), 183
Air traffic controller evaluations, 110–113
Alcohol abuse
   interventions for, 28–31
   by pilots and air traffic controllers, 111, 112
American Academy of Forensic Psychology, 185
American Association of Sexuality Educators, Counselors and Therapists (AASECT), 223

American Psychological Association (APA)
   continuing education provider approval by, 161
   conventions, 10, 32, 39
   Counseling Psychology division, 39
   Ethical Principles of Psychologists and Code of Conduct, 197
   Exercise and Sport Psychology division, 216
   income-generation survey among members of, 4
   Intellectual and Developmental Disabilities division, 126
   media referral service, 206
   Mental Impairments program workbook, 109
   National Disaster Response Advisory Task Force, 88
   Psychologists in Public Service division, 117
   as resource for parent coordination, 183
   and training for supervision, 148
American Red Cross, 98–99
American Society of Reproductive Medicine (ASRM), 68–70
Anand, Margo, 222
Anger management, 111
Anxiety
   management of, 158
   reduction skills for, 179
   and smoking cessation, 72–73
APA. *See* American Psychological Association
Applied Psychophysiology and Biofeedback, 80

Ardmore Animal Hospital, 41
ASRM. *See* American Society of Reproductive
    Medicine
Assertiveness skills training groups, 168–170
Assessments. *See also* Evaluations
    of competency, 184–186, 189
    of gifted clients, 211–214
    of men and women entering religious life,
        127–129
    for prospective adoptive parents, 37–38
    social security disability, 106–109
    software for, 202
    vocational rehabilitation, 103–105
Association for Applied Psychophysiology and
    Biofeedback, 80
Association for Mental Retardation, 126
Association for Scientific Advancement in Psycho-
    logical Injury and Law, 117
Association of Family and Conciliation Courts, 183
Asylum cases, 193
Atlanta Center for Cognitive Therapy (ACCT),
    159–161
Attention-deficit disorder (ADD), 51
Attention-deficit/hyperactivity disorder (ADHD)
    coaching for, 54–56
    neurotherapy for treatment of, 79
    psychoeducational testing for, 51, 53
Audio taping (supervision), 149
Autism
    and psychoeducational testing, 52
    and sport psychology, 216
Automated data collection systems, 201–202
Aviation psychology, 110

B
Bariatric surgery, 75, 76
Barnett, J., 4, 225, 227
Barnett, W. S., 50
Baron, R., 225
BCIA. *See* Biofeedback Certification Institute
    of America
Beck, Aaron T., 160, 161, 227
Behavior change, 29
Behavior modification, 41, 125
Benson, Herbert, 173
Best of Stress Management (audio program), 174
Beyond Words, 62
Bianco, James, 41
Billing
    for academic readiness evaluations, 49
    for ADHD coaching, 56
    for employee assistance programs, 92
    for expert witness practices, 189
    for health care organization consultation, 132
    for marriage therapy, 26
    for personal growth workshops, 221
    for pilot and air traffic controller evaluations, 112

    for pregnancy support groups, 167
    for psychoeducational testing, 53
    for public safety services, 116
    of religious organizations, 129
    for reproductive medicine, 69
    for serving as guardian ad litem, 178
    software for, 202
    for stress management, 95
    for supervision, 149
    for vocational rehabilitation assessments, 103
    for workshops, 158
    for work with developmentally disabled adults,
        124
Biofeedback Certification Institute of America
    (BCIA), 79, 80
Biopsychosocial interventions, 31
Birth-order dynamics, 98
Blue Book (Social Security Administration), 109
Booklet Categories Test, 112
Bracken School Readiness Assessment—
    Third Edition, 48
Brain maps, 78, 79
Branding
    for non-managed care practices, 11–13
    for products, 204–207
Breaking Free of Managed Care (D. Ackley), 3
Business psychology, 83–99. *See also* Finance
    employee assistance programs, 90–93
    executive leadership coaching, 83–86
    for family-owned businesses, 97–99
    stress management, 94–96
    and workplace trauma, 87–89

C
Campbell Interest and Skill Surveys, 60
Canine behavior therapy (CBT), 40–42
Capella University, 154
Career counseling. *See* Vocational counseling
Carll, Elizabeth, 226
CBT. *See* Canine behavior therapy; Cognitive
    behavior therapy
CCEs. *See* Child custody evaluators
Center for Emotional Health of Greater
    Philadelphia, 120
Center for Mind-Body Medicine (CMBM), 171, 173
Center for Mindful Eating, 76
Child custody cases, 189–190
Child custody evaluators (CCEs), 177, 181
Children
    academic readiness evaluations for, 47–50
    adoption of, 36–39
    and divorce, 32, 33, 180–182
    and expert witnesses, 188
    gifted, 211–214
    and immigration proceedings, 193
    neurotherapy for, 79
    psychoeducational testing of, 51–53

services available to, 157
social skills of, 62
and sport psychology, 216
Chronicle of Higher Education, 155
CILAs (community integrated living arrangements),
124
Clinical interviews, 37
Closed adoptions, 36
CMBM. *See* Center for Mind-Body Medicine
Coaching
for ADHD, 54–56
executive leadership, 83–86
for traders and investors, 137–139
Cognitive ability
academic readiness evaluations, 48
and U.S. citizenship examination, 193
Cognitive behavior therapy (CBT), 160
Cognitive therapy groups, 75–77
Cognitive Therapy of Depression (Aaron T. Beck), 160
Coleading, 149
Collaborative divorce practice, 32–35, 183
Colorado State Psychological Association (CPA), 148
Communication
in marriage therapy, 26, 27
and serving as guardian ad litem, 179
Community integrated living arrangements (CILAs),
124
Community outreach, 151
Competency, assessment of, 184–186, 189
Competency to Stand Trial Evaluations
(Thomas Grisso), 185
Confidence, 12
Confidentiality
in assertiveness skills training groups, 169
in premarital counseling, 23
Conflict resolution, 26, 27
Conners' Rating Scales, 51–52
Consultative examination providers, 107
Consulting
for assessment of competency administration, 185
with family-owned business, 97–99
for financial planners, 141–143
with health care organizations, 130–133
Continuous Performance Test (CPT), 51
Contracts, 118–120
The Co-parenting Survival Guide (Jeffrey Zimmerman
and Elizabeth Thayer), 183
Corporations, 94–96
Costs. *See* Fees
The Counseling Psychology, 39
Couples, 142–143. *See also* Marriage
Cox, Adam, 214
CPA (Colorado State Psychological Association),
148
CPT (Continuous Performance Test), 51
Credibility, 132
Crisis networks, 13
Crisis response services, 88–89

Culture
of care practices, 10–11
of industries, 95–96
Curran, Stephan, 227

D
Dansinger, Stuart, 226
Dass, Ram, 174
Data collection systems, 201–202
DBT (dialectical behavior therapy), 169
DD. *See* Disability Determination
Decision-making processes, 99
Delaware Valley Psychological Services (DVPS),
118–120
Department of Professional and Financial
Regulation (DPFR), 196, 197
Deportation proceedings, 192
Depression, 72–73
Developmentally disabled adults, 123–126
Developmental maturity, 48–49
Diagnostic Assessments of Reading—
Second Edition II, 48
Dialectical behavior therapy (DBT), 169
Differential diagnosis, 108
Different Minds (Deirdre Lovecky), 213
Direct marketing, 52–53
Disability
defined, 107
and developmentally disabled adults, 123–126
Disability Determination (DD), 103, 106–107, 109
Disaster response networks, 88
Disease theory, 30
Disney, 11
Distance education, 153–155
Divorce
and collaborative divorce practice, 32–35
and marriage therapy, 27
Doctoral students, 147, 148
Dogs, 40–42
DPFR. *See* Department of Professional and Financial
Regulation
Dream work, 220
Drug abuse
interventions for, 28–31
by pilots and air traffic controllers, 111, 112
Duke, Marshall, 61
DVPS. *See* Delaware Valley Psychological Services

E
Eating disorders, 77
Eating in the Light of the Moon (Anita A. Johnston),
76
Education. *See also* Psychoeducational psychology
distance, 153–155
for executive leadership coaching, 85
of gifted clients, 212, 213
and workshops for educators, 156–158
Educational testing, 53

Education.com, 49
EEG (electroencephalograph) biofeedback, 78
Egg donors, 69
eLearning, 203
Electroencephalograph (EEG) biofeedback, 78
Electronic medical records, 201, 203
E-mail
    for coaching, 55
    for making contact, 139
Employee assistance programs, 88, 90–93
Employment law, 115
The Enchanted Self (Barbara Becker Holstein), 205–206
The Enchanted Self state, 204–206
English language, 194
Equilibria Psychological and Consultation Services,
    LLC., 83
Estate planning, 138
Ethical Principles of Psychologists and Code
    of Conduct (American Psychological
    Association), 197
Ethics, 196–198
Evaluating Juveniles' Adjudicative Competence
    (Thomas Grisso), 185
Evaluations
    academic readiness, 47–50
    for ADHD, 54
    for developmentally disabled adults, 123, 124
    of egg donors, 69
    by expert witnesses, 188–189
    in health care settings, 131
    immigration, 191–194
    for pilots and air traffic controllers, 110–113
    of professionals, 195–198
    and psychoeducational testing, 51–53
    for smoking cessation, 72
    for social security disability assessments, 107
    for state agencies, 118–120
    in supervision, 148
Evidence, 178
Executive leadership coaching, 83–86
Expert services, 115
Expert testimony
    for assessments of competency, 186
    on dog behavior, 42
    in immigration proceedings, 193–194
    and serving as guardian ad litem, 178, 179
    and serving as witness, 187–190
Extended care hospitals, 132
Extreme or exceptional hardship cases, 192

F
FAA. *See* Federal Aviation Administration
Facilitating Financial Health (B. Klontz, R. Kahler,
    and T. Klontz), 142
Families, 125
The Family Court Review, 183
Family histories, 37
Family-of-origin work, 25

Family-owned businesses (FOBs), 97–99
Family psychology, 21–42
    for adoption, 36–39
    canine behavior therapy, 40–42
    collaborative divorce practice, 32–35
    premarital counseling, 21–23
    substance abuse interventions, 28–31
    teaching marriage skills, 25–27
Federal Aviation Administration (FAA), 110–112
Fee-for-service practices, 3
Fees
    academic readiness evaluation, 49
    assertiveness skills training group, 170
    canine behavior therapy, 41
    collaborative divorce practice, 34
    employee assistance program, 92
    executive leadership coaching, 83, 84
    immigration evaluation, 193
    neurotherapy, 79
    personal growth workshop, 221
    pilot and air traffic controller evaluation, 112
    psychoeducational testing, 53
    smoking cessation, 73
    social security disability assessment, 108
    sport psychology, 216
    state agency evaluation, 119
    substance abuse intervention, 29–30
    supervision, 149
    trader and investor coaching, 139
    vocational rehabilitation assessment, 105
    workshop, 158
Fielding Graduate University, 154
Finance, 137–143
    and financial planners, 141–143
    trader and investor coaching, 137–139
Financial investment, 9
Financial planners, 141–143
Flexibility, 84
FOBs. *See* Family-owned businesses
Forensic psychology, 177–198
    assessment of competency in, 184–186
    evaluation of professionals in, 195–198
    and high-conflict divorce, 180–183
    immigration evaluations in, 191–194
    serving as expert witness in, 187–190
    serving as guardian ad litem in, 177–179
Forer Sentence Completion tests, 128
Freeman, Art, 161
Froman, Frank, 227
Functional mental illnesses, 187
Fundraisers, 13

G
Gamble, Susan, 226
Gaskill, Frank, 15
Gesell Institute, 49
Gifted Child Quarterly, 214
Gifted clients, 211–214

Gilson, Mark, 227
Gordon, James, 173–174
Gottman, John, 23
Government services, 103–120
  pilot and air traffic controller evaluations, 110–113
  public safety services, 114–117
  Social Security disability assessments, 106–109
  state agency evaluations, 118–120
  vocational rehabilitation assessments, 103–105
Graduate students, 147, 148, 151
Greene, Mitchell, 226
Grisso, Thomas, 185
Group engagement, 220
Groups
  assertiveness skills training, 168–170
  mind-body skills training, 171–174
  pregnancy support, 165–167
  weight-management, 75–77
Guardians ad litem, 177–179

H
Haber, S., 3
Haldeman, Doug, 227
Hallowell, Edward, 55
Hard-sell intervention, 29
Harm-reduction model, 30
Hassan, Gina, 226
Haveren, Rick Van, 60
Head injuries, 188–189
Health care organization consultation, 130–133
Health psychology, 67–80
  neurotherapy, 78–80
  reproductive medicine, 67–70
  smoking cessation, 71–74
  weight-management groups, 75–77
Hendlin, Steven, 226
High-conflict divorce, 180–183
Higher Learning Commission, 155
Holstein, Barbara Becker, 205–206, 226
Homework, 169
Homicide, 87
Hypnosis, 72, 74

I
IACP. *See* International Association of Chiefs of Police; International Association of Collaborative Professionals
IAHB. *See* Institute for the Advancement of Human Behavior
Immigration evaluations, 191–194
Immigration Psychology Associates (IPA), 191
Income, 9
Independent clinical practice, 150–152
Infertility, 37, 67, 68
Infinity and Zebra Strips (Wendy Skinner), 214
Inheritance issues, 138
In-person contact, 139

Institute for the Advancement of Human Behavior (IAHB), 161, 162
Insurance coverage
  for academic readiness evaluations, 49
  for assertiveness skills training groups, 170
  for high-conflict divorce work, 182
  for immigration evaluations, 193
  for marriage therapy, 26
  for personal growth retreats, 221
  for pilot and air traffic controller evaluations, 111
  and practice possibilities, 3
  for pregnancy support groups, 167
  for premarital counseling, 22
  for psychoeducational testing, 53
  for psychotherapy with clergy members, 129
  and reproductive medicine, 69
  for trader and investor coaching, 139
Integrated university teaching, 150–152
Integrity, 12
Intellectual evaluation, 107
International adoptions, 36
International Association of Chiefs of Police (IACP), 116
International Association of Collaborative Professionals (IACP), 33–35
International Coaching Federation, 84, 85
International Social Work, 39
International Society for Neurofeedback and Research, 80
Internet
  marriage skills information on, 26
  and premarital counseling, 22
  referrals from, 223
  services on, 29
  and stress management, 95
  and training programs, 161
Interns, 14
Interventions
  for family-owned businesses, 98
  for high-conflict divorce, 180–181
  mind-body, 171
  for substance abuse, 28–31
Interviewing skills, 61–63, 108
Interviewing Skills Program, 62–63
Interviews
  clinical, 37
  of men and women entering religious life, 128
Investors, 137–139
IPA (Immigration Psychology Associates), 191
IQ tests
  for assessment of competency, 185
  in psychoeducational testing, 52
Ishee, Trey, 14

J
Johnson O'Connor Abilities Battery testing, 59
Johnston, Anita A., 76
Jones, Jeff, 226

Journal of Family Psychology, 23
Journal of Marriage and Family, 23
Journal of Neurotherapy, 80
Jung, Carl, 219
Juvenile justice treatment programs, 202

K
Kahler, R., 142
Kamoo, Ray, 227
Keenan, Lucille, 226
Keynote, 14
Kindergarten readiness evaluations, 47–50
Klontz, B., 142, 226
Klontz, T., 142
Klontz Consulting Group, 142

L
Law. *See also* Forensic psychology
    assessment of competency in, 184–186
    and evaluations of professionals, 197
    expert witnesses in, 187–190
    guardians ad litem in, 177–179
    and public safety services, 115
Le, Jane, 4
Leadership coaching, 83–86
Learning disabilities
    neurotherapy for treatment of, 79
    testing for, 52, 53
Learning process deficits, 185
Levinson, Harry, 59
Liability, 42
Limbrunner, Heidi, 15
Linehan, Marsha, 169
Lipkin, Nicole A., 85
Lipner, I., 3
Lipton, Marc, 227
Listening skills, 142, 179
Literacy, 48
Little, Laurie, 78, 226
Live supervision, 149
Lovecky, Deirdre, 214
Lowman, Rodney, 58
Lubar, Joel, 79
Lutz, David, 227

M
Mailings, 34
Managed care organizations (MCOs)
    and crisis response services, 88–89
    and employee assistance programs, 92
    proliferation of, 131
Manifesto for a New-Medicine (James Gordon), 173
Marketing
    of ADHD coaching, 56
    of assertiveness skills training groups, 170
    of assessments of competency, 186
    of collaborative divorce practice, 34
    of executive leadership coaching, 85

    of marriage workshops, 27
    of mind-body skills training groups, 172–173
    of neurotherapy, 79
    of non-managed care practices, 11, 12
    of premarital counseling, 22
    of psychoeducational testing, 52–53
    of sport psychology practice, 217
    of stress management, 95
    of weight-management groups, 77
    of workplace trauma counseling, 89
Marriage
    and financial planner consultation, 142–143
    and premarital counseling, 21–23, 27
    teaching skills for, 25–27
Married to the Brand (W. McEwen), 12
Maturity, 48–49
MBSG. *See* Mind-Body Skills Group
McEwen, W., 12
MCOs. *See* Managed care organizations
Mediation, 34, 183
Medication
    for ADHD, 54
    and pilots and air traffic controllers, 111
Mental health professionals (MHPs), 3
Mental Health Resource (MHR), 130
Midwifery organizations, 167
Millon Clinical Multiaxial Inventory—III, 128
Milton H. Erickson Foundation, 23
Mind-Body Skills Group (MBSG), 171–174
Mind-body skills training groups, 171–174
Mindfulness skills, 76
Minnesota Council for the Gifted and Talented, 212–214
Minnesota Educators of Gifted and Talented organization, 213
Minnesota Multiphasic Personality Inventory—2 (MMPI–2), 37, 107, 128
Money disorders, 142
Money scripts, 142
Mood disorders, 166
Morganstein, Barrie, 15
Motherhood, 165–167

N
National Association for Gifted Children, 214
National Board for Certified Counselors, 161
National Career Developmental Association, 60
National Institute for Clinical Application of Behavioral Medicine (NICABM), 173
Networking
    in executive leadership coaching, 85
    with health care organizations, 132
    with immigration attorneys, 194
    with local professionals, 120
    for supervision opportunities, 148
Neuropsychological assessment, 78, 186
Neuropsychological evaluations, 107, 118
Neuropsychology, 187

Neuroscience, 187
Neurotherapy, 78–80
New Psych listserv, 68
New York City Marathon, 217
New York State Psychological Association, 88
NICABM (National Institute for Clinical Application of Behavioral Medicine), 173
Niches for practice, 15–16, 223–224
No Mind Left Behind (Adam Cox), 214
Non-managed care practices, 8–18
    and abundance, 17–18
    branding for, 11–13
    building niches in, 15–16
    creating special experiences in, 10–11
    giving presentations in, 14–15
    referrals in, 13–16
Nonprofit organizations, 119, 120
North American Society for Psychosocial Obstetrics and Gynecology, 166
Nowicki, Steve, 61

O
Obesity, 75
One-coach model (collaborative divorce practice), 33
Online games, 27
Online teaching, 153–155
Online trading, 137, 138
Open adoptions, 36
Organic mental illnesses, 187
Organizations, 123–133
    for developmentally disabled adults, 123–126
    health care, 130–133
    nonprofit, 119, 120
    religious, 127–129
Outlook (newsletter), 213, 214

P
Pain management services, 131
Paraeducators, 157
Parents as Partners for Kindergarten Readiness, 50
Passion, 12
Patience, 179
Payment. *See* Billing; Fees
PCPs (primary care physicians), 77
Pediatric health psychology, 78
Perinatal mood disorders, 166
Perinatal Psychotherapy Services, 165
Personal growth retreats, 219–221
Personality assessment, 98, 186
Personality disorders, 41
Physicians, 79
Pilot evaluations, 110–113
Plante, T., 4
Plante, Thomas, 227
Police agencies, 114–116
Police reports, 188
Positive psychology, 211–224
    and gifted clients, 211–214

personal growth retreats, 219–221
sport psychology practices, 215–218
tantric sexuality education, 222–224
Postpartum Stress Center, 166
Postpartum Support International, 166
Power of Two Marriage Skills Workshops, 27
PowerPoint, 14, 15
PPOs (preferred provider organizations), 131
Preferred provider organizations (PPOs), 131
Pregnancy support groups, 165–167
Premarital counseling, 21–23, 27
Presentations
    for developing a brand, 205
    in non-managed care practices, 14–15
    for referrals, 13
Preventative treatment programs, 96
Pride, 12
Primary care physicians (PCPs), 77
Principals, 157
Privacy, 28
Private schools
    crisis networks for, 13
    interviewing skills for, 62
Processing software, 202
Products, 201–207
    and branding, 204–207
    social service programs software, 201–203
Professionals, 195–198
Psychodiagnostic evaluation, 107
Psychoeducational psychology, 47–63
    academic readiness evaluations, 47–50
    attention-deficit/hyperactivity disorder coaching, 54–56
    interviewing skills, 61–63
    testing, 51–53
    vocational counseling, 58–60
Psychoeducational testing, 51–53
Psychological evaluations. *See* Evaluations
Psychometrics, 112
Psychosexual evaluations, 118
Public agencies, 13
Publicity, 206
Public safety services, 114–117

Q
Quality, 12
Quantitative electroencephalograph (QEEG), 78, 79

R
Readiness evaluations, academic, 47–50
Reagan, Ronald, 98
Recognition, 132
Recovery programs, 111
Referrals
    ADHD coaching, 56
    employee assistance programs, 91–92
    for evaluation of professionals, 195, 197
    expert witnesses, 189

gifted clients, 213
high-conflict divorce work, 182
immigration evaluation, 193
marriage therapy, 26
for men and women entering religious life, 128
mind-body skills training groups, 172, 173
neurotherapy, 79
in non-managed care practices, 13–16
for personal growth retreats, 221
pregnancy support groups, 167
premarital counseling, 22
psychoeducational testing, 52
for public safety services, 116
smoking cessation treatment, 73
Social Security disability assessment, 107
state agency evaluations, 119, 120
substance abuse intervention, 29
supervision, 148
tantric sexuality education, 223
trader and investor coaching, 139
for treatment and training programs, 159
university teaching, 151
vocational rehabilitation assessment, 104
workplace trauma counseling, 88, 89
for work with developmentally disabled adults,
126
Re-forming Gifted Education (Karen Rogers), 213
Relationships, 14, 142
Religion, 22
Religious organizations, 127–129
Reports
accident, 188
for assessments of competency, 186
by expert witnesses, 189
on gifted clients, 213
on men and women entering religious life, 128
with social security disability assessments, 108
for state agency evaluations, 120
on work with developmentally disabled adults,
124
Reproductive medicine, 67–70
Reputation
for academic readiness evaluations, 49
and developing a brand, 206
in non-managed care practices, 9
Restraining orders, 181
Retreats
personal growth, 219–221
tantric sexuality, 222
Rodino, E., 3
Rogers, Karen, 213
Rosenfeld, Brad, 226

S
Sachs, Michael, 216
Saying Goodbye to Managed Care (Haber, Rodino, and
Lipner), 3
Scarcity, 17–18
School counselors, 157

School psychologists, 157
School records, 188
Self-care, 172
Self-regulation, 173
Self-worth, 205
Seminars, 157–158
Settlement conferences, 182
Seven Gateways to Happiness, 205
Sex therapy, 223
Sexual abuse, 127
Sexuality education, tantric, 222–224
Shane, S., 225
Shea, Kathleen, 226
Shebroe, Valerie, 227
Sidun, Nancy, 226
Silverman, Linda, 214
Sixteen Personality Factor Questionnaire, 128
Skills training groups, 168–170
Skinner, Wendy, 214
Smart Marriage, 27
Smoking cessation, 71–74
Social Security Administration (SSA), 107–109
Social Security disability assessments, 106–109
Social service programs, 201–203
Social skills, 62
Society of Police and Criminal Psychology, 117
Soft-cell intervention, 29–30
Software, 201–203
Southeast Psych, 10
Specialty groups, 165–174
assertiveness skills training groups, 168–170
mind-body skills training groups, 171–174
pregnancy support groups, 165–167
Sport psychology, 215–218
SSA. *See* Social Security Administration
Standardized assessment tools, 202
Stanford-Binet test, 123
Starr, David, 226
State agency evaluations, 118–120
State licensing boards, 195, 196
Stress management, 94–96, 111, 172
Students, 147, 148, 150–152
Substance abuse
and employee assistance programs, 90
interventions for, 28–31
by pilots and air traffic controllers, 111, 112
and weight management, 77
Suicide, 87
Supervision, 147–149
and ethical issues, 196
for psychoeducational testing practice, 53
of students, 150–152
Surgery, bariatric, 75
Systems orientation, 132

T
Take It Off/Keep It Off Program, 76
Tantric sexuality education, 222–224

Taylor, Tish, 226
Teachers
    and gifted children, 212
    and psychoeducational testing, 52
    workshops for, 156–158
Teaching, 150–162. *See also* Supervision
    integrated university, 150–152
    online, 153–155
    and serving as guardian ad litem, 179
    treatment and training programs, 159–162
    workshops for improvement in, 156–158
Teaching Your Child the Language of Social Success
    (Marshall Duke and Steve Nowicki), 61
Technology, 142, 201–203, 206
Telephone calls, 139
Telephone lines, 91
Testimony, expert. *See* Expert testimony
Testing. *See* Assessments; Evaluations
Thayer, Elizabeth, 183
TherapyHelp.com, 27
TheStreet.com, 137
Toastmasters International, 70
Torque Interactive Media, 25
Trade books, 205
Traders, 137–139
Trail-Making Tests, 112
Training
    for ADHD coaching, 55, 56
    for collaborative divorce practice, 33–34
    for employee assistance programs, 92
    in intervention processes, 31
    in mediation, 183
    for online teaching, 154
    programs for, 159–162
    for prospective adoptive parents, 37
    for social security disability assessments, 108
    for supervision, 148
Trauma
    and children, 188
    workplace, 87–89
Treatment programs, 159–162
Trust, 142
The Truth (Barbara Becker Holstein), 206
Two-coach model (collaborative divorce practice), 33
Two-generational family histories, 37

U
Udell, Meryl E., 118
United States Council of Catholic Bishops, 127
University counseling centers, 58
Unstuck (James Gordon), 173–174

Upside-Down Brilliance (Linda Silverman), 214
U.S. citizenship examination, 193

V
Validity testing, 107
Videotaping (supervision), 149
Vineland Social Maturity Scale, 123
Violence, workplace, 87–89
Violence Against Women Act, 193
Virtual assistants, 206
Vocational counseling, 58–60
Vocational rehabilitation (VR) assessments,
    103–105
Volunteer work, 132, 150, 152
VR assessments. *See* Vocational rehabilitation
    assessments

W
Walden University, 154
Walfish, S., 4, 225, 227
Ware, M., 4
Websites
    for developing a brand, 206
    for marketing ADHD coaching, 56
    for marketing reproductive medicine, 69
    for premarital counseling, 22
Weight-management groups, 75–77
Witnesses, expert, 187–190
Women, 204–207
Woodcock–Johnson Tests, 48, 52, 53
Workplace trauma, 87–89
Workshops
    for assessment of competency administration,
        185
    in collaborative divorce practice, 34
    and health care organizations, 133
    on high-conflict divorcing, 181
    for marriage skills, 26–27
    personal growth, 221
    for tantric sexuality education, 222
    for teachers and educators, 156–158
    on trading, 139
    for training and treatment programs, 160
    weight-management, 76

Y
Yarian, David, 226
Y in the Workplace (Nicole A. Lipkin), 85

Z
Zimmerman, Jeffrey, 183

About the Contributors

David O. Aspenson, PhD, 111 Cloister Court, Suite 100, Chapel Hill, NC 27514; http://www.davidaspenson.com; daspenson@mindspring.com

Lauren Behrman, PhD, 600 Mamaroneck Avenue, #303, Harrison, NY 10528; http://www.laurenbehrmanphd.com; laurenbehrman@gmail.com.

Elizabeth K. Carll, PhD, PO Box 246, Centerport, NY 11721; http://www.drelizabethcarll.com; ecarll@optonline.net

Myles L. Cooley, PhD, 9121 N. Military Trail, Suite 218, Palm Beach Gardens, FL 33410; http://www.drmylescooley.com; cool612@bellsouth.net

Stephen F. Curran, PhD, 29 W. Susquehanna Avenue, Suite 704, Towson, MD 21204; http://www.atlanticoccupsych.com; greenpsych@aol.com

Debbie Daniels-Mohring, PhD, 2200 Pump Road, Suite 220, Richmond, VA 23233; drdanielsmohring@comcast.net

Stuart Dansinger, EdS, 4601 Excelsior Boulevard, Suite 303, St. Louis Park, MN 55416; sdansinger@minneapolis-psychologist.com

Marla W. Deibler, PsyD, The Center for Emotional Health of Greater Philadelphia, 385 N. King's Highway, Suite 205, Cherry Hill, NJ 08034; http://www.thecenterforemotionalhealth.com; drdeibler@thecenterforemotionalhealth.com

Michaele P. Dunlap, PsyD, 818 NW 17th Avenue, Suite 11, Portland, OR 97209; http://www.michaeledunlap.com

Gary M. Eisenberg, PhD, 950 Glades Road, Boca Raton, FL 33431; gme43@aol.com

Frank Froman, EdD, 1891 Maine Street, Quincy, IL 62301; frankfroman@att.net

Susan Gamble, PsyD, Private Practice, Pasadena, CA; http://www.drsusangamble.com; info@drsusangamble.com

Mark Gilson, PhD, Atlanta Center for Cognitive Therapy, 1772 Century Boulevard, Atlanta, GA 30345; http://www.cognitiveatlanta.com; gilson@cognitiveatlanta.com

Mitchell A. Greene, PhD, http://www.greenepsych.com; mitchell.greene@comcast.net

Mary Gresham, PhD, 2801 Buford Highway, Suite 260, Atlanta, GA 30329; http://www.doctorgresham.com; mg@doctorgresham.com

Lisa R. Grossman, JD, PhD, 500 North Michigan Avenue, Chicago, IL 60611; lrgrossman@aol.com

Douglas C. Haldeman, PhD, 101 Stewart Street, Suite 1111, Seattle, WA 98101; http://www.drdoughaldeman.com; doughaldeman@aol.com

Gina Hassan, PhD, 1600 Shattuck Avenue, #200, Berkeley, CA 94709; http://www.ginahassan.com; ghassanphd@aol.com

Susan Heitler, PhD, 4500 East 9th Avenue, Suite 660, Denver, CO 80220; http://www.therapyhelp.com; drheitler@gmail.com

Steven J. Hendlin, PhD, 230 Newport Center Drive, Suite 220, Newport Beach, CA 92660; http://www.hendlin.net; baney@yahoo.com

Mitchell W. Hicks, PhD, 1655 N. Arlington Heights Road, Suite 205E, Arlington Heights, IL 60004; http://www.drmitchellhicks.com; mwhicks@drmitchellhicks.com

Barbara Becker Holstein, EdD, 170 Morris Avenue, Long Branch, NJ 07740; http://www.enchantedself.com; Encself@aol.com

Jeffrey Jones, PhD, Beyond Words Center, 1762-B Century Boulevard, Atlanta, GA 30345; http://www.beyondwordscenter.com; jeff@beyondwordscenter.com

Ray Kamoo, PhD, 2550 S. Telegraph Road, Suite 240, Bloomfield Hills, MI 48302; http://www.immigrationpsychologist.com; rkamoo@comcast.net

Lucille Keenan, PsyD, Cameron Park Therapy, 629 Oberlin Road, Raleigh, NC 27605; http://www.cameronparktherapy.com; drkeenan@cameronparktherapy.com

Brad Klontz, PsyD, PO Box 529, Kapaa, HI; http://www.yourmental wealth.com; brad@klontzconsulting.com

Marcia Knight, PhD, Private Practice, New York, NY

Nicole A. Lipkin, PsyD, MBA, Equilibria Coaching and Consultation Services, 525 South 4th Street, Suite 471, Philadelphia, PA 19147; http://www.equilibriapcs.com; nlipkin@equilibriapcs.com

Marc B. Lipton, PhD, MPA, 901 Dulaney Valley Road, Dulaney Center II, Suite 101, Towson, MD 21204; http://www.psychologistforyou.com; w2elt@comcast.net

Kirk D. Little, PsyD, Little Neurotherapy Center, 6900 Houston Road Building 500, Suite 11, Florence, KY 41042; http://www.littlepsych.com; kirk.little@littlepsych.com

Laurie Little, PsyD, Little Neurotherapy Center, 6900 Houston Road Building 500, Suite 11, Florence, KY 41042; http://www.littlepsych.com; laurie.little@littlepsych.com

David Lutz, PhD, Missouri State University, 901 South National Avenue, Springfield, MO 65897; http://www.davidlutzphd.com; davidlutz@missouristate.edu

Eric G. Mart, PhD, Highland Psychological Services, 311 Highlander Way, Manchester, NH 03103; http://www.psychology-law.com; emart@comcast.net

Kathy Martone, EdD, 1271 Lafayette Street, Denver, CO 80218; http://www.dreamagik.com; kmartone@dreamagik.com

Molly C. McKenna, PhD, 3939 NE Hancock Street, Suite 318, Portland, OR 97212; http://www.drmollymckenna.com; drmollymckenna@msn.com

Nona L. Patterson, PhD, 4425 Randolph Road, Suite 411, Charlotte, NC 28211; http://www.drnonapatterson.com; drnlpatterson@mac.com

Thomas G. Plante, PhD, Santa Clara University, Psychology Department, 500 El Camino Real, Santa Clara, CA 95053; http://www.scu.edu/tplante; tplante@scu.edu

T. J. Price, PsyD, 777 S. Wadsworth Boulevard, Building 2, Suite 103, Lakewood, CO 80226; http://tjprice.com; tj@drtjprice.com

Brad Rosenfield, PsyD, Philadelphia College of Osteopathic Medicine, 4170 City Avenue, Philadelphia, PA 19131; bradrosenfield@yahoo.com

Daniela E. Schreier, PsyD, S.M.A.R.T. Living LLC, 233 East Wacker Drive, #1607, Chicago, IL 60601; http://www.drschreier.com; drschreier@drschreier.com

Steven N. Shapse, PhD, 145 Lincoln Road, Lincoln, MA 01773; http://www.shapse.com

Kathleen V. Shea, PhD, Shea Psychological Associates, Forum Square A, Suite 9, 1117 Milwaukee Avenue, Libertyville, IL 60048; http://www.kathleensheaphd.com; sheakvphd@gmail.com

Valerie L. Shebroe, PhD, 2875 Northwind Drive, Suite #110, East Lansing, MI 48823; vshebroe@acd.net

Nancy M. Sidun, PsyD, 1195 Kamchame Drive, Honolulu, HI 96925; n.sidun@hawaiiantel.net

Genie Skypek, PhD, The Skypek Group, Tampa, FL; skypek@mindspring.com

David R. Starr, PhD, PO Box 400, Middleton, ID 83644; http://www.drdrstarr.com; unionpsychos@msn.com

Tish Taylor, PhD, 11100 Ash, Suite 202, Leawood, KS 66211; http://www.tishtaylor.com; drtish@tishtaylor.com

Peter C. Thomas, PhD, 3500 Piedmont Road NE, Suite 775, Atlanta, GA 30305; pctfocus@gmail.com

David Verhaagen, PhD, Southeast Psychological Services, 6115 Park South Drive, Charlotte, NC 28210; http://southeastpsych.com; dverhaagen@southeastpsych.com

Steven Walfish, PhD, 2004 Cliff Valley Way, Suite 101, Atlanta, GA 30329; psychpubs@aol.com

Edward A. Wise, PhD, Mental Health Resources, 1037 Cresthaven Road, Memphis, TN 38119; http://www.mhrmemphis.com; EdWisePhD@gmail.com

David Yarian, PhD, 1410 17th Avenue South, Nashville, TN 37212; http://www.davidyarian.com; dayarian@comcast.net

Jeffrey Zimmerman, PhD, 315 Highland Avenue, Suite 202, Cheshire, CT 06410; http://www.jzphd.com; drz@jzphd.com

About the Editor

Steven Walfish, PhD, is a licensed psychologist in independent practice in Atlanta. He is the associate editor of *Independent Practitioner* and has served on the editorial boards of several journals. He has published in the areas of substance abuse, weight loss surgery, and professional training and practice. He is a recipient of the American Psychological Association (APA) Division of Consulting Psychology Award for Outstanding Research in Consulting Psychology, the Walter Barton Award for Outstanding Research in Mental Health Administration from the American College of Mental Health Administration, and the APA Division of Independent Practice Mentoring Award. His first book (coedited with Allen Hess) was *Succeeding in Graduate School: The Career Guide for Psychology Students*. His second book (coauthored with Jeffrey Barnett), *Financial Success in Mental Health Practice: Essential Tools and Strategies for Practitioners,* was published by APA in 2008.

Dr. Walfish received his PhD in clinical and community psychology from the University of South Florida and has been a visiting professor at Kennesaw State University and Georgia State University. He is currently a clinical assistant professor in the Department of Psychiatry and Behavioral Sciences, Emory University School of Medicine.